Sovereignty Games

Palgrave Studies in Governance, Security, and Development

Series Editor: Dietrich Jung of the Danish
Institute for International Studies

This series contributes to the critical analysis of international affairs, linking the theoretical and the empirical, especially through comparative works. The focus is on three processes in international relations: *governance* involving both formal and informal institutions; *security*, meaning that of key actors in international society, with a focus on the distinctions and differences among security of and for individuals, groups, and states; and *development*, meaning the improvement of both political and economic conditions for individuals and groups. The links among the three will be a focus, which is pertinent given the interactions among them and among the levels of influence (from individual to global society).

Also in the series:

Aid Impact and Poverty Reduction
    Edited by Steen Folke and Henrik Nielson

Democratization and Development: New Political Strategies for the Middle East
    Edited by Dietrich Jung

Fragile States and Insecure People?: Violence, Security, and Statehood in the Twenty-First Century
    Edited by Louise Andersen, Bjørn Møller, and Finn Stepputat

State Recognition and Democratization in Sub-Saharan Africa: A New Dawn for Traditional Authorities?
    Edited by Lars Buur and Helene Maria Kyed

Religion, Politics, and Turkey's EU Accession
    Edited by Dietrich Jung and Catharina Raudvere

Sovereignty Games: Instrumentalizing State Sovereignty in Europe and Beyond
    Edited by Rebecca Adler-Nissen and Thomas Gammeltoft-Hansen

Sovereignty Games

Instrumentalizing State Sovereignty in Europe and Beyond

Edited by

Rebecca Adler-Nissen and
Thomas Gammeltoft-Hansen

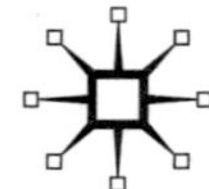

SOVEREIGNTY GAMES

Copyright © Rebecca Adler-Nissen and Thomas Gammeltoft-Hansen, 2008.

First published in 2008 by
PALGRAVE MACMILLAN®
in the United States—a division of St. Martin's Press LLC,
175 Fifth Avenue, New York, NY 10010.

Where this book is distributed in the UK, Europe and the rest of the world,
this is by Palgrave Macmillan, a division of Macmillan Publishers Limited,
registered in England, company number 785998, of Houndmills,
Basingstoke, Hampshire RG21 6XS.

Palgrave Macmillan is the global academic imprint of the above companies
and has companies and representatives throughout the world.

Palgrave® and Macmillan® are registered trademarks in the United States,
the United Kingdom, Europe and other countries.

ISBN-13: 978–0–230–60775–0
ISBN-10: 0–230–60775–6

Library of Congress Cataloging-in-Publication Data

Sovereignty games : instrumentalizing state sovereignty in Europe
and beyond / edited by Rebecca Adler-Nissen and Thomas
Gammeltoft-Hansen.
p. cm.
Includes bibliographical references and index.
ISBN 0–230–60775–6
1. Sovereignty—Congresses. 2. European Union—Politics and
government. I. Adler-Nissen, Rebecca, 1979– II. Gammeltoft-Hansen,
Thomas.

JC327.S644 2008
320.1'5094—dc22   2008015880

A catalogue record of the book is available from the British Library.

Design by Newgen Imaging Systems (P) Ltd., Chennai, India.

First edition: December 2008

10 9 8 7 6 5 4 3 2 1

Printed in the United States of America.

Contents

Part III   Horizontal Sovereignty Games

Figures

Contributors

Tanja E. Aalberts is assistant professor in international relations at the Department of Political Science, University of Leiden. Her primary research interests include the continuity and change in the sovereignty principle on which she wrote her thesis as well as the relation between politics and international law. Among her primary publications is "The Future of Sovereignty in Multilevel Governance Europe—A Constructivist Reading" (*Journal of Common Market Studies*, 2004). In 2007, Tanja E. Aalberts was awarded the European Consortium for Political Research Jean Blondel PhD Prize for her thesis *Politics of Sovereignty*.

Rebecca Adler-Nissen is a doctoral candidate at the Department of Political Science, University of Copenhagen. Her current research focuses on flexible integration in the EU, national opt-outs, socialisation in international organizations, and the transformation of diplomacy. Her recent publications include "The Diplomacy of Opting Out: A Bourdieudian Approach to National Integration Strategies" (*Journal of Common Market Studies*, 2008) and "Behind the Scenes of Differentiated Integration" (*Journal of European Public Policy*, 2009). She was awarded the Gold Medal of the University of Copenhagen for her coauthored treatise on democratic theory, hermeneutics, and the EU's Constitutional Treaty (Djøf, 2005).

Jens Bartelson is professor of international relations at the Department of Political Science, University of Lund. His fields of interest include international political theory, the history of political thought, political philosophy, and social theory. Jens Bartelson has written extensively about the concept of the sovereign state and the philosophical foundations of modern international relations. He is the author of *A Genealogy of Sovereignty* (Cambridge University Press, 1995), *The Critique of the State* (Cambridge University Press, 2001), as well as of articles in journals such as *International Studies Quarterly*, *Political Theory*, *Review of International Studies*, *European Journal of International Relations*, *European Journal of International Law*, and *International Sociology*.

Thomas Gammeltoft-Hansen is a doctoral candidate at the Institute of Law, Aarhus University and the Danish Institute for International Studies (DIIS). His research focuses on the intersection between sovereignty and international refugee law, and he works on issues regarding migration management, EU asylum policy and the Danish EU opt-out on asylum and immigration. His recent publications include "Extraterritorial Responsibility under International Refugee Law" (in Gibney and Skogly, eds., *Extraterritorial Obligations in International Law*, UPP, forthcoming), "The Extraterritorialisation of Asylum and the Advent of 'Protection Lite'" (in Guiraudon, ed., The *International Politics of Immigration*, Edward Elgar, 2008) and "Filtering out the Risky Migrant" (Amid, 2006). Besides his research, Thomas Gammeltoft-Hansen works as policy analyst for the Danish Refugee Council.

Andrew Glencross holds a PhD from the European University Institute where he is currently a research fellow at the European Union Democracy Observatory. His research focuses on European integration, especially in comparison with the US experience of evolving federal arrangements, democratization, and constitutionalism. He has published articles on these topics in the journals *Democratization* and *European Political Science*. His other research interests include the concept and practice of political representation in the EU and its member states.

Christoph W. Herrmann is assistant professor of European and international economic law at the University of Munich. He currently works on monetary sovereignty and individual rights, but he also publishes on EU law and WTO law. Among his publications are "Monetary Sovereignty over the Euro and External Relations of the Euro Area" (*European Foreign Affairs Review*, 2002) and "Much ado about Pluto? The Unity of the Legal Order of the European Union Revisited" (in Cremona and de Witte, eds., *EU Foreign Relations Law: Constitutional Fundamentals*, Hart, 2008).

Anna Leander is associate professor at the Department of Intercultural Communication and Management, Copenhagen Business School and fellow at the Hansewissenschaftskolleg (Delmenhorst). Her research centres on the role of private authority and private military service provision in global politics. Currently she works on the commercialization of the use of force and has recently published *Eroding State Authority? Private Military Companies and the Legitimate Use of Force* (Centro Militare di Studi Strategici, 2006) and "The Market for Force and Public Security" (*Journal of Peace Research*, 2005), and she is co-editor of *Constructivism and International Relations: Wendt and His critics* (Routledge, 2006).

Ole Spiermann is professor in international law at the University of Copenhagen. His research encompasses a broad range of issues within international law, including international private law, EU law, human rights law, and constitutional law. He is the author of the most comprehensive Danish reference book on international law, *Moderne Folkeret* (2006, 3rd ed.), he was awarded the Gold Medal of the University of Copenhagen for his treatise on conceptualizations of sovereignty, *Enten & Eller: Studier i suve. ænitetsbegreber* (DJØF, 1995) and the 2007 Idman price for best Nordic treatise for his Cambridge doctoral thesis titled *International Legal Argument in the Permanent Court of International Justice: The Rise of the International Judiciary* (CUP, 2005).

Neil Walker is Regius professor of public law at the University of Edinburgh. From 2002 to 2008, he was professor of law at the European University Institute. He has published numerous articles and books on EU law, aspects of sovereignty, constitutional theory, and questions of theory and method in the legal and political philosophical study of European integration. Among other books, he is the editor of *Sovereignty in Transition* (Hart, 2003), co-editor of *The Paradox of Constitutionalism* (OUP, 2007) and coauthor of *Civilizing Security* (CUP, 2007). He is currently completing a manuscript on the constitutional direction of the EU.

Wouter G. Werner is professor of public international law at Vrije Universiteit Amsterdam. His main fields of research include the philosophical foundations of international law, the legal regime regulating the use of force, and the interplay between international law and international politics. As a scholar, he manages to complement legal theory with insights from international relations and sociology. He is the co-editor of *Governance and International Legal Theory* (Brill, 2004) and coauthor of "The Endurance of Sovereignty" (*European Journal of International Relations*, 2001).

Acknowledgments

The idea for the present volume grew out of our common interest in sovereignty. This shared fascination led us to organize a conference on Sovereignty Games at University of Copenhagen, March 29–30, 2007. By bringing together both legal and political scholars working on different subject areas related to sovereignty, we had a unique chance to test and challenge our hypotheses across both disciplinary and material boundaries. The conference proved most stimulating and we would like to thank all the contributors for their enthusiastic participation and willingness to revise and submit their papers for the final book.

We would like to acknowledge Morten Kelstrup and Marlene Wind for much encouragement and the research priority area "Europe in Transition" of the University of Copenhagen for financial support in realizing the conference. We would also like to thank the discussants at the conference, Morten Kelstrup, Ian Manners, Catharina Sørensen, and Frederik Rosén, for their fruitful comments and suggestions. Moreover, we are grateful for Virginie Guiraudon's inspired contribution throughout the conference and for Finn Stepputat's insightful comments to the introductory and concluding chapters. In particular, our warm thanks go to Stefano Guzzini from the Danish Institute for International Studies who chaired the concluding roundtable and from whose ideas and thoughts, the epilogue of the final book have substantially benefited.

Furthermore, we would like to thank series editor Dietrich Jung from the Danish Institute of International Studies as well as the editorial team at Palgrave for believing in the project and great support in the publication process.

A special acknowledgment is owed to Mathias Lydholm Rasmussen who throughout the project made a heroic effort in covering all the bases that allowed the editors to focus on the substance of the text. His skilled assistance was of immense value throughout the process. In addition, we express our thanks to Rikke Nørgaard for competent assistance with the index.

June 2008

Rebecca Adler-Nissen and Thomas Gammeltoft-Hanser

I

An Introduction to Sovereignty Games

Thomas Gammeltoft-Hansen and
Rebecca Adler-Nissen

Baha Mousa was working as a receptionist at the Haitham Hotel in Basra. On the morning of September 14, 2003, he was detained by British soldiers as they suspected the hotel was used as storage for hiding illegal weapons. Mr. Mousa was taken to a nearby military base where he was subjected to harsh interrogation techniques and brutally beaten until he died from his injuries on the following evening.

The incident attracted little attention until family relatives brought it to the British courts along with five other cases concerning the killing of Iraqi civilians following shooting incidents involving British armed forces.[1] The legal questions are anything but simple when trying to sort out who, if anybody, can be held responsible. What are the rules of the game? Does British law apply to soldiers operating in Iraq? Does the European Convention on Human Rights or other international human rights instruments? And if the answer to these questions is no, does that mean that British soldiers are simply free to do outside their territory what they clearly may not do inside?

In the end, the British House of Lords took a cautious approach. While British soldiers were deemed to be responsible in Baha Mousa's case since he died in British custody, the other five cases were dismissed as British forces were not deemed to exercise "effective control" in the legal sense of the word. Although activists have expressed great concern that this may create an accountability vacuum whenever states act abroad, the secretary of defense may have sighed in relief over not having to deal with complex human rights questions in situations where it was argued that they were never intended to apply. Yet, the House of Lords ruling is merely one round in the political and legal interplay around this issue. The remaining cases are currently being appealed to the European Court of Human Rights and the result remains to be seen.

More fundamentally, the earlier case points to the way new and global modes of organization challenge some of the most firmly established principles of sovereignty. In the world of today it has become increasingly common for states to operate vital functions outside their territory; not just military, but also production, finances, and migration control. At the same time, power and competences are progressively delegated to nonstate actors, be it private military companies in Iraq or supranational organizations such as the European Union (EU).

A pressing question is how to bring order to such a world. Sovereignty prescribes that ultimate and exclusive authority is maintained by each individual state within their territory. Yet, what happens when two sovereigns are occupying the same physical space or start bartering off sovereign prerogatives among each other? And how should we deal with new polities that are brought to coexist alongside the traditional state and increasingly take over responsibilities in areas that hitherto were thought to define the essence of sovereignty? While these instances may until recently have been downplayed as aberrations or exceptions to the ordinary functioning of the Westphalian order, it is becoming increasingly clear that this is more likely a systemic feature of a globalized age.

For the political scientist it may seem as if the concept of sovereignty, or at least how we use it, is undergoing rapid changes. In many EU debates across Europe, sovereignty is invoked by both the nationalists, eager to avoid further EU empowerment, and the Eurocrats, seeking to downplay the importance of further integration. Repeatedly the concept is brought to life to serve a multitude of purposes for anyone who demands it. Similarly, lawyers have identified a struggle of the current international legal framework to adapt to this reality. While some push for the extension and reassertion of state responsibility, others are keen to move beyond the Westphalian framework and push for the development of norms that can make international organizations, private companies, or even the individuals employed by them directly accountable.

In both the political and the legal spheres, what emerges is an expansion of the playing field relating to sovereignty. Whether it be state executives looking to avoid domestic scrutiny and legal responsibility by outsourcing core functions, or diplomats entering into a tricky game to simultaneously allow international cooperation and communicate a sense of sovereignty to the domestic audience, it is the ability to successfully maneuver among the varying and overlapping claims to sovereignty and its content that remains decisive. Understanding these processes is what motivates the present volume. Together, the contributors make the argument that state sovereignty is far from waning in the context of increased Europeanization and globalization. Rather, states and other actors have become increasingly creative in instrumentalizing their use of sovereignty to reassert legitimacy, power, and control in face of new challenges.

Speaking of Sovereignty

Few words have begotten so much dispute, confusion, and opaqueness as that of sovereignty. Thus, a first task for any work so prominently claiming the word as part of its title is necessarily to try and clarify what we are talking about. In its usage sovereignty appears to be a multifaceted technical concept. For starters it is generally approached somewhat different depending on the disciplinary baggage in which it is framed. In legal terms, sovereignty sets out the material and geographical scope of polity's authority and thereby the mutual exclusive claims in a world inhabited by a plurality of states; in political terms, sovereignty signifies the supremacy and inviolability of a state's institutions, its *unboundedness* both internally and externally (Espersen, Harhoff, and Spiermann 2003, 142). As a legal-political concept, sovereignty in this sense transgresses any simple definition, but it may perhaps best be described along the continuum of its different guises. These include sovereignty as a competence, a set of legal rights toward both the peers and the subjects of the polity; sovereignty as power or control, whether envisaged in political, economic, or symbolical terms; sovereignty as legitimacy, especially since the rise of debates on popular sovereignty; and sovereignty as personality, entailing a certain number of duties and obligations for those claiming it.

In these various incarnations scholars of several disciplines have been wedded to an ongoing discussion of whether, and to which extent, state sovereignty is still a meaningful concept in today's world. In particular, those claiming that sovereignty as a property of the state is absolute and indivisible have had a hard time identifying role models of states exercising sovereignty in this ideal typical sense. Rather, several analysts have argued that sovereignty as we know it is being challenged to a point where former UN General Secretary Boutros Boutros-Ghali concluded that "[t]he time of absolute and exclusive sovereignty... has passed" (Forsythe 2000, 22). But if sovereignty is an absolute condition, either states have it or they do not (Sørensen 1999, 593). Does it really make sense to argue that a state is 75 percent sovereign? (Wæver 1995, 417).

Those skeptical of the continued importance of state sovereignty identify at least four, somewhat interrelated, developments that can be argued to erode the traditional picture of the sovereign state in Europe. Firstly, as a development of interstate cooperation after 1945, more and more sovereign prerogatives have been transferred to international institutions. Whether it be military sovereignty, as in the case of NATO, economic sovereignty, as in the case of the World Trade Organization (WTO) and the World Bank, or most extensively political sovereignty, as in the case of the Organisation for Economic Co-operation and Development (OECD), Council of Europe, and the EU, states are seemingly willingly entering into arrangements that de jure or de facto confers or "pool" substantial aspects of their sovereign power (Sassen 1995, xv). This is particularly manifest in Europe where the EU transgresses the territorial boundaries and political authority of its member states (Mattli 2000). Those arguing that European integration is fundamentally compromising state sovereignty may point to the infringements on constitutional independence, the cessation of economic and monetary autonomy, and the increasing pooling of other core sovereign competences, such as immigration, internal security, defense, and foreign policy (Wallace 1999, 96; Kelstrup and Williams 2000, 4; Tokar 2001). In its place a system of overlapping decision making is appearing in which each member state has to succumb not only to qualified majority decisions among its peers, but also to hand over the right of initiative to supranational institutions and bow to an increasingly independent European judiciary (Werner and de Wilde 2001, 304). To some, this represents an abandonment and erosion of the traditional modes of regulations (Sur 1997, 436).

Second, what we normally refer to as globalization creates an image in which global flows of capital, commodities, and people seems to make it increasingly difficult for states to assert effective jurisdiction over their borders, economic flows, and indeed human activity in general (Sassen 1995; Krasner 1999, 105; Held, McGrew, Goldblatt, and Perraton 1999). Today, even the most developed states are struggling to control irregular migration; new transnational identity groups are emerging and their currencies and government bonds are being settled on the global financial markets. The state model alone simply does not stand the test of economic Europeanization and globalization, which entails a shift of components of state sovereignty to, for instance, private transnational corporations.

Third, since the Second World War and the decolonization process many states have emerged that clearly struggle to uphold any meaningful authority within their territory. These "quasi-states" seem to exist more by the grace and support of the international community than on any capacity on the part of the governments to establish internal power (Jackson 1993; Krasner 1999, 127). Thus, today the concept of state sovereignty risks being reduced to upholding international borders and the "negative sovereignty" conveyed by the international normative framework rather than the "positive sovereignty" that emerged in the early Westphalian era of modern state building (Jackson 1999). Further, it is clear that the formal equality of all states granted by this normative frame is not matched by any meaningful substantial equality (Sørensen 1999, 600). These weak states are intimately dependent on development aid, economic support, and security arrangements provided by its more developed colleagues. In turn, it becomes difficult if not impossible for these states to refuse when more developed states require access or favors, be it for reasons of security interests, oil concessions, or migration control.

Last, it has been argued that while before 1945 international law existed primarily to keep states apart, leaving the individual state sovereign in an "almost absolute sense, exercising supreme legal authority within its jurisdiction," the emergence of EU law and human rights law has substantially altered this relation (Forsythe 2000, 22). The willingness of governments to comply with rulings from the European Court of Justice (ECJ) and European Court of Human Rights is an ultimate demonstration that states are no longer totally free to exercise power within their territory regardless of the consequences for its subjects. The ECJ challenges national social sovereignty through its far-reaching legislation on citizen rights, which means that nation states no longer control who are legitimate participants in their national political societies. The judicial dialogue between the ECJ and national courts may also change the relationship between the legislative and judicial branch inside member states (Claes and de Witte 1998). So, is this the "end of sovereignty" (Camilleri and Falk 1992)?

On the other side of the fence stand those who believe that one should not readily buy into the historical assumptions or the analytical conclusions of the earlier claims. First, some scholars have argued that the arguments above build on an implicit assumption of a "heyday" of state sovereignty that is ultimately imaginary. Thus, while the earlier observations may be correct, one should take a closer look at the history of the Westphalian state system before making too strong a juxtaposition between the world today and 50 or more years ago. Stephen Krasner argues that the four different aspects of sovereignty also identified earlier—internal authority, recognition by other states, autonomy in decision making, and control over transborder flows— have never been fully claimed by any state; indeed, the various aspects are unlikely to be possessed simultaneously, as the strive for one may fundamentally impair the other (Krasner 1999, 3, 220).

Second, even among the proponents of the earlier arguments, there seems to be a recognition that elements of state sovereignty seemingly go untouched even when put under the duress of such fundamental changes. While enticing to think so, no international organization or institution has so far managed to escape the Statist framework and the legitimacy and legal base of these institutions remains the limited powers conferred to them by independent states (Keohane 1995, 172; Sur 1998, 1). Similarly, international political economists have stressed that the state is itself the necessary institution for a globalized market and argue that the capitalist state needs borderless globalization just as much as global markets are better able to reproduce themselves within national formations (Sakellaropoulos 2007). Further, the proclamations for the rise of the international judiciary as a threat to state sovereignty needs to be moderated by the homage paid by these bodies to the institution of state sovereignty and the extensive leeway granted to states by introducing, for example, "margins of appreciation" (Sur 1998, 4; Wilde 2005, 782).

Third, while we may speak of fundamental differences in the quality of and claims to sovereignty made by weak or "failed" states, what is perhaps most surprising is the resilience of their existence, which seems to reflect the continued strength of sovereignty as an international legal concept. Indeed, the increasing number of states and attempts to claim statehood over the last half century is perhaps the best evidence of the continued popularity of state sovereignty (Sørensen 1999, 594).

This suggests that we need to temper the claims that state sovereignty is being eroded because of globalization or Europeanization. In other words, what may be changing is not the importance of state sovereignty but a transformation of the social state to a headquarters state with contracted functions—implying that some state functions are either delegated or simply erode away (Sakellaropoulos 2007).

Other authors have questioned the ontological assumptions made earlier. Both sides of this discussion on "more or less" sovereignty are all build on the assumption that sovereignty is something that can somehow be measured "out there" as a property of the state, international organizations, or something else. In contrast to this view, a number of scholars have argued that both "sovereignty" and the "state" need to be understood as social and historical constructions (Kratochwil 1989; Ruggie 1993; Hansen and Stepputat 2005, 2).

Against the "descriptive fallacy" sovereignty must be understood more fundamentally as a claim to authority or as an institutional fact for the supreme ordering of power (N. Walker 2003, 6–7). To this end it is maintained as an existential value of international political and legal life that when mobilized allows for exceptional measures (Werner and de Wilde 2001, 297). Despite the challenges set out earlier we thus need to appreciate sovereignty as a still solid claim to the ultimate ordering power that constitutes the polity (N. Walker 2003, 8). It may be that the "speech act" of sovereignty is more complex to perform in an era of globalization and constitutional pluralism, yet it remains an essential political tool in constituting the functional national and international legal orders in which power politics are played out (N. Walker 2003, 6, 19–25).

In this sense, it becomes the very nature of sovereignty to be contested. It is exactly in the struggle over differing claims to authority that sovereignty comes most to the fore. The performative moments of sovereignty are strongest in times of crisis, when the state appears to loose the ability to ensure effective internal rule and freedom from external interference (Koskenniemi 1989, 210; Werner and de Wilde 2001, 287). It is also in these moments that the inquiry of this book becomes most evident. How can we understand workings of such sovereignty claims, who perform them and under which conditions? To advance this investigation in more detail, we propose an analytical framework, which pictures the state and other actors in a web of legal, economic, political, and cultural institutions and processes. It is this web that constitutes the playing field of what we have termed "sovereignty games."

The Constituents of Sovereignty Games

In furthering the idea of "sovereignty games," one should of course be careful how far the notion is pursued. "Game" is a loaded word and may immediately lead some to think about "game theory" or other rational choice approaches in which sovereignty may be won by one, lost by another. To be clear, the notion of "sovereignty games" as employed in the present volume is merely intended as a heuristic device rather than signifying any particular theoretical heritage (N. Walker 2003, 4).[2] Where we feel the idea of "games" is useful, however, is in emphasizing and bringing analytical attention to the three necessary components of any game—*rules, players, and moves.* It is around these three themes, and in particular the interplay between them, that the contributions to present volume are anchored.

First, by emphasizing *moves* as part of sovereignty games, we hope to progress beyond the descriptive level set out earlier. The present volume does not purport to give any answers as to whether states have more or less sovereignty in today's international order. Rather than looking to measure sovereignty as something "out there," the emphasis is rather placed on how it is used, or being played out, as legal and political practices. This allows for a more nuanced analysis of the strategic ways that states and other actors use the framework of sovereignty. In this sense, the moves in the sovereignty game may perhaps best be described as claims to authority and the social practices that surround them. Claims may be more or less institutionalized or settled, and more or less successful in bringing about change in the configuration of this authority (N. Walker 2003, 6–9; Werner 2004, 133). This explains why sovereignty continues to be such a coveted "property" at a time where state authority seems increasingly under pressure; it is in a time of crisis that what is ordinarily taken for granted needs to be most vigorously defended (Werner and De Wilde 2001, 287). Second, it opens for an analysis of how different moves may be made to achieve different outcomes, both in the horizontal games of claiming and relinquishing authority between states and in the vertical game of allocating competence between sub-state, state, and EU actors.

Further, our proposition by emphasizing the notion of sovereignty games is that these moves may be seen to have a strategic dimension, a skilled use of sovereignty claims. Indeed, a closer look at the different dimensions of sovereignty and how they are used to assert certain conceptual ideas, suggests that states are becoming more instrumental in their claims to sovereignty and skilled in adapting it to the challenges that they face. Just as much as the EU and its interaction with globalization and international legal regimes constrain the exercise of sovereign power for the individual state, it also provide new opportunities for exploiting the relationship that sovereignty establishes between states, institutions, and individuals.

Second, implicit in the notion of sovereignty games is the presupposition that someone is playing them. Who are then these *players*? Compared to scholars anxious to relocate sovereignty somewhere else, with sub-state entities or suprastate institutions, our particular perspective, or prism, keeps the sovereign state system and states in focus. By this we mean that even though changes in the world may create a window of opportunity for those looking to claim authority from other positions than that of the state, the contributions in this book generally affirm the homage paid in any articulation of sovereignty to some conceptualization of the state. Although ideas of "late sovereignty" (*Neil Walker*) and the possibility of "global community" (*Jens Bartelson*) both hint toward some kind of emancipative potential in relinquishing the statist optic, the state is still reaffirmed as an epistemic starting point that is inherently difficult to change.

This is not to say that states are the only players of sovereignty games. First, opening up the state "box" the contributions of the present volume also hope to shed light on how these games are played out at different levels, be it state executives (*Rebecca Adler-Nissen*), national banks (*Christoph Herrmann*) or individual lawyers (*Ole Spiermann*). Second, one should realize that playing the sovereignty game is not necessarily tied to a *personal* claim to sovereignty, but it may involve anyone seeking to influence or invoke such claims. This may be seen in both the outsourcing of security and migration control functions to private companies and third states (*Anna Leander and Thomas Gammeltoft-Hansen*) and in the role played by international courts and EU institutions (*Andrew Glencross*). Although these dynamics generally reaffirm state sovereignty at the discursive level, they nonetheless play a vital role in the interpretation and development of sovereign rights and duties.

Last, the idea of sovereignty games entails the existence of certain game *rules*. These rules may be understood at several levels. To some scholars, the conceptual content of sovereignty is simply that—game rules. Within international law, state sovereignty has been described as shorthand for a definite set of competencies, claims, and duties (Ross 1961, 42–56; Koskenniemi 1989, 197). Similarly, within international relations, sovereignty has been equated with a certain *doxa* of international political life, first and foremost the principle of nonintervention (Jackson 1999, 423f).

The struggle within both disciplines to determine the exact rules flowing from the concept, especially at a time when even core principles seem to be revised, has lead several authors to dismiss the concept entirely as, at best, superfluous and, at worst, directly misleading (Kelsen 1928, 320; Koskenniemi 1989, 198; Clapham 1999, 522; Henkin 1999). Yet, in the continued importance of the term in international life, what this critique may be pointing to is perhaps rather a need to probe deeper into the structures of sovereignty games. If we want to understand why both states and academics are still concerned with sovereignty, we need to examine how the concept works for those using it. In this sense, the "rules of the game" may not only be thought of as legal prescriptions or the principles of power relations but also reflect nonexplicit rules that structure the way we think and act in the name of sovereignty (Kratochwil 1989, 83).

To this end, the present volume begins with three contributions probing into the epistemic, ideological, and systemic foundations of sovereignty games. *Neil Walker* opens by arguing that while the rules of the sovereignty game at the ideological and systemic levels may be changing and relocating, the core epistemic functions on which these rules are premised remain intact. As long as we can identify something called the state, sovereignty will serve a key role both in conceptualizing the state and in conditioning its peer relations. For this purpose, we may employ the language of "late sovereignty" as a way of describing the way that states and other actors relate to and interpret sovereignty to reassert control, power, and legitimacy in changing contexts. Sovereignty games thus become strategic maneuvers through which sovereignty is claimed and reinterpreted to simultaneously protect autonomy and enhance influence on the international scene (see also N. Walker 2003, 19–25; Werner 2004, 131). Faced with globalization, transnational political activities, legal or illegal, and current strategic uses of traditional territorial understandings of sovereignty, for example, the US detentions at Guantanamo, it has been argued that it no longer makes sense to see sovereignty as a purely territorial phenomenon, as a spatially bounded concept. Rather, sovereignty can and should also be defined functionally, that is, by its effects and scope, which may allow for both Cuban and US sovereignty (and hence responsibility) to be exercised in different ways in the same territorial space (Raustiala 2005).

Following on from this, *Jens Bartelson* argues that we need to step back and take a critical look at the current academic debate for and against state sovereignty if we want to understand the analytical and normative significance of this concept in the future. A fair share of this debate comes down to an underlying conflict between those who maintain a semantic view to the concept of sovereignty as referring to something "out there" and those who take the nominalist position that sovereignty is simply a label through which we order the world. While under the former view, conflict continues to rage as to what exact norms and facts sovereignty denotes, the concept itself remains largely unaffected to changes at this level. More recently, however, studies in sovereignty have been drawn toward the linguistic turn. At first glance, much of this analysis would seem to suggest that the meaning sovereignty is wholly contingent on the political and discursive practices through which we claim it. Yet, the trap of such approaches, however much they may help our understanding of how the meaning of sovereignty may change in different contexts, is the irrefutable temptation to inject some assumptions and meanings to the concept by the researcher to meaningfully structure the analysis. In this sense, "the linguistic turn has brought us full circle" as any analysis of concepts and their referents necessarily presupposes some idea of what we are talking about. In each view sovereignty is thus reproduced and only a radical break with our conceptualization of the world as *international* will ever see it whither away.

Last, a more formulaic approach is presented, in which sovereignty must necessarily be analyzed through a double optic. For *Ole Spiermann* the basic rule of any sovereignty game is that something takes superiority over something else. Yet, this "something" is not fixed but dependent on a preliminary, material choice (Spiermann 1995, 320). In other words, sovereignty games become a question of which descriptive frame to employ.

Within national law, the framing has traditionally been based on the Bodinian concept of sovereignty as the absolute and perpetual power of a commonwealth, whereas in international law the state is poised as an international law subject. These frames may seem fundamentally at odds but are nonetheless both present and continue to play themselves out in the international adjudication of, for example, the European Convention on Human Rights and the ECJ. For the international lawyer it becomes a daily quest to operate between the two, and each frame may be used to emphasize different normative implications.

An underlying question for these first three contributions is the potential for change in the more deep-seated and epistemic levels. How does the playing out of sovereignty games affect the rules of the game? Here the contributors sketch out rather different scenarios. While to Ole Spiermann the input to the sovereignty game is open, and thus adaptable to new contexts and cases, the fundamental structure, the double structure, is unlikely to change. Nor will lawyers easily rid themselves of the historical frames in which the concept of sovereignty has been posited. Jens Bartelson, on the other hand, seems to suggest at least a transformative potential at the epistemic level of the sovereignty game. However far away such a world may seem, a fundamentally post-Statist order is fathomable. Between these stand Neil Walker who by employing the language of "late sovereignty" suggests a fundamental continuity even in the light of current changes and transformations in the actors and shapes of sovereignty games which points to an epistemic core that, while in principle not immutable, is likely to remain with us for the time being.

Playing the Games

To understand how these intriguing games of sovereignty are played out in practice, the theoretical and conceptual insights developed in the first part of the book are applied to a range of empirical cases in the remaining part of the book. These chapters are structured around two dimensions of the instrumentalization of claims to authority, which seem to be particularly striking in the European context: the horizontal and the vertical sovereignty games. In both dimensions, various actors aim at simultaneously enhancing autonomy and legitimacy by playing strategically on the discursive and legal structure of sovereignty.

The vertical dimension of the sovereignty games are played out as authority is passed strategically up and down between different political and legal levels to enhance political autonomy. International and regional organizations provide a particularly useful playing ground for such strategic moves and sovereign claims become instrumental to carve out new spaces for inter- and transnational decision making. In vertical games, political and administrative elites are playing on the different legal and symbolic structures related to sovereignty to enhance their autonomy in both the domestic and the international arena.

In comparison, horizontal sovereignty games are characterized by the conceptual stretching of sovereignty to cover activities outside the area traditionally reserved for exercises of ultimate authority—the national territory. Facilitated by international institutions and private companies, everything from immigration policies to military interventions can be exercised far away from where the decisions were originally taken, but with the crucial legitimization built into the language of sovereignty. By tactically shifting sovereignty outside the national territory and to nonstate actors, political autonomy is enhanced and maybe even justified as it is brought to bear on particular problems stemming from globalization.

Vertical Sovereignty Games

The second part of the book deals with vertical sovereignty games. This type of game emerges when states, often driven by national executives, are playing on the legal and symbolic arsenal provided by the conceptual framework of sovereignty to enhance their autonomy in both the domestic and European or international arena. Sovereignty seems to shift up and down from levels above and below the state. Thus, the handing over of formal powers to the EU or other international organizations may be instrumental in reasserting both domestic and international control.

Recent decisions taken by states regarding the delegation of their monetary sovereignty is analyzed in the chapter by *Christoph Herrmann*. Traditionally, the right of coinage has been considered to constitute one of the core elements of sovereignty of modern nation states. However, hardly any other "core element" of sovereignty demonstrates a greater variety in its usage and its failure alike. Some states have deliberately no currency of their own; others adopt foreign currencies or bind their own tightly to them. The Euro zone with 13 member states have transferred their monetary sovereignty to a supranational institution, while other states put extreme pressure on their citizens to protect the currency and to enforce its use, often without success. These decisions are part of a vertical dynamic where monetary sovereignty is passed around between the domestic and international layers of authority.

States play out sovereignty games to maximize their power drawing on the exact same processes of Europeanization and globalization that are seemingly constraining them. The main actors gaining autonomy however are not states per se but one particular branch of the state—national executives. *Rebecca Adler-Nissen* demonstrates how opt-outs from the EU and EC Treaties obscure the degree to which statehood is changing because of regional integration. In international and regional cooperation, sovereignty claims are made by national politico-administrative elites in what may be termed a "two-dimensional sovereignty game." Hence, the controversial opt-outs from common currency and the cooperation on immigration, asylum and civil law granted to the United Kingdom and Denmark with the Maastricht Treaty in 1992 allow the mediators to preserve the figure of an autonomous state despite its entanglement in the European integration process. Serving the purpose of legitimizing continued EU membership to the Euroskeptic domestic audiences, the diplomatic strategies of opting in and out articulate a game, an "organized duplicity" that allow states to pick and choose from the buffet of new EU legislation. The game, however, easily gets out of control as the opt-outs are translated into diplomatic routines and popular guarantees are challenged. This demands a continuous reinterpretation sovereignty to fit the two dimensions where it is exercised.

In his chapter, *Andrew Glencross* examines the democratic consequences of the European sovereignty games, which are driven by both ideological motivations and strategic calculation. Glencross argues that the EU is a hybrid polity combining federal and confederal principles, which is why member states and the EU share the claim and burden of representing citizens. The balance of confederalism and federalism can be seen as a tacit sovereignty game between two antagonistic principles. States have asserted aspects of sovereignty (through the treaties, domestic, and EU politics) to manage expectations about integration in the face of unexpected supranational developments. The problem of controlling the course of integration to the satisfaction of states and citizens constitutes a sovereignty game with dramatic consequences for democracy. Responses to this "democracy game" include democratizing the EU or redefining democracy to make it compatible with the representation of states. Both responses are problematic and the chapter suggests that the impact of sovereignty games on democracy is still not fully understood. There is no simple solution for ensuring that these games do not take democracy as a hostage.

Horizontal Sovereignty Games

In the remaining part of the book, three chapters are devoted to the analysis of how claims to sovereignty transform our sense of geography as sovereign functions are outsourced or privatized. The contributors explore how states engage in conceptual stretching because they increasingly experience that they are constrained by domestic and international legislation restricting their exercise of power. Policies to disconnect state power from the sovereign territory, understood as the locus of these responsibilities, are therefore starting to grow increasingly fashionable. Most well-known is the US administration's argument that because the offshore detention facilities at the Guantanamo base lies in Cuba and is not part of the sovereign US territory, certain responsibilities toward the detainees can be avoided. However, similar arguments are heard in Europe, as member states assert that legal obligations such as the Refugee Convention cannot be made applicable to migration control conducted in international waters. These arguments are illustrative of recent attempts to "reconstruct" the notion of sovereign treaty responsibilities, such as human rights obligations, as something solely pertaining to the sovereign territory and separate from the extraterritorial acts of states. Whether or not one accepts such arguments, it is evident that sovereign power conducted "out of sight" of national judiciaries, media, and civil rights groups is likely to substantially affect access to rights otherwise owed to those subjected to that power.

This horizontal broadening of the concept of sovereignty is particularly intriguing in the processes of legitimization of the use of armed force in new circumstances and locations. *Tanja Aalberts* and *Wouter Werner* examine how sovereign claims have been used to push the boundaries of self-defense. Originally, the right to self-defense was included in the UN Charter as a limited and temporary exception to the prohibition on the use of force. Paradoxically, however, the attempts to outlaw the use of force results in the creation of several new discursive spaces to legitimize the use of force: armed force could (and should) now be justified in terms of exceptions, as exceptional measures aimed at restoring and protecting sovereignty and normalcy. This discursive practice already started in the late 1940s but gained new momentum after the 9/11 attacks. Werner and Aalberts demonstrate how the recent attempts to further stretch the limits of the sovereign right to self-defense is linked to large-scale reconstructions of domestic societies where "the enemy" can be found both inside and outside the national borders.

An opposite but related trend in this horizontal stretching of sovereignty claims is the commercializing of state functions such as the legitimate use of force. *Anna Leander* explores how states delegate security provisions to private actors. Leander argues that when private actors take the use of force into their own hands, be it as terrorists or as mercenaries, this does not weaken the state "monopoly" on the use of force. The outsourcing and privatization of the use of force strengthens security establishments and those who share their interests both within the field of security but perhaps more importantly in relation to actors of other fields. The commercialization of the use of force is hence not undermining sovereignty as much as it is altering its meaning. Security establishments have effectively extended their say in how sovereignty is understood and have given security a greater place in sovereign practices, sovereignty is "secured" not undermined.

A similar argument of the horizontal broadening of sovereignty can help to gain an understanding of how the global migration pressures are countered by the emergence of global migration control regimes. *Thomas Gammeltoft-Hansen* explores the sovereign function of migration control as it is "extra-territorialized" and "commercialized" in Europe. He demonstrates how and why the traditional picture of the refugee arriving at the border and surrendering herself to the authorities uttering the magical word, "asylum," is increasingly seldom. Rather, migrants and refugees are sought intercepted before they arrive, either by EU states acting extraterritorially or by private or third state partners. Over the last years, the EU has radically expanded its migration control on the high seas and forged a range of cooperation agreements with North African countries to ensure their cooperation in naval interdiction operations. By moving migration control outside their territory, states are not acting beyond the law; rather they exploit the conceptual dualism and interpretative space inherent in the notion of sovereignty and jurisdiction. This has allowed states to play on more territorial understandings of jurisdiction or shift legal regimes to perform migration control while simultaneously shifting corollary human rights obligations to its southern neighbors. As such, this chapter demonstrates how the deliberate delegation of traditional sovereign rights through horizontal sovereignty games is often countered by an increase in the actual capacity to exercise control.

Together, the contributions on horizontal and vertical sovereignty games demonstrate that state sovereignty is not just eroding with processes of Europeanization; rather, the application of sovereign power takes new creative forms as states play sovereignty games. The main argument brought forward is that states and other political and legal actors are not just observing passively how economic flows transgress their borders or how the national legal order is subjugated to international and supranational EU law. Instead, they engage in new practices and modify understandings of their own sovereignty, which, paradoxically, may end up strengthening their position vis-à-vis other actors not only in Europe but also on the global scene.

How these practices may affect the institution of sovereignty in the longer run remains to be seen. How stable is the present situation? Revisiting once more the theoretical debate, the concluding chapter attempts to draw together and reflect on the insights provided in the analysis carried out earlier. The sovereignty games described may certainly carry a transformative power, yet one should be careful when discussing where such transformations occur. Thus, we present a new model to conceptualize three layers of sovereignty and the dynamics between them. The most visible layer constitutes sovereignty as everyday *practices*, be they social, legal, political or symbolic, and it is at this layer that the most obvious sovereignty games are played out. In playing these games, however, reference is inevitably made to a second layer, namely the concept of sovereignty as legal and political *authority*. This is the layer from where norms and rules are derived and where contestation is increasingly referred as sovereign practices probe the boundaries of hitherto established principles. Below these is the *epistemic* layer. This is where sovereignty simultaneously constitutes and is reconstituted; here sovereignty represents a way of thinking of the foundation and structure of the political and legal world.

Although at the level of practices, sovereignty appears relatively open to change, it is a more intricate question whether new practices trickle down to the deepest layers. Sovereignty skeptics argue for the emergence of either an empire or a cosmopolitan commonwealth, yet our analysis does not support any radical break to a post-sovereign order. Sovereignty may find new guises and adapt to changing conditions, but as a foundational institution it is likely to remain with us for the time being. Thus, the contribution of the present volume is rather centered on the analysis of how this powerful concept operates today and we hope that the following chapters will provide a set of tools for both practitioners and academics to continue reflection on this topic.

Notes

1. *Al-Skeini and others v. Secretary of State for Defence.* June 13, 2007. House of Lords. UKHL 26.
2. To be certain, the metaphor of "sovereignty games" is not original to this volume. In particular, it has been employed by Robert H. Jackson in his seminal book *Quasi-States: Sovereignty, International Relations and the Third World*

(Cambridge: Cambridge University Press, 1993) and by Georg Sørensen in "Sovereignty: Change and Continuity in a Fundamental Institution" (In *Sovereignty at the Millennium*, ed. Robert Jackson, Oxford: Blackwell and Political Studies Association, 1999). We are indebted to these authors at the nominal and conceptual level; however the idea of "sovereignty games" as developed in the present volume does not build in any large part on the theorizations in these works.

Part I

Theoretical Perspectives

2

The Variety of Sovereignty

Neil Walker

Introduction: Relocating Sovereignty

This chapter seeks to engage simultaneously with three related sets of challenges to sovereignty in contemporary understandings and with three questions of sovereignty's "relocation" that issue from these challenges. First, and at the highest level of abstraction, "relocating" conveys the search for something that has been lost. It suggests that for whatever reason or combination of reasons, the conceptual relevance of sovereignty is no longer apparent—because either it is simply redundant or it has become such a protean concept as to be meaningless—and that active efforts have to be made to rediscover this sense of relevance. Second, by "relocating" sovereignty we may have in mind a less definitive but still fundamental theoretical project, for even if, as the present chapter urges, we resist the idea that sovereignty is in mortal conceptual danger, we should avoid the opposite mistake of its conceptual reification. We should instead acknowledge that it may require to be repositioned and reordered within our conceptual cartography—that the role of sovereignty in the mental map through which we make sense of our legal, social, and political world(s) has to be readdressed. Third, and final, "relocating" carries a more basic spatial connotation. If sovereignty has traditionally been viewed as an attribute of states and of relations between states, then in a less state-centered world we have to be aware of the various new sites—subnational, supranational, and functional—at which sovereignty or its equivalent may be located, or at least where the attributes of sovereignty may be shared with traditional state sites. What is more, we are likely to discover that it is in significant part this third spatial sense of relocation that underpins the conceptual discontinues and challenges suggested by the first two, nonspatial senses of relocation.

Thinking about Thinking about Sovereignty

Even to think about rethinking—and relocating—a concept so basic to our traditional understanding of the social world as sovereignty requires some prior appreciation of the reasons why it occupies such a basic place and of the dangers thereby posed. Two clusters of threshold questions in particular will be addressed.

In the first place, as sovereignty has traditionally been associated with ideas of a special kind of power—one that is both final and presumptively legitimate—it is no surprise that there is much contestation as regards the things that are deemed the appropriate subject of sovereignty and as regards the modalities through which they are recognized as sovereign. Should we associate sovereignty with individuals or, as is commonly the case, with forms of social organization? If the latter, are we concerned only with holistic forms of social organization such as states, or with specific dimensions of social organization, such as those concerned with money, security, border control, or the environment? Through what register of regulation is sovereignty best conceived—legal, political, or economic, or some combination of all? Is the sovereignty prize something that by its nature must be exclusive or distinctive to the party who wins it, or can it be shared around? And however we define the subjects and modalities of sovereignty, how much if any of it can be found in today's world, or will remain in any future possible world? All of these are deeply contested questions, and all admit of deeply diverse answers. In the face of this, how, if at all, can we hope to lend any order or coherence to the debate over sovereignty? Where, in other words, are we to begin to locate or relocate the concept of sovereignty in the first and second senses referred to earlier?

Secondly, if sovereignty is such a basic idea, how do we understand the connection between the second order question as to the nature and existence of that quality of "basicness" and first order questions that take that basic quality for granted? How, in other words, do we relate the question whether sovereignty is an inescapable and irreplaceable feature of the social world as opposed to a category of social thought that is in danger of becoming obsolete (as the first meaning of "relocating" suggests), to other questions concerning its particular and contingent manifestations? In turn, this subdivides into two forms of inquiry and two types of difficulty—one to do with the normative or evaluative dimension of sovereignty and the other concerning its explanatory dimension. In normative terms, what is the relationship between the irreducible core of sovereignty, if there is such a thing, and its ideal form? If sovereignty is an inevitable social category, or at least a highly resilient one, does it make sense to ask whether and how it may be shaped differently, and just how differently may it be shaped without it ceasing to be sovereignty? In explanatory terms, how do we think of such a deeply embedded concept as sovereignty in a dynamic mode? How, in the face of the pressures we mentioned under the third, spatial, sense of relocation suggested earlier, do we avoid the danger of conceptual rigidity, and so either of ignoring the evidence and reifying sovereignty as something that is entirely immune from change or of too easily conceding its redundancy or obsolescence? Alternatively, how in the face of these same pressures do we avoid the opposite danger of conceptual vacuity, of treating sovereignty as stretched in various different directions but essentially unbreakable—as a highly contingent and event-sensitive category whose resilient causal significance is lost and whose continuity is reduced to the merely nominal (Bartelson 2006)?

These two prior considerations—the question of finding *any* common ground within sovereignty's highly contentious politics of definition, and the question of the relationship between a sovereignty "core" on the one hand and, on the other, its evolved "superstructure"—inform the way in which the present chapter proceeds. In what follows we seek to address the problems that they pose and the issues that they raise through a conceptual apparatus that grounds sovereignty in certain conditions of possibility that are sufficiently historically and politically grounded to exclude certain modalities of authority but flexible enough to allow meaningful variations on a theme. A key move in this exercise is to separate sovereignty into different dimensions of significance, thereby allowing us to address it as a concept that exhibits internal *variety* rather than one that comes in different *varieties*. These dimensions are, in turn, epistemic, symbolic, and systemic.[1]

The Dimensions of Sovereignty

Epistemic

In a basic epistemic sense, sovereignty may be seen as a particular way of knowing, representing, and ordering the social and political world, as something that "silently frames the conduct of much of modern politics" (Jackson 1999). Unlike medieval forms of authority linked to and divided in accordance with a myriad of statuses, functions, and locations, sovereign authority implies the existence and, indeed, describes the form of a specialized species of political authority, one developed through a sharp differentiation of public and private domains and subsequent generalization of the public domain (Loughlin 2003, ch. 5; Grimm 2005). First and foremost through the modern state and in terms of its claim to hold such specialized public-political authority comprehensively within a particular territory, sovereignty involves conceiving of the possibility of creating an ultimately authoritative "unity [out] of a manifold" (Lindahl 1997). The perspective of sovereignty is a perspective that imagines and identifies discrete polities or political communities that can organize and act in the name of an undifferentiated collective notwithstanding an internal diversity of interests, values, and wills. Given its framing properties, the perspective of sovereignty is epistemically before both politics and law and does not necessarily privilege either. Rather it is a process of imagining the polity that enables a form of politics and a form of law both within and between such polities.

What does this basic epistemic framing of politics and law imply for our understanding of the potential of both? As regards politics, while what is enabled through the sovereignty frame is by no means *all* of politics, sovereignty is certainly the organizing template for two key types of politics (Huysmans 2003). First, politics self-defined by their key actors as "constitutional politics" (i.e., politics within that legal-constitutional framework of the polity that is presupposed and sustained under the authority of the "sovereign"); second, politics self-defined by their key actors as "international" or "transnational" politics (i.e., politics between thus created and sustained polities on the basis of the doctrine of "sovereign equality"). This leaves at least two other forms of politics that are not directly framed by sovereignty. First the very politics of sovereignty assertion that precedes and always underpins the successful "sovereign" frame are themselves not structured by the sovereign frame, except as an aspiration (see e.g., Tierney 2005). Indeed, these politics of "sovereign becoming" point us toward the well-known paradox of sovereignty as both *pouvoir constituant* and *pouvoir constitué,* as ruler and ruled, creator and created, political and legal, Schmitt and Kelsen.Second, there are these diverse forms of national or transnational politics that ignore or resist the framing of constitutional or international law. These politics will also be a form of collective action, and thus of political agency—whether we are dealing with transnational civil society or the Al-Qaeda terror network. Accordingly, to be effective actors, and indeed, to be identifiable as distinct actors, the bearers of these political forms need to be organized, however fluidly, so as to assume and construct their own sense of unity (Lindahl 2003). However, beyond this basic epistemic common ground, resistance does not imply imitation. Whether because their defining purpose is critique, destabilization, or destruction, or because they envisage a new kind of political authority, they do not claim the comprehensiveness or continuity of decision making authority required for sovereign polity constitution and maintenance.

If some politics remains capable of being conceptualized other than under the sovereign frame, it is more contentious whether any law does. For many legal positivists, all domestic law flows from the command of the sovereign. Even those who would modify or reject a traditional Austinian or Kelsenian conception of positivism in favor of a conception of law as a complex form of custom or social practice (see e.g., MacCormick 1993; Wade 1996) or as a matter of natural (Finnis 1980) or socially constructed and contended (Dworkin 1986) right or obligation, are apt to trace the formal pedigree of law—if certainly not its moral credentials—back to the sovereign creator (although there is also a robust tradition of legal pluralism that would reject even this formal pedigree in favor of a more diverse sourcing of original legal-normative authority in other sites of social and political power such as indigenous communities, the workplace, and even the family (see e.g., Santos 1995). Of course, such is the self-referentiality of law—the claim of law to provide its own final source of authority, that even the sovereign creator is typically reconceptualized within legal discourse as a construction of law, and, it often follows, as something that can be modified by law—for example, through the commonly available technique of amending the constitution, and so changing the form of the "sovereign" law-giver, by virtue of a mechanism provided for in the constitution itself. In other words, within domestic legal discourse "law" is seen as before "politics," even if it remains palpably the case that the effectiveness of law is sustained or complemented by an underlying political commitment to sovereignty assertion and maintenance.

What of international law? Clearly this too presupposes sovereignty, in that sovereignty identifies the salient actors of international law. Yet there is a hint of paradox here. Given that its overriding purpose is to establish and sustain the identity of the polity qua polity, does the very sovereignty claim that makes *international* law possible not also, in its resistance to any external claim that might compromise that purpose, render international *law* impossible? As Koskenniemi (1989) famously suggested, is not the very idea of law *between* sovereigns oxymoronic? Or, can we, with Kelsen (1960), claim to rescue the purity of international law either by positing it as having its own independent and super-ordinate sovereign source, or more modestly, by understanding it as emerging and stabilizing itself at the point of coincidence between various national sovereign wills?

To summarize then, in epistemic terms, sovereignty frames much of politics and, arguably, all of law. It does so by limiting and constraining the space for both other than in its own terms, while simultaneously problematizing one aspect of the field of law that it helps to create.

Symbolic

Here we are concerned with sovereignty as a symbol of power—as an expressive claim to authority. The claim to sovereignty is important in providing a distinctive discursive register in which the bid for ultimate or supreme authoritative unity is made. That is to say, that the claim is made to *sovereignty* rather than, say, to *representation* or *agency* more generally, involves a certain type of signification. The invocation of sovereignty involves a "speech act" (see e.g., Austin 1961; Searle 1969; Werner and de Wilde 2001) with not only locutionary and illocutionary force but also *perlocutionary* force. It has real effects on social and political practice, and these effects are inseparable from sovereignty's particular history and present constellation of meaning associations. If ideology is about the ways in which meaning is constructed to facilitate domination, then sovereignty is a deeply ideological category.

For example, if we look to the internal or intra-polity dimension of sovereignty, the sovereign label is often reserved for a particular type or degree of unity of institutional arrangements over and above the basic epistemic unity of a polity; namely, a vertical and rigidly hierarchical political architecture, which may be contrasted, often unfavorably, with a more horizontalized and heterarchical system of "governance" or "network" arrangement. Equally, the language of split or divided sovereignty, or even post-sovereignty, is often used of federal states where the basic epistemic unity of the polity under the federal constitution remains undeniable but where there is a strong territorialized division of institutional authority. Adjectives are also important here, with, for example, the parliamentary sovereignty/popular sovereignty divide tracking diverse claims as to the preferred mode of democratic legitimacy and organization of the polity. Here, in the domestic domain, there is undoubtedly a degree of fluidity and contestation around sovereignty, often reflecting particular historical compromises in state-building and state-sustenance. Crucially, however, behind this diversity there has remained a deeper common ideological assumption that ultimate authority over the internal operation of the polity is exhausted by these internal sources and modes of expression and that there is no remainder available to external sources.

If we turn now to external sovereignty, there are two salient and connected ideological uses of sovereignty, both of which reaffirm the predominance of the state in the international domain. Here, strikingly, the use of the language of sovereignty is less fluid and more hegemonic. One pattern of usage concerns the deep resistance to the conceptualization of any entity other than the national or pluri-national state as a unity that can be legitimately represented as sovereign. In other words, the title of sovereign is never granted by states to nonstate entities, and indeed rarely even claimed by nonstate entities (other than entities that themselves aspire to statehood), even in the case of the most mature and "state-like" nonstate polity—the European Union (EU), and even though the EU in many of its other claims such as "supremacy" or "primacy" and "direct effect" of laws seems to presuppose and affirm its own epistemic unity (de Witte 1995; de Burca 2003). The second concerns the resilience of the language of sovereignty as a code for understanding the connection between states—the idea that relations between states are essentially relations between indivisible sovereigns with exhaustive title to represent these states, regardless of the internal division of authority within each state. In other words, the existence of a strong currency of thought within a federal state such as the United States to the effect that its internal authority may be split or divided, tends not to translate in ideological terms into a self-conception and self-projection as anything other than unqualifiedly sovereign in the external domain (Keohane, 2002). In turn, this close fit between the internal and the external claim to sovereignty is made possible by the conviction, already referred to, that the plenitude of ultimate authority over internal affairs, however diversely institutionalized and however contested its legitimate mode of expression, continues to reside within the polity. This equation of internal and external sovereignty as both implying an exhaustive *internal* authority sharply highlights the difficulties of binding such self-referential units of authority to the stable discipline of international rules.

Systemic

International relations theorists often use the language of "system"—as in the "system of states" or the "Westphalian system" (see Jackson 1999). Sovereignty is again important in accounting for this systemic quality. Apart from its epistemic and symbolic dimensions, sovereignty speaks to an idea of system or structure—of wholeness and self-regulation, of latency and self-reproduction. The very systemic qualities of the sovereignty configuration make for a degree of path dependency. In the final analysis, however profound the epistemic difficulties of establishing a stable legal order between sovereign states, the deeply iterative pattern of their mutual recognition as the key actors of the international system provides a stability to the general enterprise of international law and the general practice of international relations, if not necessarily to some of their particular manifestations. Conversely, if we look beyond the state form, the same systemic qualities resist other forms of recognition.

The example of the EU again points us toward one of the significant ways in which recognition is rendered problematical. The difficulty for a nonstate polity, even one as powerful as the EU, to break into or break up the sovereignty frame is exacerbated by the fact that in the world of discrete territorial states each claiming supreme authority, just because the dominant ideological mode of that claim has been one of exclusive authority within the relevant territorial domain, the claim of other putative sovereigns, to be plausible as supreme claims within the default system, also have to be exclusive claims over territory. If, instead, a new claim were to countenance competing claims of "old sovereigns" within the same territorial domain, then, since any such competing prior sovereignty claim would by definition be exclusive, that prior claim would be incapable of the mutual and reciprocal act of recognition of the sovereign title of the new claim. If coexistence within the one territorial domain is not permitted, in short, then the systemic logic of sovereignty tends to drive toward new claims themselves being made in territorially exclusive terms. The EU tries to escape this bind by claiming a kind of "functional" authority (as do other supranational organizations, if to a lesser extent)—one that is not a claim to ultimate authority over all matters within a territory, but only as regards the particular functions that fall within its asserted jurisdiction. It seeks thus to decouple the claim to finality (or originality) of authority—of nondependence on any other authority—from the stronger claim to exclusivity (N. Walker 2003). But as we have seen, the EU shies clear of the explicit language of sovereignty in describing this "sovereign-like" claim, and its member states would certainly emphatically deny in their dominant political discourse that the EU is a rival sovereign (de Witte 1995).

So a kind of zero-sum strategic logic attaches to sovereignty, competing claims tending to be framed in the same exclusive language or not at all. We are used to that in the language of domestic politics, in contexts of secessionist or other nationalist movements (Tierney 2005). In the transnational context, this zero-sum systemic logic joins with the ideological difficulty of nonstate entities claiming sovereignty to create a situation in which nonstate entities tend to be doubly resisted. The logic of the system makes it difficult for them to make a claim to independent or original authority without also making the stronger claim to exclusivity, but in any case the stronger and more systemically orthodox claim to sovereignty would be strongly denied them on ideological grounds unless they were also to make—and succeed with—the claim to statehood. Accordingly, however plausible and effective the "sovereign-like" claims of a body such as the EU, there remain a degree of systemic and ideological drag impeding their full acceptance.

Beyond claims to independent polity status by nonstate entities, the conservative quality of the systemic logic can also be seen at work in the broader unfolding of international relations and international law. On the one hand, there is no deep structural reason why nonstate actors should not have some kind of "title" or agency or personality in international law short of sovereignty, and indeed in recent years we have seen a substantial growth in this, with NGOs and other nonstate actors increasingly allowed standing before international tribunals and in international legislative contexts (see e.g., Jackson 1999; Held 2004). On the other hand, there are structural or systemic limits to this of three sorts. First, as the historically dominant actors of the international system, states will not lightly use their sovereignty to reduce their own authority. Second, and reflecting this, many of the substantive precepts of international law such as equality, noninterference, sovereign immunity, and the like have a conservative quality, a disposition to maintain the formal internal and external sovereignty of states that is the starting point of international law—the international "state of nature" (Knop 1993; Kingsbury 1998). Third, the point or purpose of having title crucially depends on whom you can claim to legitimately represent and whom you can effectively commit. Since, in the first place, notions of legitimate representation are developed in the image of the state and, in particular, the population of the state is deemed to be the relevant community of attachment—the object represented—and since, in the second place, the monopoly or at least the preponderance of the means of effective implementation lies in the hands of the states as the sole domestic sovereigns, again this marginalizes nonstate actors.

The Primacy and Resilience of the Epistemic Core

So while sovereignty is far from being a purely nominal category—a loose container of many and quite distinctive *varieties*, sovereignty is nevertheless a multilayered idea, one that displays considerable internal *variety*. We can distinguish between the core epistemic features of sovereignty that furnish the idea with its basic integrity on the one hand, and its secondary symbolic and systemic properties on the other. The symbolic and systemic features are finally contingent—all ideology is contestable and all systems are more or less open to transformation. If we recall our two prior questions of deep definitional contestation and of finding a balance between immutability and excessive deference to changing geopolitical circumstances, we should focus on both the practical interweaving and the analytical separation of these different layers or dimensions. The effects of the sovereignty frame cannot be fully appreciated without understanding the close relationship between the epistemic on the one hand and the symbolic and the systemic on the other. Yet the space for transforming while still retaining the sovereignty frame depends on the possibilities of reimagining and asserting the symbolic and systemic dimensions differently from their dominant traditional formulations against the backdrop of an unchanging epistemic core. The limits thereby set are both sociological and normative. They ask both to what extent it is plausible to alter the contingent symbolic and systemic dimensions against a background where the epistemic remains constant, and how and in what circumstances this may be done in a justifiable manner—one that redeems the promise of self-legislation, rights protection, and popular accountability contained in many claims of popular sovereignty (Habermas 1996) rather than reverting to older sovereign-associated traditions of peremptory top-down power or community reification (Yack 2001).

Elsewhere, I have coined the term "late sovereignty" (N. Walker 2003) to try to capture the domain of possibility of such internal transformation. The label serves two main purposes. Positively, the idea of late sovereignty seeks to capture both the force of the sociological dynamic and the flexibility of the normative possibilities that is reflected in the shift in the ideological and systemic superstructure of sovereignty. Late sovereignty, with its uneven, often resisted but gradually self-reinforcing openness toward forms of "sovereign-like" authority beyond the state does appear to be increasingly distinct from and discontinuous with earlier forms of Westphalian sovereignty. The global configuration of authority of 2008 looks very different from the postwar world into which the emphatically state-centered United Nations was born only 60 years ago.

Negatively, the idea of late sovereignty also suggests the resilience of this new phase. On the one hand, late sovereignty is probably irreversible. Once categories of "sovereign-like" authority have been conceded or successfully claimed beyond the state, it is hard if not impossible to imagine the circumstances under which we might rewind to the old world of purely or predominantly state sovereignty. This is not to say, of course, that we cannot imagine the powerful reassertion of uncompromising sovereign authority by states in certain times and places—think of the United States in the period after the cold war, and, more forcibly still, since 9/11. Rather, it is to suggest that the cumulative force of the changing systemic imperative and of attendant shifts in the ideological climate militates against any general reversal in these terms.

However, we should not assume that the late phase of sovereignty is also a terminal phase. Indeed, the burden of proof points in the opposite direction. This is so because anyone who questions the continuing robustness of the sovereignty frame and is skeptical of the sustainability or acceptability of transformation within that frame of the sort outlined earlier—and so contemplates the final breaking of the frame of sovereignty, must ask an even more formidable set of questions of any more fundamental alternative. Having given up on the task of "relocating" the lost or disappearing world of sovereignty, they must commit themselves to replacing sovereignty at the epistemic level. They must ask how, if at all, to conceive of an alternative matrix of political agency in which sovereignty no longer figures prominently, or perhaps at all. Then they must ask the same sociological and normative questions that we ask of sovereignty. At the level of social praxis, is such an alternative framing, whatever form it might take, strategically possible and plausible? At the normative level, would this alternative framing produce more just answers to questions of the overall pattern and distribution of normative power relevant to the ordering of social relations?

What this makes clear is that whether it is possible to replace the epistemic frame of sovereignty, and to do so in a manner that meets the threshold of sociological plausibility and normative adequacy—are deep questions—by definition *epistemological* questions about the very possibility of other ways of knowing and ordering the world—and ones that have never yet convincingly been answered in the positive (Huysmans 2003). Indeed, on this epistemically grounded view of sovereignty, it would appear that what passes for empirical claims or predictions or normative aspirations concerning the demise of sovereignty and the reinvention of politics by other means—whether they focus on the growth of politically intelligent forms of sub-state and cross-state nationalism, or on the rise of regional systems such as the EU, or on the intensification of transnational economic power and its invigilation by bodies such as the World Trade Organization, or on the emergence of a new American "empire"—typically tend to speak only to internal movements in the ideological and systemic superstructure (N. Walker 2003; 2006; Van Roermund 2003) of the sort that precisely seem to fit within the container of late sovereignty.

This is not, of course, to rule out the demise of sovereignty in the more fundamental sense. It is merely to indicate that most contemporary writing on sovereignty, even if it may seek to reject the language of sovereignty as undesirable (see e.g., MacCormick 1993; 1999), is in fact concerned not with utopian (or dystopian) alternatives. Rather, it is concerned with how gradual shifts in that part of the modern "social imaginary" (Taylor 2004) that addresses our understanding of the domain of politics are informed by and in turn may (re)inform the myriad transformative opportunities, dangers, and limitations located at the symbolic and systemic levels of our still sovereign-coded global configuration (Fraser 2005).

Note

1. For an earlier attempt to develop this scheme, see Walker 2006.

3

Sovereignty Before and After the Linguistic Turn

Jens Bartelson

Is the sovereign state here to stay, or is it withering away? Frequently posed in terms of the consequences of globalization, this question has been one of the main sticking points within academic international relations and international law during the past decades. Unsurprisingly, the answers provided by different authors display a considerable variety, both in terms of their basic assumptions about the nature of sovereignty, as well as in terms of their conclusions about its future prospects (see e.g., Ayoob 2002; Cohen 2004; Agnew 2005; Sassen 2006). On the one hand, we find those scholars who remain convinced of the staying power of state sovereignty. To them, those new forms of political authority that are believed to challenge the predominance of the sovereign state are ultimately derivative of state sovereignty, and therefore indicative of its endurance rather than anything else. Thus, when properly defined and understood, the concept of sovereignty is likely to retain its analytical and normative relevance even in the future. On the other hand, we find scholars who argue that the state is unlikely to remain the main locus of sovereignty in the future. Sovereign statehood is challenged by new forms of political authority that eventually will transform the international system into something new and different. The concept of sovereignty should either be abandoned, or at least understood very differently, to make better sense of these new constellations.

As I would like to argue in this chapter, a fair share of this disagreement is generated by underlying philosophical differences about concepts and their relationship to the world. To some extent, the question of endurance does not even concern the actual makeup of the political world and what kind of entities this world might be composed of. Rather, as I shall suggest, this debate is kept alive by profound and underlying disagreement about the ontological status of concepts. This problem has largely been neglected by those who have participated in the debate about the endurance of sovereignty. Indeed, many of these scholars are blind to the implications of their own tacit assumptions about the ontological status of concepts. To my mind, a fair share of the disagreements about the endurance of sovereignty derives from a selective uptake of insights from the *linguistic turn* within the legal and political sciences.

One would have suspected that the linguistic reorientation within political and legal science had reduced the question of endurance to a quibble over the meaningful usage of the term sovereignty. But judging from the contemporary debate on sovereignty, the linguistic orientation has made the problem of endurance look more enduring that ever. As I shall argue below, the belief that sovereign statehood is here to stay has been nourished by a *semantic* view of concepts and their meaning, while the belief that sovereign statehood is undergoing profound changes has been greatly facilitated by a *nominalist* view of concepts. According to the former view, concepts derive their meaning from a capacity to refer to classes of objects that exist independently of our efforts at classification and description. According to the latter view, concepts are nothing but general names that we use to constitute objects into distinct classes, the resulting classificatory schemes being means of which we literally create the world. For reasons of simplicity rather than historical accuracy, I shall use the term "linguistic turn" to describe the transition from the former view to the latter (see e.g., Toews 1987; Wagner 2002; Bartelson 2007).

For obvious reasons, I will not embark on the impossible task of assessing the validity of these different views of concepts and their meaning. Instead, I shall focus on their implications for how the problem of endurance has been formulated and resolved within some exemplary texts on sovereignty. These considerations will lead me to make a further point. Not only does the contemporary debate on sovereignty revolve around factual questions, such as the makeup of the political world, but there is always also a short step from explaining political phenomena to actually justifying them. As I would like to suggest, the contemporary debate on sovereignty can equally well be viewed as a question of the legitimacy of various forms of political authority as well as the larger political order of which they are part. As I contend, one unintended consequence of the selective and sometimes distorted uptake of insights from the linguistic turn has been to make sovereignty look as an inescapable precondition of political authority and order. Doing this, I shall proceed in three steps. In the first section that follows, I shall first describe the view according to which concepts do have stable meanings by virtue of their referential capacity, and then go on by exemplifying how this view has found expression in some contemporary studies of sovereignty. I shall then go on to describe the more recent view according to which concepts derive their meaning from their function and usage within different linguistic and historical contexts, and then assess the implications that this view has had for the ways in which the question of endurance has been formulated and answered. Third, I shall discuss how these different views of political concepts might hang together, and finally indicate what I take to be the proper way to resolve the tension between these views for the benefit of a more coherent understanding of the problem of sovereignty and its endurance.

Sovereignty Uncontested

At least since Plato's *Republic*, (1955, 299–325) the question of the ontological status of concepts has been intimately connected with problems of political order and authority. In Book Six of the *Republic*, the independence of universals turn out to be a condition of possible order as well as the ontological foundation on which all claims to legitimate political authority ultimately rest. But even if few people today think that concepts exist independently of their instantiations, many people believe that they must be defined to be of any value when making logical inferences or making sense of the world. According to a reasonably modern version of this view, concepts do have a life of their own only to the extent they refer to classes of objects. As such, concepts are essentially predicates, and as such, they are necessarily concepts of something, and hence cannot exist independently of that something. Concepts are conditions of objectivity insofar as they put us in touch with things, and this referential capacity is in turn a condition of their possible meaning. The logical properties of concepts imply that their meanings are universal and timeless (Frege 1984a, 1984b; see also Ogden and Richards 1936; Russell 1962). Since empirical analysis presupposes the prior analysis of conceptual meaning, we could expect the outcome of empirical analyses to reflect this view of concepts as well.

As long as this background understanding remained unchallenged within political and legal science, one of the main problems encountered was how to define the term "sovereignty" in ways that made further inquiry possible and fruitful. Although scholars agreed that the concept of sovereignty had to refer either to political facts or legal norms, this was no easy since this concept had been repeatedly recycled throughout the history of modern political and legal thought and thus had accumulated a manifold of sometimes incompatible connotations. As Kelsen once lamented, "the term 'sovereignty', while denoting one of the most important concepts of the theory of national and international law, has a variety of meanings, a fact that causes regrettable confusion in this theory" (1969, 115). As Benn then concluded, "it would appear to be a mistake to treat 'sovereignty' as denoting a genus of which the species can be distinguished by suitable adjectives, and there would seem to be a strong case for giving up so Protean a word" (1969, 85). But many others were more optimistic about the usefulness of the concept of sovereignty. Hence Hinsley could argue with impeccable logic that "this concept has involved the belief that there is a final and absolute authority within the society. Applied to the problems that arise in the relations between political societies, its function has been to express…the principle that internationally, over and above a collection of societies, no supreme authority exists" (1969, 275). Accordingly, it becomes very hard to see how sovereignty ever could change profoundly or wither away completely, since "the concept of sovereignty is the inescapable justification of the authority of the state in an integrated community; and as long as there is an international system it will be made up by territorial communities" (Hinsley 1969, 287).

Similar semantic sensibilities are still very much in evidence in the literature on sovereignty. Despite widely divergent assumptions about the nature of sovereignty and the causes of its mutability, there is an underlying agreement about the relationship between concepts and objects among more empirically oriented scholars. As Krasner states, "any theoretical perspective must make some assumptions about the nature of the world; that is, about the units that are the subject of study" (1999, 45; 2001b). By the same token, to Jackson, "the traditional academic approach to sovereignty is usually driven by the aspiration to organize into more systematic and coherent terms that are evident from international political activity, past and present" (1999a, 3). Finally, to Philpott, "it is both the contemporary global prestige and its urgent need of definition that merits sovereignty such an involved discussion" (2001, 19).

But while their Platonist predecessors regarded sovereignty as an immutable foundation of modern political life, recent authors have emphasized its mutability and flexibility. To some extent this emphasis has been made possible by an early offspring of the linguistic turn. The concept of institutional facts (Searle 1995) and the idea that they depend on our linguistic conventions for their existence has been crucial to many of these attempts to account for changes in sovereign statehood. Yet even to those who admit that the institutional fact of sovereignty is capable of historical change, sovereignty retains a hard and immutable core that itself seems rather unaffected by institutional transformations. As Reus-Smit claims in his broad survey of different international systems from antiquity to the present, "these systems have all been organized according to the principle of sovereignty; their member states have all claimed supreme authority within their territories, and these claims have been deemed legitimate by the community of states" (1999, 10).

So while Krasner (2001) concedes that some of the more basic meanings of sovereignty within an international system of states frequently have been compromised by the activities of those states, he is able to conclude that the basic institutions of sovereignty have displayed such a remarkable durability precisely because of their inherent flexibility and ability to accommodate those compromises. As we learn from Spruyt, "it was the concept of sovereignty that altered the structure of the international system by basing the political authority on the principle of territorial exclusivity" (1994, 3). Hence, to him "there are serious impediments to changing the de iure nature of the state system" (1994, 193). Given similar starting points, it becomes easy to conclude that "notwithstanding its very real limitations and imperfections, to date the *societas* of sovereign states have proved to be the only generally acceptable and practical basis of world politics" (Jackson 1999b, 34; see also James 1999). While both the theory and practice of sovereignty have undergone major transformations since the early-modern period, "we can yet view the revolutions in sovereignty as part of a common movement toward a global system of sovereign states, and the revolutions in ideas as part of an unfolding logic of liberation" (Philpott 2001, 253).

Although these scholars sometimes disagree sharply about the meaning of the concept of sovereignty, and consequently also about its political and legal implications, they are in agreement that the concept of sovereignty indeed does have a set of stable core connotations that make theoretical and empirical inquiry possible and meaningful. They are also inclined to believe that the sovereign state will remain the main source of political authority in the future, and that phenomena that appear to be indicative of a world beyond that of states in fact are dependent on, if not reducible to, what goes on within an international system of states. Thus, and at least partly as a consequence of their underlying commitments to a semantic view of concepts, these authors are likely to conclude that however profound and lasting the changes in the *institution* of sovereignty, sovereignty *itself* remains essentially the same since it is constitutive of the international system of states as a domain of inquiry. These authors are then left with the difficulty of finding a way to tell under which conditions we would be entitled to say that we have left this international system behind for good, and entered into a new political universe that supposedly knows nothing of the concept of sovereignty. Thus, from this point of view, sovereignty appears to be an immutable condition of modern political life, as well as a necessary condition of its intelligibility. But if my diagnosis is correct, sovereignty appears to be necessary only to the extent that stable conceptual meaning is perceived to be a necessary condition of further inquiry. And such stability in turn appears to be a condition of possible inquiry by virtue of conceptual meaning being based on the capacity to refer to a class of objects, in this case states.

Contesting Sovereignty

One main upshot of the linguistic turn has been to claim that our concepts are actively involved in the constitution of legal and political reality, rather than merely being descriptive of norms and facts. But as Ian Hacking has argued, most such arguments presuppose a nominalist view of concepts and their meaning (Hacking 1999, 80–84). Such a view entails the belief that concepts are nothing but names that we use to label individual objects, thereby lumping them together in categories of our own making. As Locke puts it, "since all things that exist are only particulars... Words become general by being made the signs of general *ideas*; and *ideas* become general by separating them from the circumstances of time and place" (Locke 1991, 212). Consequently, in a more modern version, "we reject any statement or definition... if it commits us to abstract entities." (Goodman and Quine 1947, 105; Goodman 1978, 1–22). When these objects also are things of our own creation—such as practices and institutions—naming them indeed becomes a way of making them. Since concepts themselves do not enjoy any existence independently of their usage, their meaning cannot be timeless and universal. Instead, since they are likely to be used in different ways and for different purposes in different linguistic and historical contexts, their meaning is likely to vary across these contexts as well. Conceptual meaning thus only remains stable as long as the linguistic conventions governing their usage within these contexts remain stable.

Such a view of conceptual meaning is very evident in much recent scholarship in international law and international relations theory, within which the concept of sovereignty has become a major bone of contention. Much of this contestation has been achieved thanks to the linguistic reorientation within the social and legal sciences, and the sense of conceptual relativism it has brought. From having been a preoccupation mainly of critical theorists within the discipline of international relations, many scholars now start out from the assumption that the meaning of sovereignty is wholly contingent on its usage, and that this usage in turn is governed by a blend of linguistic conventions and rhetorical intentions. Rather than assuming that the concept of sovereignty has any timeless or universal meaning, a recent wave of scholarship has focused on its changing meaning and function across a variety of historical and political contexts. This has led scholars to raise questions about how and why the meaning of this concept changes across time and space, and under what conditions these changes might spill over into relocations of political authority to agents other than states, and perhaps even into a wholesale transformation of the international system into a global society.

When this contestation started, much attention was focused on how sovereignty had been constituted in fundamental opposition to anarchy within international relations theory, and in what ways this distinction was involved in the legitimization of power politics. As Ashley observed, sovereignty is "conceived as a transcendental origin of power that is not itself a political power because it is also the timeless and universal source of all that can be meaningful and true in history" (Ashley 1995, 103). Political realism and the practices of power politics were held to be responsible for the bifurcation of modern political life into two distinct and opposed spheres of thought and action (Ashley 1987). Similar lines of inquiry were vigorously pursued by Walker, who argued that the "conventional history of state sovereignty, while conformed by practice and offering a persuasive resolution of the most basic political and philosophical questions about the nature and location of political community, must also be understood as a reification" (R. Walker 1990, 171). In an attempt to understand how sovereignty had been reified into a constitutive principle of modern political life through practices of intervention, Weber argued that "sovereignty marks not the location of the foundational entity of international relations theory but a site of political struggle. This struggle is the struggle to fix the meaning of sovereignty is such a way as to constitute a particular state... with particular boundaries, competencies, and legitimacies available to it." (Weber 1995, 3). Finally, as I argued myself back then, "[t]o say that sovereignty is contingent is to say that it is not necessary or essential, but that its central and ambiguous place in modern political discourse is the outcome of prior accidents" (Bartelson 1995, 239).

When these authors disputed the allegedly timeless and universal meaning of sovereignty, they did so by questioning the underlying notion that concepts and their meaning could be understood independently of their actual usage in concrete linguistic contexts. But in this first wave of contestation, there was little agreement as to the ultimate sources of conceptual meaning and conceptual change beyond the point that they were intimately connected to those practices and institutions that conditioned the meaningful usage of this term. Neither had these authors very much to say about the actual changes the concept of sovereignty had undergone as a result of having been employed in different ways in different contexts, by different agents and for different rhetorical purposes. Despite the almost ritualistic emphasis on the contingency of sovereignty, the first wave of contestation arguably strengthened the sense of entrapment by equating conceptual change with the possibility of total transcendence of the international system, and then denying the possibility on the former on grounds of the impossibility of the latter. Yet the first wave of contestation undeniably opened up a new domain of inquiry: few people in the trade today doubt that sovereignty is what human beings make of it.

More recent scholarship has done a lot to improve our understanding of how the concept of sovereignty and its meaning change as a consequence of its different use in different contexts, and how these changes in turn provide legitimizations of different constellations of power. As Werner and de Wilde have argued, "the question as to what state of affairs corresponds to the meaning of the term 'sovereignty' should be replaced by questions like—in what context is a claim to sovereignty likely to occur?" (Werner and de Wilde 2001, 3). Suggestions such as these have been taken seriously by many scholars. Thus, in an attempt to make sense of the constitutional pluralism of the European Union (EU), Walker defines sovereignty as a discursive claim concerning the existence and character of a supreme ordering power for a particular polity. He then goes on to argue that such a conception indeed is indispensable to understand and justify the transition from good old Westphalian sovereignty to our present condition of late sovereignty. The constitutional pluralism and multidimensional order characteristic of late sovereignty display considerable continuity with the old order in the way they handle the tension between law and politics, yet they have some distinctive features of their own. Boundaries are no longer territorial, but they have become functional to the effect that "it becomes possible to conceive of autonomy without territorial exclusivity" (N. Walker 2003, 23). If we are to believe this account, there is no way back from this new world, only a way forward: not only is the condition of late sovereignty here to stay, but it also contains the seeds for a piecemeal transformation of the international system into a global society within which political authority is decentralized and dispersed.

In a similar vein, Huysmans has recently raised the question whether transnational practices really make any difference to the logic of sovereignty in international politics, or if they merely constitute one of its many reproductive circuits. Rather than simply reiterating any of the standard views about the corrosive effects of transnational practices on state sovereignty, Huysmans reformulates this problem in terms of how these practices might affect the *matrix* of sovereignty, understood as the way in which the question of the political conventionally has been formulated in terms of a territorialized distinction between the domestic inside and the international outside. From this perspective, transnational flows "fragments the international society of sovereign states into functionally defined arenas and consequently challenges the neat fix that territorialized the tension and the gap that characterize the matrix of sovereignty" (Huysmans 2003, 220). The existence of such practices thus opens up the possibility of envisaging politics in terms of pluralization instead of unification, making it possible to rework the matrix of sovereignty and thus to align it closer with a democratic ethos.

In another recent volume, Beaulac focuses on the constitutive functions of the concept of sovereignty within early-modern legal and political discourse, and he tries to make sense of the concept of sovereignty and the myth of Westphalia in the shaping of the modern society of states. As he aptly phrases the role of such a myth in international life, it "triggers reality to become larger than life" (2004, 39). Hence words and myths have the power not only to describe and represent reality, but also to actively create and transform it. What appears to be universalistic and timeless connotations are in fact constituted through the changing employment of the term sovereignty across different contexts, but for what turns out to be similar ideological purposes.

Finally, Malmvig has studied how the concept of sovereignty takes on different meanings depending on its different usages in justifying practices of intervention and nonintervention in the international system. One upshot of this analysis is to show that sovereignty and intervention not only are mutually constitutive concepts, but also hierarchically arranged insofar that sovereignty can be regarded as normal only by virtue of intervention being considered pathological, and vice versa. At first glance, such an analysis would seem to reinforce the belief that the meaning and applicability of the principle of sovereignty are wholly contingent on political and legal practices, and that there is no hard core of meaning left that could function as an uncontested foundation of those practices. When sovereignty simply is what we make of it through our discursive practices, any attempt to define the meaning of this concept independently of those practices is nothing but a concealed attempt to seize the rhetorical initiative, and thereby a chunk political power as well. So sovereignty is not only what we make of it, but equally that which constitutes the identity of its makers by virtue of being at stake in their recognition games (Malmvig 2006).

This brings us over to the fundamental problem faced by those scholars who have taken the linguistic turn. Although these authors readily have accepted some version of nominalism and hence believe that concept are but general names by means of which we shape our world, they have nevertheless felt compelled to attribute at least some basic meanings to the concept of sovereignty for their inquiries into its actual usage to get off the ground. Much like those scholars who are trying to make sense of the institutional realities of sovereignty earlier, those who are trying to make sense of the language games of sovereignty are equally compelled by scholarly conventions to convey some sense of what they are talking about, if not by means of definitions so at least by consistent usage and coherent implication. The very possibility and relative immutability of such meanings in fact condition further contestation, insofar as these meanings constitute a baseline agreement about what interlocutors meaningfully can disagree about, in and out of the academy. Not only are many of those who have taken the linguistic turn inclined to believe that sovereignty is likely to remain a permanent feature of international and global political life for a foreseeable future, but they arguably do also unwittingly contribute to its reproduction as a consequence of their adherence to those linguistic conventions that happen to govern their particular sovereignty game.

Sovereignty Decontested

So taking the linguistic turn appears to have brought us full circle, since it turns out that underlying even the most radical attempts to contest the concept of sovereignty in academic debates we find assumptions about the conceptual identity of sovereignty and its basic meanings, being safely removed from contestation. The tension between a semantic and a nominalist view of concepts turns out to be that which keeps the debate on sovereignty alive, and hence what makes the topic of sovereignty so salient in contemporary legal and political thought. This order of things also correspond neatly to the way the concept of sovereignty is supposed to function outside the academic debate, where the constant contestation of its meaning supposedly reinforces those incontestable core connotations that make contestation possible in the first place, and its endurance more likely in the second. Thus sovereignty seems to remain an inescapable part of modern political life and a condition of its intelligibility, not despite but rather because of the above attempts to historicize and denaturalize its meaning.

Many scholars today would agree that we live in a world in which the territorial differentiation into distinct and bounded political communities like states is being challenged by new constellations of political authority and community. In this world, new claims to sovereignty by new kinds of agents can be justified with reference to several competing normative frameworks. The traditional framework of international relations and law has been challenged, first by universal human rights and pleas cosmopolitan democracy, and then by emergent claims to imperial authority made by the United States and its allies (Cohen 2004). These latter challenges are notoriously hard to separate from each other, so that each attempt to justify the exercise of authority with reference to a global demos is likely to be seen as little but a concealed expression of imperial ambition. But even if we would agree that sovereignty is in the process of being relocated from states to supranational entities, this kind of conclusion seems possible to reach only against the backdrop of some idea of what sovereignty basically is or means.

But this is hardly the end of the story. If the earlier analysis is correct, the tension between different conceptions of sovereignty has more to do with our view of concepts in general than with our view of the concept of sovereignty in particular. In that case, the reason why sovereignty appears to be a condition of its own contestability has little to do with the concept of sovereignty itself or its range of connotations, but it is rather the outcome of a lingering tension between different attitudes to concepts and the contradictory sensibilities they engender within academic and political discourse. Whereas a semantic view of concepts seems to be a necessary condition of inquiry insofar as we need to know and convey what we are talking about, a nominalist view of concepts seems necessary to understand how concepts shape and transform those things we are trying to talk about as a consequence of our very trying. To these different attitudes to concepts thus corresponds two distinct dimensions of language within which the contestation of sociopolitical concepts like sovereignty can take place. According to Skinner, the first of these "has conventionally been described in the dimension of meaning, the study of the sense and reference allegedly attaching to words and sentences," while "the other is best described…as the dimension of linguistic action, the study of the range of things that speakers are capable of doing in (and by) their use of words and sentences" (Skinner 2002, 3–4).

But as the earlier analysis has made plain, it seems not possible to speak of concepts and their referents within any of these dimensions without presupposing that about which one speaks. This implies that these two dimensions of language indeed are fundamentally interdependent, insofar as the activities undertaken within one of these dimensions will determine what kind of activities that can be undertaken within the other. Not only do practices of definition provide the baseline for further disagreement and contestation, but disagreement and contestation also generate those connotations that make attempts at definition possible and necessary. The fact that the two dimensions of language are interdependent further points to a more fundamental fact of language, namely that the use of language invariably involves making presuppositions about those things we speak about, while simultaneously allowing us to speak about those presuppositions. The thing itself—in this case sovereignty—only exists within language as a consequence of being spoken about, yet it is possible to speak about sovereignty only by presupposing it (Agamben 1998b, 27–38).

But by presupposing things we also remove them from contestation. As Freeden has described this practice, "[w]e can only access the political world through decontesting the contested conceptual arrangements that enable us to make sense of that world, and we do so—deliberately or unconsciously—by imposing specific meanings onto the indeterminate range of meanings that our conceptual clusters can hold" (2006, 19). According to him, by removing certain concepts from contestation we also turn their meanings into starting points of political ideologies, and these ideologies are then used to legitimize the very same conceptual arrangements. This brings me over to my final and concluding point. If talk about sovereignty always and invariably implies presupposing sovereignty, and if presupposing sovereignty implies decontesting sovereignty, and if decontesting sovereignty implies turning it into ideology, we might as well wonder what kind of political order thereby is legitimized? This kind of question is certainly no news to those who have taken the linguistic turn, and much energy has been spent answering it during the last decade. To the first wave of critics, sovereignty was regarded as intimately involved in the justification of the practices of power politics and the imposition of Western values globally. The critical upshot of these contentions was to dispute the moral legitimacy of sovereignty on the basis of its undesirable implications for mankind as a whole. In the second wave of linguistically oriented scholarship, students of sovereignty have focused more on its function in legitimizing particular claims to power by specific agents within delimited political and historical contexts. One important consequence of these inquiries has rather been to demonstrate in some empirical detail how sovereignty has been reproduced through these practices, and why the concept of sovereignty remains an indispensable rhetorical resource to those who want to raise successful claims to power in international politics.

Yet a more obvious but more disturbing conclusion has been avoided by most of the authors discussed earlier. To my mind, the most basic ideological function of the concept of sovereignty is not to legitimize particular claims to power by specific agents, but rather to legitimize the very political order within which those claims can be made and understood as meaningful by the agents involved. Actual claims to sovereignty can only make sense in a political world within which political authority and community already have been thoroughly particularized, such as within the modern international system of states. The concept of sovereignty helps us to make sense of a world—and only makes sense within a world—in which the division of mankind into distinct peoples is regarded as an inescapable and perhaps even desirable condition. Before that world came into being sovereignty made no sense, yet the reason why sovereignty makes sense within this world is because that world was brought into being by sovereignty. When that world has withered away, so will sovereignty.

4

Playing with Sovereignty: Examples from the Theory and Practice of International Law

Ole Spiermann

Positioning Public International Law

International law represents an expansion of the rule of law beyond the confines of national law to, in the first place, what is traditionally phrased relations between states.

Many lawyers seem to know that international law maintains a somewhat uneasy relationship with bindingness, in Hans Kelsen's phrase *Das Problem der Souveränität* (Kelsen 1928; and e.g., Sukiennicki 1927, 55; Hart 1994, 220). However, the true problem is not whether international law is binding, but whether relations between states—and other issues taken to affect the interests of a plurality of states—may be subject to law at all. Relations between states are located outside the conceived confines of national law for the simple reason that each national legal system is linked to a particular, sovereign state and, therefore, inapt to govern issues involving other equally sovereign states. Once an issue has been defined as involving the interests of a plurality of states, for whichever reason, tradition or otherwise, national law no longer recommends itself, not even to national lawyers. It is recognized that states are not only sovereign; they are also independent.

Whether law is excluded from certain areas of life is a philosophical conundrum of considerable intellectual depth. Suffice it to say that the positioning of international law on the periphery of law adds an idealistic, if not missionary, flavor to international lawyering, even today. More significantly, lawyers confronted with specific cases generally recognize the need for as well as the possibility of law also in situations related to the interests of more than one state. Reconciling sovereignty of a state with the binding character of international law has been more agreeable than a Hobbesian vision of the state subjecting other sovereign states to its national legal system in contradiction with their sovereignty and independence. In this light, bindingness presents itself as the lesser of two evils. To put it differently, the cardinal dichotomy, national versus international, does not at its most fundamental level translate as internal versus external, but as one national sovereign versus more national sovereigns, or single versus plural.

It is rather trivial, to a practitioner at least, that international law is binding; and to look for the explanation in international law, and so to assume the system to be self-referential, is certainly a misconception. Nevertheless, in theory it has been rather more difficult to overcome *Das Problem der Souveränität*. Martti Koskenniemi has taken the view that international law is indeterminate. This is because, "[o]n the one hand, we seem incapable of conceptualizing the State...without reflecting on the character of the social relations which surround it" and "[o]n the other hand, we cannot derive the State completely from its social relations and its liberty from an external (and overriding) normative perspective without losing the State's individuality as a nation and the justification for its claims to independence and self-determination" (Koskenniemi 1989, 193). This argument emphasizes an external perspective on the state. However, when considering situations related to the interests of more than one state, lawyers do not start out with a perspective that is external to both or all states. Lawyers start within a national legal system and so with a perspective that is internal. It is possible with the internal perspective to reject, or at least be critical of, the notion of another sovereign (another state), or its representative, being a national law subject. What follows is a need for law other than national law, law that is common and international and within which the perspective on sovereignty is external. But this external perspective on interstates relations is generated by, and is dependent on, the internal perspective of national legal systems mastered by one state. For the same reason, the most fundamental conception of sovereignty is not external or international; it is internal or national.

A seed sown by Kelsen and nursed by Alf Ross is instructive (Kelsen 1928, 308). This is the view that the "current" definition of international law is circular. Referring to a definition of international law as "the body of legal rules binding upon states in their relations with one another,"

Ross wrote: "The term 'International Law' is defined with reference to the term 'state' and the definition of the term 'state' again refers back to the term 'International Law'. A definition thus biting on its own tail is circular. The consequence is that on the point in question the definition is in reality a blank" (Ross 1947, 12). This vicious circle was on the basis of the following definitions: "(1) A definition of International Law as the law valid between states; (2) A definition of the state by the concept of sovereignty; and (3) A definition—explicit or implicit—of sovereignty as sole subjection to International Law" (Ross 1947, 12, note 1 and 41). According to Ross, the circle could be avoided by changing the conception of state. Ross substituted the term "self-governing community" for the term "state" and held that "a legal community is called self-governing when and in so far as it is the highest legal power in relation to its individual members" (Ross 1947, 15). Ross's analysis impressed some Continental scholars (Verdross 1950, 10; Antonowicz 1966/67, 195; see also Koskenniemi 1989, 262, note 279). On a closer look, however, what Ross had changed was better described as the conception of sovereignty (Spiermann 2003, 680–682). The external perspective on sovereignty that takes part in the circular definition (sovereignty being independence, or the state only being subject to international law) had been exchanged for the internal perspective on sovereignty echoing Jean Bodin's definition of sovereignty being the absolute and perpetual power of a commonwealth, or supreme and absolute power over citizens and subjects. Leaving aside Ross's seemingly relentless pursuit of iconoclasm and his claim, obviously unfounded, that the dichotomy between external and internal was a novelty, Ross's circle and the way in which it was undone illustrates the importance to international law of the internal perspective or the national conception of sovereignty. Disregarding this Bodinian conception and international law cannot be fully appreciated.

This is not to say that the national conception of sovereignty is sufficient for purposes of international law. Quite to the contrary, additional meanings or conceptions of sovereignty—external perspectives—have to be introduced to reconcile sovereignty with bindingness and public international law. The resulting complication has dogged international lawyers till this day. On the one hand, the national conception is the *raison d'être* of international law. It is exactly because national law is seen as a projection of supreme and absolute state power that national law is inadequate when a plurality of sovereign states are involved; instead, international law has been envisaged as a complementary and residual, common legal system to which issues affecting the interests of more than one state may be referred. On the other hand, although international law may only be properly conceived against the background of the national conception of sovereignty (which determines the scope of internationalism), when engaged with international law, and its content, lawyers are in need of international conceptions of sovereignty. To put it shortly, international lawyers need to be familiar with and yet distance themselves from the national conception of sovereignty.

The outside observer struck by state sovereignty being presented as the very basis of legal reasoning, internationally as well as nationally, has taken the first step toward understanding the limited role that is entrusted to law and the consequent distinctions between political theory, day-to-day realities, and (international) law. When misguided theorists go the whole hog and strike the pejorative word "sovereignty" off the vocabulary of international law, they confirm the importance of the word, at least to legal reasoning: nobody would care about striking off an irrelevant word (e.g., Téson 1992, 54 and 92; MacCormick 1994, 1; Henkin 1995, 8; Franck 1995, 5).

The Wimbledon

The Wimbledon was a case decided in 1923 by the newly established Permanent Court of International Justice, the predecessor of the present International Court of Justice. Essentially, the case raised the question whether Germany had put itself under an obligation, pursuant to the Versailles Treaty, to give access to the Kiel Canal to vessels carrying weapons intended for a belligerent. The position of the German Government, as reproduced in the judgment, was that an obligation to this effect would be contrary to Germany's obligations as a neutral toward other belligerents as well as Germany's sovereignty and, for these reasons, not obligatory. The Permanent Court rejected the latter argument in what has been referred to as the classical statement of a governing axiom (Schwebel 1980, 188):

> The Court declines to see in the conclusion of any treaty by which a State undertakes to perform or refrain from performing a particular act an abandonment of its sovereignty. No doubt any convention creating an obligation of this kind places a restriction upon the exercise of the sovereign rights of the State, in the sense that it requires them to be exercised in a certain way. But the right of entering into international engagements is an attribute of State sovereignty.[1]

What the Permanent Court contemplated was the national conception of sovereignty, that is, the conception of the state as a national sovereign, on which "an obligation of this kind places a restriction"; and the Permanent Court invoked, as a counter-argument, an international conception of sovereignty that may be termed the conception of the state as an international sovereign: "the right of entering into international engagements is an attribute of State sovereignty" (Spiermann 2005, 180). This is a famous dictum, and it makes a nice quotation. It has impressed generations of international lawyers. Referring to the theoretical dichotomy between sovereignty and bindingness as "the sovereignty dilemma," Jan Klabbers has concluded as follows (1998, 364):

> Instead of being plagued by the sovereignty dilemma, the *Wimbledon* court had managed to make a virtue out of a vice; it had squared the circle, and its solution has been with us since 1923, internalized as probably no other international legal dogma has become internalized in the collective mind of the "invisible college of international lawyers."

Still, it all boils down to international lawyers not being secure in the normative status of public international law and the much less sophisticated argument, articulated by the Permanent Court the year before, that the provision in question "is part of the Treaty and constitutes an obligation by which the Parties to the Treaty are bound to one another."[2] The subsequent *dictum* pronounced in *The Wimbledon* appeals to those not willing to rely on bindingness, or the other international conception of sovereignty, which may be referred to as the conception of the state as an international law subject.

The Lotus

A parallel example is the following famous, some would say infamous—and certainly provocative—paragraph taken from *The Lotus*, which involved jurisdiction to legislate in relation to a collision between a Turkish and a French vessel on the high seas. In 1927, the Permanent Court held:

> International law governs relations between independent States. The rules of law binding upon States therefore emanate from their own free will as expressed in conventions or by usages generally accepted as expressing principles of law and established in order to regulate the relations between these co-existing independent communities or with a view to the achievement of common aims. Restrictions upon the independence of States cannot therefore be presumed.[3]

The question arises what is the exact implication of the last sentence. This has not been a "game" played within the Permanent Court, but between the majority of the Permanent Court and the readers of its judgment.

Often the last sentence has been read against a background colored by the national conception of sovereignty to the effect that "independence" has been taken to be synonymous with sovereignty and that the Permanent Court has given support to a presumption against international law: *in dubio pro libertate*, or when in doubt the state is free, as the Turkish Government had been arguing.[4] Indeed, most lawyers work and think on the basis of a national legal system; they rarely pay regard to international law and see the national legal system as being self-contained, capable of solving on its own disputes and other issues as they present themselves. But it would have been truly extraordinary had a newly established international court favored this national principle of self-containedness over international law. Nor was it the intended meaning. The sentence relates to the conception of the state as an international, as opposed to a national, sovereign (Huber 1928, 47–48; De la Grotte 1929, 387; Huber 1936, 84–85; Anzilotti 1958, 58). When put in its own context, the sentence implies that a state is not bound by international law unless it has agreed so: "The rules binding upon the States therefore emanate from their own free will." No state may legislate with binding effect on another state, or at least this cannot be presumed. This follows from what the Permanent Court had referred to earlier as "a fundamental principle of international law," in French "la base même du droit international,"[5] that is, independence (Huber 1974, 277).

The Double Structure of International Legal Argument

The analyses of *The Wimbledon* and *The Lotus* suggest that in the context of international law, the internal perspective on sovereignty and the conception of the state as a national sovereign is fundamental but not sufficient. International conceptions of sovereignty are needed, together with a clear distinction between them: in relation to the making of international law the state is to be seen as an international sovereign (*The Lotus*), and in relation to the application of international law as an international law subject (*The Wimbledon*).

In consequence, international legal argument is erected upon not one, but three different conceptions: the (national) conception of the state as a national sovereign, the (international) conception of the state as an international sovereign, and the (international) conception of the state as an international law subject. The main question is not one of choosing between the intentions of the different conceptions, but one of extensions and the categorization of issues within the structures of international legal argument.

There are two main structures. One of them, the basic structure, advances from the national principle of self-containedness (and the conception of the state as a national sovereign) to general or customary international law (the international law of coexistence) (still mainly the conception of the state as a national sovereign); the line dividing the two categories reflects national lawyers' needs for a common legal system that supplements the several national legal systems in respect of issues involving conflicting state interests (thus also based on the conception of the state as a national sovereign). The other, dynamic structure advances from treaty law (the international law of cooperation) (and, at least as a starting-point, the conception of the state as an international law subject) to the residual principle of sovereignty (the conception of the state as a national sovereign), the dividing line being generated by treaty making (reflecting the conception of the state as an international sovereign). What makes each of the two structures normative is that, in practice as well as in principle, lawyers do not have a free hand in categorizing issues. It is not left with the individual lawyer to decide whether there is such a clash between the interests of national sovereigns that it triggers international law. Nor can it be said to be a matter of the individual lawyer's will whether international law has been made by concluding a treaty, explicitly or implicitly.

The two structures of international legal argument are in a sense the opposite of each other: the basic structure advances from the national to the international and the dynamic structure from the international to the national. Each and every issue may be categorized within both structures, often with different results. Accordingly, even if accepting that each structure taken on its own is normative, the question remains whether choosing between the structures is governed by international law. An answer in the negative and this model of international legal argument would reproduce well-known indeterminacy arguments (Kennedy 1987, 29–54; Koskenniemi 1989, 42–50). But the claim ingrained in international law is precisely that international law remains essential also when choosing between the basic and the dynamic structures of international legal argument. Thus, there is not merely two structures of international legal argument, but a double structure of international legal argument in which the two structures are hierarchically ordered. The questions where in each structure to categorize a specific issue, and which structure to treat as the hierarchically privileged, form a pertinent and sometimes difficult task confronting, for example, the members of an international court. Categorizing specific issues within the double structure may be uncertain; obviously, categorizations may also change over time. Nevertheless, it takes a distortion of international law, alienating it from national as well as international lawyers, to conclude that lawyers may choose between the two structures at will as if moving in vicious circles.

Taking the two structures together as a double structure of international legal argument, discussions of a general hierarchy between sovereignty and bindingness are misconceived. From the international lawyer's point of view, sovereignty does not carry a fixed, general meaning, nor are sovereignty and international law mutually exclusive. Sovereignty is neither *passé* nor all-embracing. In respect of issues coming within the national principle of self-containedness, it can be said that sovereignty restricts, if not excludes, international law (sovereignty *contra legem*), while the international law of coexistence may furnish examples of international law determining sovereignty (sovereignty *infra legem*). In yet other cases, those that fall under the international law of cooperation, international law can indeed be said to have gone beyond sovereignty, thus the conception of the state as an international law subject, which implies that sovereignty is not, prima facie, relevant in treaty interpretation. In respect of issues that do not fall under the international law of cooperation, while belonging to the same dynamic structure of international legal argument, there is a residual principle of state freedom that makes sovereignty supplement international law (sovereignty *praeter legem*). In addition, sovereignty determines international law in the sense that states are free to conclude treaties. The variety of meanings given to sovereignty emphasizes the importance of the hierarchical relationship between the two structures of which the double structure consists.

Some of the most notable illustrations of international legal argument in recent decades have emerged within regional courts in Europe established under treaty regimes which states, as international sovereigns, have extended to individuals. Thereby, international law has been brought to comprise not only relations between states, but also relations between state and individual. In respect of the latter, both the European Court of Human Rights and the European Court of Justice (ECJ) have experienced serious difficulties in substituting the conception of the state as an international law subject for the conception of the state as a national sovereign, or in other words to accept the dynamic structure of international legal argument as hierarchically privileged, just as in *The Wimbledon*.

The European Court of Human Rights

It is common for institutions operating under human rights instruments like the European Court of Human Rights to make observations such as the following: "Unlike international treaties of the classic kind, the Convention comprises more than mere reciprocal engagements between contracting States. It creates, over and above a network of mutual, bilateral undertakings, objective obligations which, in the words of the Preamble, benefit from a 'collective enforcement'."[6] As individuals may invoke responsibility and bring claims of their own before the European Court of Human Rights, the court also found that in "interpreting the Convention regard must be had to its special character as a treaty for the collective enforcement of human rights and fundamental freedoms."[7] Ultimately, involvement of individuals led the court to the language of constitutionalism, as well as supranationalism. Lawyers have evidently been taking advice from national law in conceptualizing the human rights movement.

In applying the European Convention of Human Rights to specific cases, it has been of some significance that, from early on, the court defined its own task as one of reviewing the decisions of national authorities rather than itself subsuming facts of the case under the relevant provisions of the convention. The first case in point, *Wemhoff v. Germany*, raised the question whether the length of detention before trial was "reasonable" as required under Article 5(3) of the convention. In previous cases, the Commission of Human Rights, the original supervisory body of first instance, had defined a set of seven criteria on the basis of which to assess the length of detention. The court took a different position:

> The Court does not feel able to adopt this method. Before being referred to the organs set up under the Convention to ensure the observance of the engagements undertaken therein by the High Contracting Parties, cases of alleged violation of Article 5 (3) must have been the subject of domestic remedies and therefore of reasoned decisions by national judicial authorities. It is for them to mention the circumstances which led them, in the general interest, to consider it necessary to detain a person suspected of an offence but not convicted. Likewise, such a person must, when exercising his remedies, have invoked the reasons which tend to refute the conclusions drawn by the authorities from the facts established by them, as well as other circumstances which told in favour of his release.
>
> It is in the light of these pointers that the Court must judge whether the reasons given by the national authorities to justify continued detention are relevant and sufficient to show that detention was not unreasonably prolonged and contrary to Article 5 (3) of the Convention.[8]

Responding states only having to provide "relevant and sufficient" reasons in what resembled a doctrine of misuse of powers, the approach was equal to admitting states a "margin of appreciation," as the court would put it.

Power to fill gaps in open texture is not a privilege granted to subjects of international law generally. The articulation of a margin of appreciation could hardly be anything but a witness to state authorities, the supposed subjects, being seen as the more appropriate master of individuals, very much in accordance with the internal perspective on sovereignty. Admittedly, the court's approach also stressed the role of national courts in applying the convention before local remedies having been exhausted. But the margin of appreciation was more than a symbolic gesture intended to bring national judges around, nor simply an expression of interinstitutional comity. Being a margin indeed, this doctrine has regularly, though erratically, served to lessen the burdens imposed on the state precisely by stressing the sovereignty of the latter and not emancipating the individual fully from its curb. In Waldock's phrase, "[t]he doctrine of the 'margin of appreciation'... is one of the more important safeguards developed by the Commission and the Court to reconcile the effective operation of the Convention with the sovereign powers and responsibilities of governments in a democracy" (Waldock 1980, 9).

It might be difficult today to imagine human rights jurisprudence, in Europe and elsewhere, without the doctrine of a margin of appreciation. It facilitates the functioning of overburdened systems, and it is familiar to many national legal systems, not least in the areas of constitutional and administrative law. On the other hand, bearing in mind that states come to an international court as, in the first place, subjects of international law—as opposed to national sovereigns—it is not self-evident that an international court less impressed by state sovereignty would have ended up with the same general doctrine justified by the nature of the supervisory system, as distinct from the interpretation of specific treaty rules.

The European Court of Justice

The ECJ, which is an integral part of the European Union (EU), has stated that "[t]he essential characteristics of the Community legal order... are in particular its primacy over the law of the Member States and the direct effect of a whole series of provisions which are applicable to their nationals and to the Member States themselves."[9]

This pronouncement echoed some of the most celebrated moments in the court's own making of the community legal order. As for "the new legal order," the phrase had been coined in 1963 in the first judgment on direct effect of treaty provisions on individuals. "The EEC Treaty," the court had noted, was "more than an agreement which merely creates mutual obligations between the contracting states."[10] In a famous statement, the court had declared that "the Community constitutes a new legal order of international law for the benefit of which the states have limited their sovereign rights, albeit within limited fields, and the subjects of which comprise not only Member States but also their nationals." Direct effect made the community legal order "new" because, in the court's view, individuals were not subjects of international law and, accordingly, international law did not have direct effect. As the European Economic Community (EEC) Treaty, in addition to the member states, counted individuals as its subjects, the legal order set up by the treaty was "a new legal order of international law." The phraseology of a "new legal order" endowed the study of Community law with self-confidence. Thirty years after the decision in *Van Gend en Loos*, Judge G. Federico Mancini wrote: "But if the European Community still exists 50 or 100 years from now, historians will look back on *Van Gend en Loos* as the unique judicial contribution to the making of Europe" (Mancini and Keeling 1994, 183).

The other "essential characteristics" mentioned by the European Court in 1991, in addition to direct effect, was "primacy over the law of the Member States." This principle was articulated by the court in what was essentially its second judgment on direct effect, *Costa v. ENEL* from 1964. On this occasion, it was stated that the community had "real powers stemming from a limitation of sovereignty or a transfer of powers from the States" because the community legal order was "a body of law which binds both their nationals and themselves."[11] For this reason, the court juxtaposed the EEC Treaty with international law: "By contrast with ordinary international treaties, the EEC Treaty has created its own legal system which, on the entry into force of the Treaty, became an integral part of the legal systems of the Member States and which their courts are bound to apply." The Community legal order was no longer, as in *Van Gend en Loos*, "a new legal order of international law." It was now "an integral part of the legal systems of the Member States," a new legal order of national law, as it were.

The rationale was as straightforward as it was antiquated: because of its direct effect, community law was not merely applicable to relations between states, and consequently the community legal order was part of national law, as opposed to international law. This was a consequence of the national conception of sovereignty. In this light, it was only logical that the court should take seriously the Italian Government's national law argument that the Italian act of ratification had been overturned by a new Italian act. This misplaced argument would have carried no weight in international law. But the court saw the community legal order as belonging to the very system that bred the argument, namely Italian national law. Although the "new legal order" phraseology had convinced Community lawyers that international law had been left behind, the principle of precedence equipped them with a new understanding of the community legal order: Community lawyers began to talk about constitutionalism, with the EEC Treaty being a constitution. This was so even though the ultimate basis for precedence was trivial, as made clear in a passage in which the court was hardly carried away by its own eloquence:

> The integration into the laws of each Member State of provisions which derive from the Community, and more generally the terms and the spirit of the Treaty, make it impossible for the States, as a corollary, to accord precedence to a unilateral and subsequent measure over a legal system accepted by them on a basis of reciprocity.[12]

As a matter of principle, precedence stands as a poor translation of *pacta sunt servanda*, yet the exceptional gesture toward the state, its sovereignty and national law, might have more than one explanation. *Van Gend en Loos* and *Costa v. ENEL* were preliminary rulings requested by national courts. Framing the court's decisions in a language familiar to national lawyers might add to the trenchancy of community law. A national court envisages not only the treaty but also national law and thus potential conflicts between treaty rules and national law, making a principle of precedence more appealing than simply *pacta sunt servanda*. That being said, *Van Gend en Loos* and *Costa v. ENEL* were clearly not only about rephrasing ordinary principles of international law. It can safely be said that community lawyers, judges, and readers alike, were themselves attracted by the national conception of sovereignty, a key value of national law that captivates any lawyer distancing himself or herself from international law. Had the new legal order phraseology been merely a rhetorical device for purposes of seeking a higher degree of autonomy in adjudicating future disputes, members of the court would hardly have chosen a language and a discourse so familiar to that conception of sovereignty.

It is instructive that, as certain human rights lawyers, community lawyers have tended to assume that international law contains a general, sovereignty-based principle of restrictive treaty interpretation (Riese 1966, 27; Donner 1974, 135; Kutscher 1976, 31; Mancini 1989, 596), an assumption that certainly says more about their own preference for state sovereignty than it does about international law. Equally misconceived are community lawyers who express doubt about the European Court's style of interpretation on the assumption that treaty interpretation is confined to the text, or to the original intention of the

Contracting Parties (Rasmussen 1986, 25–33; Hartley 1999, 22–42). Still, most lawyers familiar with Community law have not appreciated the evident defects in the court's self-acclaimed new legal order. For when seen against the national conception of sovereignty, and the national principle of self-containedness, the court's making of the community legal order has appeared innovative, even though it did not quite come up to the promises contained in the Community treaties.

Concluding remarks

The analyses of *The Wimbledon* and *The Lotus* suggest that in relation to the making of international law the state is to be seen as an international sovereign and in relation to the application of international law as an international law subject. These form the international conceptions of sovereignty needed for purposes of international law.

The analyses of the European Court of Human Rights and the ECJ suggest that this is a lesson that cannot be learned once, a hindrance that international law could not simply overcome in the golden age of international adjudication. Rather, it is a daily quest for international lawyers. International law being a complementary and residual legal system that owes its existence to national law, there is always the risk that the international lawyer fails to restraint the national lawyer, and accompanying conceptions, lurking within him or her.

From this perspective, lawyers may be said to be engaged in a game of sovereignty that, albeit never-ending, produces losers and perhaps also winners each and every day.

Notes

1. *Case of the SS Wimbledon*, PCIJ Series A No. 1 (1923) at p. 25; the "axiom" had been expressed earlier: for example, *Cession of Vessels and Tugs for Navigation on the Danube*, Reports of International Arbitral Awards, vol. 1 (1921) at p. 103.
2. *Nomination of the Workers' Delegate to the International Labour Conference*, PCIJ Series B No. 1 (1922) at p. 19.
3. *The Case of the SS Lotus*, PCIJ Series A No. 10 (1927) at p. 18; see also the similar pronouncement in *Affaire des biens britanniques au Maroc espagnol*, Reports of International Arbitral Awards, vol. 2 (1924) at p. 699.
4. PCIJ Series C No. 13-II at pp. 150–151.
5. *Status of Eastern Carelia*, PCIJ Series B No. 5 (1923) at p. 27.
6. *Ireland v. United Kingdom*, ECHR Series A No. 25 (1978) at para. 239.
7. *Soering v. United Kingdom*, ECHR Series A No. 161 (1989) at para. 87.

8. ECHR Series A No. 7 (1968) at para. 12.
9. *Draft Agreement Relating to the Creation of the European Economic Area*, Opinion 1/91, [1991] ECR I-6079 at paras 20–21.
10. *Van Gend en Loos*, Case 26/62, [1963] ECR 1 at 12.
11. Case 6/64, [1964] ECR 585 at 593.
12. Ibid.

Part II

Vertical Sovereignty Games

5

Play Money? Contemporary Perspectives on Monetary Sovereignty

Christoph W. Herrmann

Introduction

The more books one reads on money, the more one gets confused and frustrated about one's incapacity to grasp the very essence, the idea of what constitutes money. Yet one can derive at least some comfort from the fact that even Nobel Prize laureate economists such as John Maynard Keynes or famous bankers such as Baron Rothschild—almost coquettishly—admitted to know only two or three people who actually understood money, but unfortunately disagreed about its nature (Ingham 2005, xi). Rephrasing slightly another quote of unknown origin, one could say that there are three roads to madness: love, ambition and the study of money (Chown 2003, 5).[1] I am still undecided whether me being a lawyer by training—and therefore allegedly equipped with a natural confusion about numbers[2]—will make me go down that road even faster or rather slower.

The disagreement as to the nature of money is not restricted to the different disciplines that deal with money: Economics, Law, Sociology, Political Science (and even Geography[3]), but also manifests itself in the economic discipline.[4] To some extent, the difference in thinking about money reflects the diverse interests the disciplines have in the subject and is of no relevance to the others: Economists do not necessarily have to consider in their treatment of monetary theory that money is a symbolic medium and a precondition of modern detached lifestyle from a sociological point of view.[5] Nor does a lawyer always have to consider what is used in practice as money when he has to answer the question as to the legal tender of a given country.[6] However, thinking about monetary sovereignty means thinking about the nature of a relationship between the state, the individual, and the economy.

According to the still important "State Theory of Money," formulated in 1905 by G. F. Knapp, money is "a creature of law" (Knapp 1923, 1)[7], law being identified with the modern state. The key argument of this theory is the existence of debt. The state provides its power of enforcement of contractual debts, but defines what serves as satisfaction of the debt through the definition of legal tender. This definition is always a historic one, on the basis of a recurrent link to the former currency in which old debt may have been denominated (Knapp, 9–20).

However, this legalistic understanding of money is widely rejected in economic circles, which tend to define money in a functional way ("money is what money does") and emphasize the actual acceptance as payment by economic entities as being decisive for something to become money. According to this view, money bears the functions of unit of account, means of exchange, standard of deferred payments, and store of value. An item that fulfils all these functions will normally be considered by economists as "money" with the medium of exchange function given supreme importance by mainstream economists (the so-called commodity theory of money).[8] This view may have been correct in the past, that is, from early ancient times until the beginning of the twentieth century. In those times, money stuff were predominantly precious metals (or banknotes and state-issued paper currencies convertible into metal), and accordingly the acceptance of money was on the basis of the appreciation the money stuff itself enjoyed as a commodity.

However, things have changed. Change began more or less one and a half centuries ago with the development of true nonredeemable paper currencies and found its ultimate completion with the breakdown of the Bretton Woods System in 1971, when the remaining indirect link between all currencies and gold was given up. It is obvious that in our times money cannot simply be—as it has widely been believed for thousands of years—the most fungible commodity available anymore, even though this may have been the historical origin of money. It would contravene the ordinary meaning of the word "commodity" to use it for money that is made of a substance that has no practical use whatsoever, or at least no real value that comes even close to the exchange value it normally embodies.[9] It holds even truer for book money that nowadays may be transferred electronically and has no bodily existence at all or for E-Money[10] or virtual currencies such as the Linden Dollars used in the virtual world of Second Life.

Hence, the nature of money must be something different. As Georg Simmel has correctly pointed out in his *Philosophy of Money* (1900), money rests on the trust of individuals who accept it as payment only because they believe that other individuals will accept it in their turn in the future (Simmel 1930, 162). The very core of this societal relationship is that of credit. According to that view, money embodies a negotiable claim on society to receive goods and services of real value in the future in return for it. It certifies that its owner has made a real contribution to the economy for which he has received only the money stuff and no real goods or services. This view does neither contradict with the functions ascribed to money by economic monetary theory—Schumpeter developed a very similar position later in his writings on the nature of money (Schumpeter 1917, 627–715; 1970) and the credit theory of money, on which these thoughts were based, dates back to John Law's writings at the beginning of the eighteenth century (cf. Schumpeter 1954, 321–323)—nor does it necessarily conflict with the state theory of money. Claims may very well be traded as commodities and trust in social and legal institutions has an extremely close relationship with the state and the law. It is a necessary sociological precondition of all legal institutions and of community as such. The importance of "credibility" of monetary policy and the need for a "culture of stability" are nowadays also widely accepted among monetary economists; hence, the persistent call for independent central banks.

It has been purported in academic writings that the two defining features of "national currencies," that is, their distinctness and exclusivity in a given territory, are under threat by different trends: denationalization, regionalization, and virtualization of money (cf. Gilbert and Helleiner 1999). In the following, we will try to tackle the question what monetary sovereignty is and what use states make of it at the beginning of the twenty-first century.

Monetary Sovereignty in Public International Law

The power over money has persistently been regarded as one of the core elements of statehood, institutionalized with the notion of "sovereignty" by Jean Bodin (1583, 211). The emergence of national currencies as such, that is, money that is distinct and exclusive to the territory of a state, is seen as closely related to the formation of nation states in modern times (Helleiner 2003) and the use of the respective legal tender has often been coerced by authorities upon citizens (Simmel 1930, 173). Money is considered a symbol of national independence as well as integration and identity. However, national money is not always appreciated. In the words of John Stuart Mill:

> So much of barbarism still remains in the transactions of the most civilized nations, that almost all independent countries choose to assert their nationality by having, to their own inconvenience and that of their neighbours, a peculiar currency of their own. (Mill 1909, 615)

The presumption that an independent state would normally also have its own currency is also implied in the Statute of the International Monetary Fund (IMF). At its conclusion in 1944, it seemed rather unrealistic that an independent country could opt for not having a currency of its own (Gianviti 2005b, 817–821).

Sometimes, the relationship between a nation and its money can have almost obsessive, even erotic traits, as may, for example, be the case with us Germans and the British. Calls for a "Denationalization of Money" (Hayek 1977) have therefore—leaving aside the amazing introduction of the Euro—neither been very frequent nor have they gained a great deal of support. Even liberal economists, for example the ordo-liberal Freiburger School of Walter Eucken and Franz Böhm, tend to take the state monopoly over money for granted or at least accept it.

Public International Law reflects this general acceptance of the state power over money. According to an often quoted decision of the Permanent Court of International Justice (PCIJ) in 1929,

> [...] is [it] indeed a generally accepted principle of public international law that a State is entitled to regulate its own currency. (PCIJ 1929, 44)

The key legal consequence derived from this *ius cudendae monetae* (right to issue money) is that the definition of a state's currency to which a reference may be made in contracts, is solely described by the law of that state, the *lex monetae*. That means that national courts have to respect measures taken by other states in exercise of their monetary sovereignty (Proctor 2005, 331–347, 499–520). It becomes relevant first and foremost in cases of a currency reform or reconstruction such as the introduction of the Euro.[11] Furthermore, given the lack of specific treaty obligations, there will normally be no basis for a legal challenge of another state's measures to organize its monetary system or of its conduct of monetary policy as long as this does not interfere with the monetary sovereignty of another state, for example, by state-controlled counterfeiting of foreign currency (cf. Proctor 2005, 531–538).

Elements of Monetary Sovereignty

Monetary sovereignty encompasses a number of sovereign rights as well as policy tools.[12] Internally, the state is free to define its unit of account, to issue banknotes and coins and to declare them legal tender, to impose criminal sanctions on counterfeiting, to prohibit the use of other currencies inside its territory, to regulate the money supply and the banking system, and to determine and change the value of its currency.

Given its impact on the effective demand for a currency, one should also consider the definition of the means of payment for taxes and state debts as forming part of the monetary sovereignty of a state (van Dun 1998, 47). Regarding the external dimension of their currency, states may decide to impose exchange restrictions and controls on the flow of capital and payments, opt for a floating or fixed exchange-rate regime and define the exchange-rate vis-à-vis other currencies.

Limitations to Monetary Sovereignty Deriving from the IMF Statute

The sovereign rights of a state are limited by the provisions of international agreements it has entered into. Relating to monetary sovereignty, the main source for such limitations is the Articles of Agreement of the IMF.[13] With its 185 member countries, the IMF constitutes the virtually universal legal framework for the exercise of monetary sovereignty.[14] However, it must be emphasized that every country is free to join and to leave the IMF,[15] that is, membership is not an exogenously imposed restriction on sovereignty, but a deliberate self-restraint, something that is sometimes forgotten in the discourse about the waning of sovereignty in the times of globalization.

For the present contribution, there are two main aspects of the rules of the IMF that deserve mentioning:

- First, since the second amendment to the Articles, which came into force in 1978 and was designed to adapt the legal framework to the practice of freely floating exchange-rates that had emerged with the breakdown of the par value system in the early 1970s, members of the IMF are free to decide to fix or float the exchange rate of their currency against other currencies (art. IV Sec. 2 [b] IMF). Even though one of the main purposes of the IMF is "to promote exchange stability, to maintain orderly exchange arrangements amongst members and to avoid competitive exchange depreciation" (see art. I [iii] IMF), there is "no clearly defined and self-standing legal duty to maintain stable currencies" presently laid down in the IMF Articles (Proctor 2005, 564). Even the most substantive "hard obligation," to "avoid manipulating exchange rates or the international monetary system to prevent effective balance of payments adjustment or to gain an unfair competitive advantage over other members" (art. IV Sec. 1 [iii] IMF) has turned out to be not very effective and has therefore been subject to changes most recently.[16]

- Second, the introduction of restrictions on the making of payments and transfers for current international transactions[17] without the approval of the Fund is prohibited (art. VIII Sec. 2 (a) IMF). Whether a member is allowed to restrict the transaction itself is a matter not for international monetary law, but for international trade law to decide. Under the World Trade Organization (WTO) regime, which applies to the trade of its 152 member countries, quantitative restrictions on trade in goods are generally prohibited (with some exceptions), but may for example, be imposed in case of balance-of-payments problems (see art. XII, XV GATT, art. XII GATS). Contrary to payments for current transactions, the IMF members are under no obligation to liberalize international capital transfers (art. VI Sec. 3 IMF). Efforts in the 1990s that were aimed at introducing disciplines in that regard have lost momentum following the Asian crisis of the late 1990s.[18]

The Waning of Monetary Sovereignty

It is one of the prominent and fashionable tenets of our time that the sovereignty of states is diminishing owing to the process of globalization. The same claim is being made regarding "monetary sovereignty." According to Treves, the statement of the PCIJ nowadays is a mere figure of speech. However, Treves writings also reveal the source of much of the misunderstandings in the debates about the waning sovereignty in the post-Westphalian world order. According to him, sovereignty is a factual question, not a question of a right. However, this is exactly where legal understandings of sovereignty and political concepts differ significantly. From a purely legal point of view, sovereignty erodes only where obligations for a state may arise and be enforced without or even against the consent of that state. Sovereign is who is not subject to legally enforceable commands from a third party. From a traditional political science perspective, sovereignty is often taken to mean absolute and factual independence. The problem with the latter view of course is that there is no state that possesses absolute independence in that sense—not even nuclear super powers—and that there was none in the past.

As regards the alleged waning of monetary sovereignty, the usual suspects are the "global capital markets" that have taken control and can bring down currencies, financial centers, and governments. Indeed, capital markets have a great influence on domestic economic policies. However, they operate only within a legal framework established and upheld by states. Free movement of capital is nothing that markets have imposed, but something that has been made possible by states because it is seen as economically beneficial. It is for every state to decide whether it wants to benefit from or engage in economic globalization including foreign capital investments or whether it wants to take the "Cuban" or "North Korean" road to the detriment of its people. Sometimes it seems that those who bemoan an alleged inability of political actors rather feel dissatisfaction about the substantive outcome of the political process, since it does not concur with their view of "good policies."

At this point, one factual limitation of all monetary sovereignty choices should not be overlooked: According to what economic theory commonly calls the "impossible trinity," "impossible triad," or the "trilemma," it is impossible in the long run to combine free movement of capital, fixed exchange rates, and an independent monetary policy (Bernanke 2005, 1–12).[19] One must always be sacrificed. The problem described by the trilemma in my view is not a question of sovereignty. It is simply a matter of factual limits to state power as they have always existed. States have at all times been unable to provide certain goods to their people, be it security, economic welfare, health, and so on and the more they tried to provide, the less they delivered. It is a mere truth of life that one has to make choices between different opportunities all the time, and it holds true for states—even the most "Hobbesian" ones—as well. As long as they still exercise effective control over their territory and the people living there, they remain free to make such choices as they deem appropriate, but they have to live with the consequences.

Monetary Sovereignty "Games"

States can use their power over the currency in many different ways. Money can be and has been used as a coercive means of politics in the past (Kirschner 1995). Monetary policy can allegedly also be the trigger of military conflicts. So it has been argued that the 2003 War on Iraq was mainly owing to Iraq's decision to switch from US Dollar to Euro in its oil trade

(Clark 2005). These matters fall of course into the sphere of International Relations theory and International Political Economy. However, they are not subject of the present contribution, which is focused on "sovereignty games" as referring to a less aggressive, lighter behavior of states regarding their sovereignty, including states' decisions not to make use of what is considered to be their lawful sovereign right.

Every state, in principle, is free not to accede to or withdraw from the IMF. However, given the large number of members and the relatively low level of commitments resulting from membership in the IMF, I will confine the following submissions to strategic options that can be pursued notwithstanding IMF membership, since they do not conflict with its legal rules.

As pointed out earlier, a member of the IMF is free to choose between a floating and a fixed exchange rate arrangement and is only obliged to ensure the convertibility of its currency for payments for current account transactions. In fact, this leaves quite some leeway for policy choices and the states widely use them. Given the obligation to allow convertibility at least for current account transactions, the key element of every monetary strategy is the exchange rate arrangement a country chooses. According to the degree of flexibility, the possible options embrace a freely or managed floating currency, a (crawling) currency peg (against one other currency or a basket of currencies), a currency board or a fully fledged "dollarization," or a monetary union with other countries (Proctor 2005, 794–816).[20]

As of July 2006[21], of the member countries of the IMF:

- 25 countries let their currency float,
- 50 countries had a floating exchange rate without a specific exchange value target,
- 5 countries had installed a crawling peg system,
- 10 countries (mainly European Union [EU] member states not [yet] participating in Stage 3 of European Monetary Union [EMU]) were involved in a system of fixed exchange rates with a narrow band of floating (ERM II[22]),
- 51 countries had another conventional fixed exchange rate,
- 5 countries had a currency board in operation,
- 33 countries were member of a currency union, and
- 9 countries were using another country's currency (to this, countries such as Andorra,[23] Liechtenstein,[24] Vatican City,[25] or the Principality of Monaco[26] must be added, which also have no currency of their own, but use either de jure or de facto the Euro or the Swiss Franc).

The most liberal regime of course is that of floating exchange regimes, where the determination of a currency's exchange value is left to the market and interventions of public authorities are rare. This approach is mainly found in major industrial countries (e.g., the United States, Canada, Japan, Australia, New Zealand, South Korea, Norway, and the United Kingdom) and countries already very well integrated in the world economy (e.g., Brazil, Chile, Israel, Mexico, and South Africa). Of course, the Euro as the common currency of the 13 countries already participating in stage 3 of EMU is a floating currency as well.[27] Needless to say that for an exchange rate to be really floating both currencies must be floating.

A pegged currency is characterized by a fixed exchange rate against either—far more frequently—one specific currency (e.g., the US Dollar or the Euro) or against a basket consisting of different currencies (only five countries as of July 2006). A variation of a pegged currency is a "crawling peg," that is, the currency is pegged against another one, but the exchange rate is adjusted according to a previously announced scheme.[28] In these cases, the internal money supply is not contingent on the foreign anchor currency nor is the balance-of-payments equilibrium automatic. Moreover, the monetary policy must be pursued according to the principle of exchange rate targeting. It is this aspect in which a currency board deviates significantly from a mere pegged currency. A currency board is a monetary authority that issues a domestic currency that is backed up by a foreign reserve currency, normally with a backing of at least 100 percent, and that is legally obliged to exchange the domestic currency against the reserve currency on demand (Chown 2003, 16; Ize 2003, 645; Proctor 2005; 801). Contrary to a central bank, a currency board does not pursue any kind of "monetary policy" since it has no policy choices to make as regards the money supply. The significant impact on monetary policy independence is quite clear in such a case, but it becomes literally much more visible for everybody in case of a complete[29] "dollarization," that is, a substitution of the domestic currency with a foreign currency, which may take place officially as an exercise of monetary sovereignty. In such case, the foreign currency would be made either sole legal tender or circulate alongside the persisting domestic currency. The degree of dollarization will also depend on the policy chosen by the issuing country, which may passively accept, actively encourage, or actively resist the use of its currency by another country,[30] even though there are no legal rules contained in the IMF Articles that prohibit a dollarization.[31] An active support would, for example, include the conclusion of an international agreement granting the adopting country coinage rights, access to payment systems and central bank credit.

A dollarization can of course also take place unofficially as a consequence of behavior of private individuals.[32] In the latter case the domestic currency—if one ever existed—may in analogy to the notion of a "failing state" be described as a "failing currency," since it remains legal tender but is not used anymore in daily life, even though the respective state may try to suppress the dollarization.[33] The foreign currency does not necessarily need to be the US Dollar. In fact it may indeed be the Euro, in which case it becomes more and more common to speak of "euroisation" (cf. Gruson 2003, 629–640).

An equally extensive but still quite different restriction (or surrender) of monetary sovereignty is associated with the establishment of a currency union. Besides the Euro Area, two of them are found in Africa,[34] another one in the Eastern Caribbean,[35] and the Golf Cooperation Council plans to establish a customs union.[36] Also in that case, the institutional design can be quite different.

The Logic of Monetary Sovereignty "Games"

For many centuries, the main purpose of the state monopoly over money was to raise revenues for the government through seignorage profits on coinage and through inflation taxes, thereby protecting the financial power of rulers necessary to finance war against foreign enemies. Regarding the exchange regime, the maximization of gold or silver accumulation corresponds to this role of money.

With the emergence of managed paper currencies without any metal base restricting the money supply, more effective taxation systems and other fundamental changes brought about by the nineteenth and twentieth centuries, however, the goals of monetary policy shifted. Keynes (1935) General Theory suggested that governments could use cheap-money monetary policy and deficit-spending to stabilize economic activity and to actively fight unemployment if they accepted some inflation that was seen as a necessary instrument to overcome nominal wage rigidities that prevented a downward real-wage adjustment in economic downswings and therefore caused huge unemployment. It also accepted a consequential decline of the external value of the currency because of its additional price-effect on real wages.

However, the ideology of intervention did not survive for more than 30 years and with the monetarist counter-revolution led by Milton Friedman, a policy preference for stable currencies has become almost unanimously supported around the globe (see Helleiner 2003, 230). The benefits ascribed to a stable currency are pretty well-known: they are the preconditions for money to fulfill its fundamental functions of unit of account, means of payment, and store of value. Inflation leads to intransparent prices, misallocation of resources, and disguised property transfers from creditors to debtors. Furthermore, a constantly inflating currency will be under constant pressure to devaluate externally, and it will become increasingly difficult to attract foreign capital investment. Generally speaking, a stable currency has a major overall economic welfare impact in the long-term perspective (cf. Ferguson 2006, 223–230; Levy 2006, 231–242). It is against this backdrop only that the different ways in which states exercise their monetary sovereignty can be understood. To achieve economic growth and welfare, states will nowadays normally try to integrate into the world economy by encouraging cross-border trade and investment. To do so, they have to provide

- a stable economic environment including a stable currency, that is, one which is not inflating at high speed and whose exchange rate is not under constant pressure to devaluate;
- (more or less) free convertibility of the currency not only for current account transactions, but also for capital account transactions.

"Monetary sovereignty games" can only be understood against this backdrop. As pointed out earlier, the key decision for the monetary sovereign to take concerns the exchange rate arrangement it wants to follow. All of the options described have advantages and disadvantages and to choose between them will depend on a great deal of different economic and social circumstances prevailing in the country making the choice.[37]

The main advantage of floating exchange rates is seen in the relative gain in internal monetary policy independence, which enables the competent authority (i.e., normally the respective central bank), to focus on the control of inflation and economic growth inside the country.[38] At the same time, a floating exchange rate will always ensure an equalized balance-of-payments, however at the cost of private businesses that have to live with changes in their international competitiveness and transaction costs caused by the need to hedge the inherent exchange rate risks. Furthermore, floating exchange rates do not attract speculation against the currency as may happen in case of a currency that is pegged against another one at an exchange rate higher or lower than the market rates and the central bank is consequentially under no pressure to intervene. This policy choice, as pointed out earlier, is prevalent in industrial countries and there is no obvious reason to abandon it within the foreseeable future, especially for the "Big Three" United States of America, Japan, and the Euro Area (Corden 2002, 255). They have established credible commitments to low inflation, large open economies and only little to gain from more exchange rate stability, since the existing exchange risks are hedged by functioning financial markets (Eichengreen 1994, 134).

For the rest of the world, matters are by far not as straightforward. For most of these countries, a stable currency is still a rather difficult goal to achieve. The reasons for inflation are still very poorly known, even though some key factors have been identified: an independent central bank, low level of conflict between capital and labor, and decentralized forms of governments in federal systems (Busch 2003, 234).[39] For the last decades, the increasing integration of low-cost producer countries such as China and India into global markets and the general competitive pressures deriving from the opening-up of national markets are also deemed to have contributed to the lower inflation over the last 25 to 30 years (Levy 2006, 234).

Whatever the reasons of inflation are, once an economy has been infected, it becomes very difficult and economically very costly to get rid of the disease. The weaker the state and its government in general are the less likely a successful reconstruction of a sound monetary system with a stable currency is. In such a situation, it may be the most promising way to "import monetary stability" by surrendering political monetary sovereignty, which in itself is an exercise of legal monetary sovereignty. The key options then are a pegged currency, a currency board, or a complete dollarization. However, these options have quite different impacts and the conditions that must be fulfilled to maintain them vary. Generally speaking, a simple currency peg, that is, a fixed but adjustable exchange rate will be difficult to operate without capital controls and its likely breakdown creates huge political and social costs as demonstrated by Britain's exit from the ERM I and the Asian crisis of the late 1990s. This is why this kind of exchange rate regime is frequently ruled out as a policy option in economic literature. The remaining choice between a more flexible exchange rate and a more credible commitment to exchange rate stability (i.e., nonadjustable) will consider the following arguments that are put forward in favor of and against flexible exchange rates or currency board or dollarization solutions (Eichengreen 1994; IMF 1999; Corden 2002; cf. Baliño 2003, 613–628; Schuler 2005)

- Proponents of flexible exchange rates usually put forward the greater domestic macroeconomic policy flexibility that remains under a flexible exchange regime as well as the shock-absorber function of flexible exchange rates that allow for easier and less burdensome adjustments than a deflationary domestic policy in case of economic shocks.

- Proponents of currency boards and dollarization emphasize the credibility-import that is associated with currency boards and dollarization and the desired consequential loss in domestic policy discretion, but point also to the reduction of transaction costs and the likely stimulation of trade and investment.

Which of these arguments are more convincing in a given situation will depend on circumstances such as the size of the economy, the credibility of the political institutions involved in monetary and fiscal policies, the development and regulation of the financial sector, the degree of openness of the economy, and so on. Furthermore, the loss of seignorage profits in case of a fully fledged dollarization may play a role as may the need to have a national currency for symbolic integrative purposes, for example, for newly independent states. States having gone through a conflict of a military kind may need a complete reconstruction of the monetary and financial system in which a currency board may be a quick solution to establish credibility.[40] What decision is being taken will of course also depend on policy preferences of domestic politicians, possible alliances between major political groups, and long-term strategic monetary goals such as accession to the Euro Area.

The creation of a monetary union such as the Euro Area seems to have rather different reasons. Of course, the whole scale of arguments against and in favor of fixed exchange rates also applies to a monetary union, but to reap its benefits, it suffices to fix the exchange rates of the participating countries irrevocably. A common currency is not a necessary element of a monetary union, as was made clear by the Delors Report that outlined the way to EMU and it also imposes costs on private individuals, for example, in connection with the change of the unit of account. However, it is equally clear that a common currency further reduces transaction costs, bolsters the credibility of the commitment to "exchange rate" stability, and has a significant symbolic meaning for the creation of a common identity among the citizens of the participating countries.[41] In the case of EMU, it is also commonly asserted that the other European countries intended to benefit from the credibility of the Deutsche Bundesbank and import the stability of the Deutsche Mark. In addition, as it has been pointed out, the introduction of the Euro has the potential to challenge the role of the US dollar as the predominant international currency (for payments as well as reserve purposes), a role that is accompanied by significant economic benefits such as seignorage profits from the currency circulating abroad or the benefit of borrowing in domestic currency (see Wegner 1998).

Conclusions

What is left then of "monetary sovereignty" at the beginning of the twenty-first century and how do states use it strategically in their "sovereignty games"? This chapter has tried to demonstrate that monetary sovereignty is a generally accepted element of state sovereignty and that it consists of a number of different sovereign rights including the definition of a unit of account, the issuing of banknotes and coins, and the establishment of an exchange rate arrangement. The most important international monetary agreement, the IMF Articles of Agreement do hardly confine the rights of its members to opt for the monetary regime they deem appropriate, except for the obligation to guarantee the convertibility of their currency for current account transactions. In fact, there are numerous options from which states can "choose."

However, in making their sovereign choice, states are confronted with a practical "trilemma" according to which exchange rate stability, domestic macroeconomic policy discretion and free movement of capital cannot coexist for a long time. Whereas in the past monetary sovereignty was mainly used for raising revenue (seignorage and inflation tax), the emergence of irredeemable paper currencies brought about new perspectives. During the reign of Keynesian macroeconomic policies, efforts were made to use loose monetary policies and public deficit spending to fight unemployment and economic stagnation. When the outcome after first successes was inflation plus stagnation and unemployment ("stagflation"), the monetarist counter-revolution struck back. As a result, stable noninflationary currencies are nowadays universally considered the primary goal of monetary policy. However, stable money has a lot to do with credibility of policy and with trust into institutions and society, something not all governments are able to generate and to build upon. In such situations, a deliberate restriction of domestic macroeconomic policy discretion by means of a credible exchange arrangement or a complete dollarization may be the most effective and efficient way to restore a sound monetary system and may generate further benefits such as the stimulation of trade and foreign investment. Further reaching restrictions of monetary sovereignty such as they are conjoint with the creation of a monetary union will normally have a rationale that goes beyond pure economic reasons, but will also rest upon political goals, in particular the creation of an identity beyond the nation state.

Whatever decision a state may take, the implications for its economy, society and political system will be significant and failure may be extremely costly in economic as well as in political terms. In this sense, there is no such thing as a "monetary sovereignty game," since the consequences are normally too serious, the stakes too high.

Notes

1. See also Marx's reference to a statement made by Gladstone in a parliamentary debate on Peel's Bank Act of 1844, who observed that "not even love has turned more men into fools than has meditation on the nature of money" (Marx 1970, 64).
2. According to a common mistranslation of the principle *iudex non calculat*, lawyers are not able to calculate. The original meaning was that arguments, evidence, and witnesses are not simply counted, but considered according to their merits.
3. For a geographical approach to the study of money see Cohen (1999, 121) with further references.
4. For an account of the different positions see Ingham (2004).
5. For sociological perspectives on money see Simmel (1930); Ingham (2004, 59–68); Zelizer (1994).
6. For a legal definition of money see Proctor (2005, 5–70).
7. The authors own translation of "Geld ist ein Geschöpf der Rechtsordnung."
8. For an account of this "mainstream" economic view see Ingham (2004, 15–22).
9. Probably, the practical value of paper money is exhaustively described by the following usages: sniffing cocaine through it, accelerating a fire with it, and using it as wallpaper or toilet paper.
10. For a definition of electronic money in european law see Directive 2000/46/EC of the European Parliament and of the Council of September 18, 2000 on the taking up, pursuit of and prudential supervision of the business of electronic money institutions, OJ 2000 No. L 271/39.
11. In such a case, foreign courts must apply the changeover from the national currencies to the Euro when claims denominated in those currencies are brought before them, see Lenihan (1998).
12. On these elements see Gianviti (2005a, 1); Lastra (2006, 22–23); Proctor (2005, 500–501).
13. On the law of the IMF in general see Lastra (2006, 371–445); Lowenfeld (2002, 529–564); Proctor (2005, 557–581).
14. A list of the members can be consulted at http://www.imf.org/external/np/sec/memdir/members.htm.
15. See Art. XXVI, Sec. 1, IMF.
16. See Decision of the IMF Executive Board of June 15, 2007 on Bilateral Surveillance of Members' Exchange Rate Policies, available at http://www.imf.org/external/np/sec/pn/2007/pn0769.htm (July 10, 2007).
17. The term "Payments for current transactions" is defined in Art. XXX (d), IMF. On this topic see Elizalde (2005, 20–22).
18. On this topic see Fischer (1999); Gianviti (1999); Hagan (1999); Gianviti (2003).
19. It may be possible in a case like China's Yuan, which is under constant pressure to appreciate. In theory, it would be possible for the Bank of China to

meet any demand of its currency. At a certain point, however, the increased amount of money in China would lead to increased inflation and the central bank would have to change its policies.

20. These categories are also used in practice, see for example, IMF (1999, 23); Deutsche Bundesbank, *Devisenkursstatistik Februar 2007*, pp. 50–51 (accessible at http://www.bundesbank.de/download/volkswirtschaft/devisenkurs statistik/2007/devisenkursstatistik022007.pdf).

21. See Deutsche Bundesbank, *Devisenkursstatistik Februar 2007*, pp. 50–51 (accessible at http://www.bundesbank.de/download/volkswirtschaft/ devisenkursstatistik/2007/devisenkursstatistik022007.pdf). Data for 2007 may be found in IMF (2007, xxv–xxvii).

22. Agreement of March 16, 2006 between the European Central Bank and the national central banks of the member states outside the euro area laying down the operating procedures for an exchange rate mechanism in stage three of Economic and Monetary Union, OJ 2006 No. C 73/21.

23. Andorra has no currency of its own. Nowadays, the Euro is used, but on an unofficial basis. Negotiations between the EC and Andorra with a view to entering into an exchange agreement similar to those entered into with the Principality of Monaco, the Vatican City, and the Republic of San Marino have not led to any outcome so far.

24. See Monetary Agreement of June 19, 1980 between Liechtenstein and Switzerland, *Liechtensteinisches Landesgesetzblatt* (1981 No. 32), p. 1. Liechtenstein had already been using the Swiss Franc for more than 50 years before the agreement was entered into.

25. Monetary Agreement between the Italian Republic, on behalf of the European Community, and the Vatican City State and, on its behalf, the Holy See, OJ 2001 No. C 299/1.

26. Monetary Agreement between the Government of the French Republic, on behalf of the European Community, and the Government of His Serene Highness the Prince of Monaco, OJ 2002 No. L 142/59.

27. However, the Council could enact guidelines for the conduct of monetary policy that the European Central Bank would have to take into account in the day-to-day operation of the Community's external monetary policy, cf. Art. 111 (2), EC Treaty.

28. Normally, a regular devaluation occurs to accommodate for differences in the targeted or real inflation rate between the anchor currency and the pegged currency.

29. A currency board is sometimes referred to as "quasi-dollarisation," see Altig and Nosal (2005, 807).

30. For a discussion of the perspective of the issuing country see Altig and Nosal (2005, 807).

31. For a discussion of this point, see Gianviti (2005b, 817). The situation is different regarding the EU member states that not yet participate in stage three of EMU. They are under an obligation to stay in the ERM II to fulfill the Maastricht Criteria on the basis of which the ultimate decision about their

accession to the Euro Area will be taken. That is one of the reasons why the ECB has shown resistance to the idea of an accession country's unilateral euroisation.

32. The degree of an unofficial dollarization may vary in different countries, depending on whether the foreign currency is used only as unit of account and store of value or also for (large or even smaller) daily payments, see Baliño, "Dollarization: A Primer" in IMF (ed.), *Current Developments in Monetary and Financial Law*, Vol. 2 (Washington 2003).

33. That is, for example, the case in Cuba, where the use of US Dollar was legally prohibited in November 2004.

34. West African Economic and Monetary Union. (UEMOA from its name in French, Union économique et monétaire ouest-africaine; Member states: Benin, Burkina Faso, Côte d'Ivoire, Mali, Niger, Senegal, Togo, and Guinea-Bissau) and the Economic and Monetary Community of Central Africa (or CEMAC from its name in French, Communauté Économique et Monétaire de l'Afrique Centrale; Member states: Cameroon, the Central African Republic, Chad, the Republic of the Congo, Equatorial Guinea, and Gabon).

35. Eastern Caribbean Currency Union, part of the Eastern Caribbean Common Market (Member states: Antigua and Barbuda, Dominica, Grenada, Saint Kitts and Nevis, Saint Lucia, and Saint Vincent and the Grenadines and the two British overseas territories: Anguilla and Montserrat).

36. The following quote has been taken from the official Web site of the GCC: "[The cooperation] is also designed to unify banking and monetary regulations and laws, as well as increase coordination between monetary agencies and central banks, including the initiation of one currency in order to further economic integration." (available at http://www.gcc-sg.org/cooperation.html#coop5).

37. Of the abundant literature on different exchange rate policies and their pros and cons see Corden (2002); Eichengreen (1994); Sweeney, Wihlborg and Willett (1999).

38. If, however, monetary has only very limited effects on real economies, monetary sovereignty (understood as policy sovereignty) is indeed "useless," cf. Schwartz (2004, 107–121).

39. Busch, "Die politische Ökonomie der Inflation" in Obinger/Wagschal/Kittel (eds.), *Politische Ökonomie* (Opladen 2003), pp. 175–197.

40. On this particular problem, see Lönnberg, "Restoring and Transforming Payment and Banking Systems in Postconflict Economies," in IMF (eds.), *Current Developments in Monetary and Financial Law*, Vol. 3 (Washington 2005), pp. 725–753.

41. On the costs and benefits of currency unions see Tavlas (2004, 89–106); Yeager (2004). See also Jonung (2004, 123–149).

6

Organized Duplicity? When States Opt Out of the European Union

Rebecca Adler-Nissen

Introduction

As part of a grand plan to make the European Union (EU) more popular, Margot Wallström, Commissioner for Institutional Relations and Communication Strategy, posted a short video on the Web site YouTube showing eighteen couples having sex. The conspicuous video (which promotes EU support for European films) ends with the couples' orgasms and the double entendre "Let's come together." Untraditional methods to convert the skeptical European publics into convinced Europeans are invented as the EU faces various forms of contestations of its supremacy from the member states. In the last decades, doubts over the benefits of Union membership have given rise to controversial national opt-outs (exemptions) from EU and EC treaties, which indicate that selected "outsiderness" may be preferred to being a full member of the Union. Opt-outs are interesting because they postulate that it is possible to reconstitute the boundary of the state in face of European integration. Opt-outs draw a line in the sand, as it were, and establish an area where the state is to remain sovereign. To the degree that statehood is fundamentally changing because of international and regional integration, national opt-outs will be a good indicator of how far this process has gone.

Existing research has largely interpreted opt-outs from the EU Treaties as safeguards of national sovereignty (Pilkington 1995, 109; Wallace 1997; Hedetoft 2000, 300; Padoa-Schioppa 2006, 86–87). In this chapter,

I propose an alternative interpretation: opt-outs demonstrate the difficult mediation between the domestic and the international sphere in the context of regional integration. When the other member states accepted to grant Untied Kingdom and Denmark opt-outs to avoid a stalemate in treaty negotiations, they were opening what I will call a "two-dimensional sovereignty game." Although opt-outs may help preserve the symbolic figure of an autonomous state to the domestic audience, in Brussels the opt-out protocols are translated into temporary measures and are politically circumvented to fit the European context. This "organized duplicity" is becoming increasingly more awkward as two different understandings of sovereignty—the national and the international—collide openly and question the value and effect of opting out. The clashes between domestic and European discourses surrounding the opt-outs unsettle the idea of a sovereign state protecting itself from outside interference and demonstrate how both the national and the international concept of sovereignty is changing with the constitutionalization of the EU.

The Two-Dimensional Sovereignty Game

The dynamic of opting out reveals the Janus-face of sovereignty in the sense that it demonstrates that claims to sovereignty in the context of international cooperation are often made before two different audiences at the same time—the national and the international. To understand this two-dimensional sovereignty game, I propose to explore the roles of the two audiences and the players who mediate between them.

Sovereignty as a Claim to Authority

Sovereignty is a discourse, which promotes a certain political order as the authoritative and prescribes certain actions and rights as legitimate (Biersteker and Weber 1996b; N. Walker 2003). By emphasizing sovereignty as a claim, the emphasis is placed on how it is used, or being played out, in legal and political practices. This approach implies an important difference between claim and control. The discourse of sovereignty can be an effective way to produce "ordering power," but only if the relevant audience accepts this claim (N. Walker 2003, 6–7). Following this line of thought, state sovereignty is produced through sovereignty practices. To be a state you need to fabricate effective symbols of legitimacy and representations of sovereignty. In a Foucauldian perspective, that is, a logic of representation, sovereign foundations are symbolic signs that make representational projects possible and allow sovereignty to refer to some original source of truth (Delcourt 2006, 49). The foundation of sovereignty changes over time and from place to place. Hence, for instance, "the people" is a sign, which does not exist naturally, or objectively, it has to be produced as the foundation of sovereignty to be politically represented. The main idea advanced here is that the two-dimensional sovereignty game is constituted by the increasingly problematic relationship between the national and the international. Neither side may be able or willing to understand how sovereignty is conceived by the other. This increases the pressure on the mediators who have to come up with legitimate and acceptable ways to bridge the tension.

The Internal and the External Audience

At the outset, the concept of sovereignty builds on a division between an internal and an external dimension. Internally, sovereignty is usually taken to mean the ultimate or highest authority within a political order and often it indicates that a government is the ultimate or exclusive authority within specified borders. In turn, sovereignty implies a hierarchic relationship between the sovereign and the subordinates, whoever they may be (Lake 2003, 304). Popular sovereignty represents one vision of this relationship, where the social contract binds the political authority and holds it accountable to the people who are the original sovereign (Besson 2004, 11). Externally sovereignty implies that the authority of the state is recognized as such by other legally equal entities (Hobson and Sharman 2005, 65) and that they respect claims to freedom from external interference. The two dimensions fit like a glove and one can argue that a "sovereign state is all of a piece" (James 1999, 464). In short, this division constitutes two different audiences for sovereignty claims—the internal audience (to whom the claim to sovereignty is a claim to supreme or ultimate authority) and the external audience (to whom a claim to sovereignty is a claim to independence and freedom from external interference) (Werner and de Wilde 2001).

However, in a "late sovereign" context of European integration, both the idea of national and international sovereignty is under pressure (N. Walker 2003). Domestically, it has become difficult to preserve the image of the autonomous "people" as the foundation of ultimate sovereignty because of transferral of competences away from national parliaments and governments to international organizations. States have accepted dramatic limits on their authority in return for the development of regional organizations. Also international sovereign claims are modified. Externally, the sovereign claim to independence is increasingly contested and reconfigured to a right to influence, an entitlement to participate or even intervene in the affairs of others (see also Sørensen 1999, 602–603). Through the very process, which limits national sovereignty, states may regain actual control of the policy areas where they have handed over competences and gain the possibility to influence the internal affairs of other states (Werner and de Wilde 2001, 295). So the "speech act" of sovereignty, be it national or international, is more complex to perform when conflicting claims to authority from states as well as nonstate polities such as the EU are the dish of the day.

Mediating between Two Spheres

It is safe to argue, without reifying a flawed picture of the state, that a particular group of people still enjoys a special status as mediators between the domestic and the international sphere. Governments and diplomats are the main players in the two-dimensional sovereignty game, because they have been granted formal authority to represent and manage the state politically and legally when it engages with inter and supranational organizations such as the EU. While companies, interest groups, and local and regional actors have contributed to turning the EU into a system of "multilevel governance" in which the state is only one actor among many others, for governments, the EU represents a clearly different level of negotiation, demarcated from the domestic. British officials still have to take the train or flight to Brussels for working group meetings and they do not come empty-handed (or –headed), but they bring instructions from London about specific objectives and national interests that they are expected to defend during the meetings. In Brussels, the EU appears of course not as an ordinary international setting, but more as a quasi-federal system, where supranational actors such as the European Commission and the European Parliament play an important role in changing the intergovernmental logic of cooperation (Forster 2000, 57). Nevertheless, ministers and diplomats are still the key mediators in the two-dimensional sovereignty game. Their task of mediation is further complicated by the fact that the national and international audiences are not homogenous entities; they rather consist of different sub-audiences. The domestic audience in democratic states includes not only parliament, but also the broader public and media, which perceive national sovereignty in sometimes markedly different ways. The international audience does not merely assemble other states, but increasingly also international and supranational organizations and courts.[1] This diversity makes mediation more difficult, but it also opens up a strategic room for discursive maneuvers.

Picking and Choosing from the European Buffet

In international and supranational organizations, states opt out of certain policy areas and functions, be it a common currency or common immigration policies, not out of territorial demarcated areas. In this sense, opt-outs represent an era of constitutional pluralism where boundaries of legitimate political authority are no longer solely understood in territorial terms, but also in a functional language. However, this has not made traditional understandings of sovereignty obsolete, indeed, opt-outs are domestically seen as symbols of national sovereignty and hence democracy reflecting what Neil Walker refers to as an ideological assumption of ultimate authority over the internal operation of the polity (N. Walker 2003).

With the Maastricht Treaty (1992), the United Kingdom was accorded an opt-out clause, meaning that it would not be required to adopt the single currency.[2] Furthermore, the United Kingdom negotiated an opt-out from the so-called Social Chapter.[3] These opt-out clauses were one of the conditions to be met if the British government were to give its approval to the treaty as a whole.[4] The opt-outs were drafted to assure that the treaty was in line with a British conception of Europe, not challenging its constitutional institutions and conventions such as parliamentary sovereignty (Hansen and Scholl 2002, 4). A few years later, the United Kingdom was granted an opt-out from the Schengen agreement (abolishing controls and checks at national borders between EU member states) and the new Title IV TEC dealing with "visas, asylum, immigration and other policies related to free movement of persons."

Denmark was also a reluctant negotiator in Maastricht, but having being granted a protocol on the European Monetary Union (EMU), the government had accepted the treaty when it was unexpectedly rejected in a dramatic referendum held in June 1992. Following the referendum, the Danish Parliament drafted a common negotiation position for the government. It focused on the most dominant issue in the Danish referendum debate—the transfer of national sovereignty to the EU (Hansen 2002).[5] The Danish "no" led to four key reserves attached to the treaties, which imply that Denmark has not adopted the euro, will not accept to replace national citizenship with EU citizenship; cannot participate in the development of a common European defense; and cannot participate in supranational cooperation in the field of Justice and Home Affairs. In this chapter, I focus particularly on the controversial British and Danish protocols on the euro, common borders, and Justice and Home Affairs.

Domestically, the opt-outs have two functions. First, they produce a fiction of national unity and fabricate a united domestic audience despite apparent political disagreements over the EU issue. As such, the opt-outs are not just defining a relation between the state and the EU, but also mediating between the different sub-audiences. Second, opt-outs present sovereignty as a fixed capital, given and known, and all it takes to reestablish it is to annul those decisions that have led to its careless dissipation (Rosanvallon 2000, 427–428; Morefield 2005). Seen from the United Kingdom and Denmark, opt-outs constitute bulwarks against European integration; underpinning an image of the state with full political and legal authority over people, territory, and money. This gives them an almost sacred character. During the negotiations on the Constitutional Treaty, the UK government continuously spoke of how the opt-outs would not be touched by what former State Secretary Jack Straw called a "simple tidying-up exercise" (Church and Phinnemore 2006, 8). The Danish Prime Minister Anders Fogh Rasmussen likewise promised that the opt-outs would be safeguarded and that the Danish people would remain in full control,

> There will be no trickery. There will be no cherry picking. The opt-outs will stand clear and clean in the new treaty. And the Danish people shall decide on this treaty including the opt-outs [...][6]

Things look differently from the perspective of the external audience. Opt-outs threaten the uniform application of EU law and thus the coherence of the Union's legal order (Curtin 1993). In the quest for European unity and constitution-building, differentiated integration is an unwanted obstacle (de Witte 2002, 236).[7] The most engaged actors in the European audience in relation to handling the opt-outs are the European Council secretariat, the European Commission, and the Council Presidency. In particular, the European Commission, acting as "guardian of the Treaties and defender of the general interests," is hostile toward the idea of opting out.[8]

To conform to the contradictory expectations of the national and the international audiences, the mediators (governments and diplomats) advance two different images of state authority, playing a double game. Mediation between the domestic and the international is not a neutral exercise; mediation is translation and hence modification of meaning. On the domestic scene, the players try to uphold a representation of opt-outs as legal and political safeguards of an independent national democracy. On the European scene, they negotiate with the other member states and EU institutions to reduce the exclusionary effects of the opt-outs and ensure that United Kingdom and Denmark act as credible partners and gain influence on the European decision-making process. In doing so, they articulate exemptions as temporary measures that are not aimed at

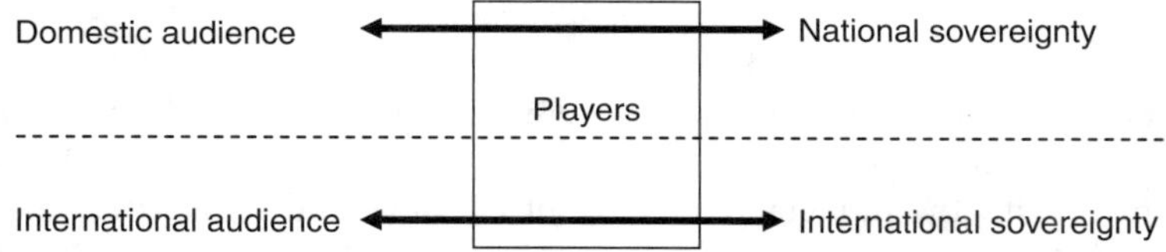

Figure 6.1   The two-dimensional sovereignty game

reducing the consistency of the EU *acquis* as a whole.[9] In this way, the players try to make sure that the domestic and European understandings of the opt-outs (and sovereignty) are kept separated. They work hard, on the one hand to ensure they are never accused by the domestic audience of manipulating while on the other hand struggling not to be seen as disloyal by the European audience. From this perspective, the British and Danish experiences of opting out give flesh to Steven Krasner's proposition that state sovereignty is "organised hypocrisy" (Krasner 1999). The game is illustrated in figure 6.1 and in the following, I will explore how it is played out in relation to the euro and Justice and Home Affairs. Building on this analysis, the chapter moves on to explore the dynamic nature of this game; as control of the mediation process is close to impossible, we see constant reinterpretations of the sovereignty, which the opt-outs were meant to protect.

Monetary Sovereignty?

Constitutional bodies of any kind, whether governments or central banks, have very limited influence in a world of deregulated currency markets and global financial movements. Monetary autonomy has clearly diminished because of the integration of the world's capital markets (Goodman 1992, 5). Nonetheless, widespread slogans such as "keep the pound" or "bevar kronen" reveal that in the United Kingdom and Denmark money is closely associated with sovereignty. In both countries, the minting of coins and printing of chapter money is (still) regarded as "sovereignty-producing practices" (Doty 1996, 143). Despite continued attempts by both British and Danish governments to "de-sovereignize" the euro, and regardless of the increasing difficulties of imagining and practicing monetary autonomy in a globalizing world, both the UK and the Danish euro protocols represent symbolic contracts between government and people; the latter is promised an ultimate (and sovereign) decision qua the referendum guarantee. Because the opt-outs represent what monetary sovereignty can mean today: a symbolic manifestation of statehood, it is very difficult to abolish them.

United Kingdom

A particular doctrine of national sovereignty in monetary affairs thrives in the United Kingdom; it is centered on ideas of a domestic political control with the monetary instrument (Gamble and Kelly 2002). In a speech to the House of Commons in January 1991, the Chancellor of the Exchequer explained that safeguarding the "sovereign right of Parliament" would be one of his four priorities in the forthcoming inter-governmental conference on the EMU.[10] Indeed, the United Kingdom has been granted a protocol on the single currency, which guarantees that it is for the UK government and parliament alone to initiate procedures for adopting the euro. Furthermore, the United Kingdom is not subject to the provisions on excessive deficits and it is not part of the European System of Central Banks (ESCB) and the European Central Bank (ECB). With the election of a pro-euro Labour in government from 1997, this firm position was forged into a "prepare and decide" policy. This attempt to push the United Kingdom closer to joining the euro was welcomed by the European audience (Miles and Doherty 2005), but domestically, it was a tricky move, because it questioned the domestic understanding of sovereignty over monetary affairs. To resolve this problem, the Labour government presented the choice to change from pound to euro as a purely economic decision with no political implications (Hughes and Smith 1998; Miles and Doherty 2005, 101). In October 1997, it announced five economic tests, which must be met before any decision to join can be made,

1. Sustainable convergence between United Kingdom and the economies in the euro area;
2. Whether there is sufficient flexibility to cope with economic change;
3. The effect on investment;
4. The impact on British financial services industry; and
5. Whether it is good for growth and employment.[11]

To label these checks "economic" demands stretching the meaning of the word "economy," but it is a necessary linguistic exercise because it allows for the view that British sovereign status is safeguarded despite flirting with the idea of replacing the pound with euro. In the two-dimensional sovereignty game, the tests serve a double purpose: to the European audience they demonstrate British commitment to joining the single currency (when it is in the United Kingdom's interests). To the domestic audience the tests contribute to the idea of a sovereign choice and underlines that in questions related to the euro the United Kingdom acts under instructions of no other nation or international actor. However, the "tests" are so elastic that anyone could claim that they have not been met.[12] Not surprisingly, when the government completed its initial assessment of the tests on June 9, 2003, it concluded that at this time the euro did not pass.[13] This almost ritual process of evaluation has been repeated in the subsequent years.

The attempt to present the euro as merely a question of economic calculations has not proved to be effective. The domestic audience (in particular parliament and the Euroskeptic media) has established a discursive consensus that the euro is one of the major political questions related to the fate of the United Kingdom as a sovereign state (Risse 2003; Howarth 2007). Consequently, to further assure the anxious public, both Labour and opposition have promised that a decision to recommend joining the euro zone should not only be put to a vote in parliament, but also a referendum (Miles and Doherty 2005, 104). In this way, the attempts to convince the predominantly euro-skeptic domestic audience to surrender the opt-out has contributed to a significant (if only partial) change in the political discourse and practices on monetary sovereignty in the United Kingdom, locating ultimate sovereign decisions (qua the referendum guarantee) with the British people rather than parliament and government. This change illustrates that opting out is not a one shot affair, the players continuously adapt to the audiences, thereby revealing that the exact meaning of a sovereignty claim such as an opt-out is negotiable.

Meanwhile on the European scene, the United Kingdom has followed a strategy of "economic and political hitchhiking" (Miles 2005, 16). This means that the British political and administrative elites have actively followed the developments of the monetary policy development in the EU despite the British opt-out (Miles and Doherty 2005, 201). The treasury has established a Euro Preparations Unit to work out a National Changeover Plan to prepare the different parts of the UK economy to manage a changeover to the euro. The Euro Preparations Unit also publishes guides for business managers, develops frameworks to protect consumers in the event of a changeover, and hosts a Web site to inform the public. Although treasury officials admit that this work is about sending the right signals to Brussels and building up credibility around the government's "prepare and decide" policy, substantial institutional reforms have also been initiated.[14] The decision over monetary sovereignty has been shared with the population through the promise to hold a referendum, but parallel to this development, the Bank of England has gained its formal independence from the parliament with the *Bank of England Act* (1998). This institutional change brought the United Kingdom more or less into line with the practice of those states, which were planning to adopt the euro at the outset (Schmidt 1997, 35). This change primarily reflected an adjustment in the conception of how monetary matters should be governed and was less due to preparations for joining the euro. However, by removing monetary policy from the competences of parliament, the act challenges elements of the ideological foundation of the euro opt-out. In the light of these contradictory moves, one could argue that the UK euro opt-out has not guaranteed the continuation—but has played a part in the transformation—of the domestic doctrine on monetary sovereignty.

Denmark

The Danish exemption from the euro formally locates the choice to join the euro zone with the Danish people because it guarantees the population a referendum. At the end of the 1990s, a clear majority among Denmark's mainstream political parties favored euro adoption and began to prepare the Danes for the single currency. The domestic audience was divided, but less euro-skeptic than the British. During the campaign leading up to the referendum of September 28, 2000, the government followed the same rhetorical strategy as the UK government, articulating the "yes" as sound business spirit and stressing the importance of "a place at the table" at the Governing Council of the ECB (see Marcussen and Zølner 2001). In May 2000, as opinion polls began to show falling support for the euro, Prime Minister Poul Nyrup Rasmussen desperately attempted to appease doubters by asserting that Denmark could join the euro zone and withdraw at a later date if it wanted, thus arguing that Danish sovereignty would be fundamentally untouched by the decision to surrender the opt-out, sovereignty could be taken back, so to speak. This followed the domestic logic behind the opt-outs. However, Nyrup Rasmussen's statement gave rise to confusion when it was contradicted by Commission President Romano Prodi who said that joining the EMU was "by definition permanent," thereby articulating the constitutional character of the EU treaties and the principle of solidarity. Mr. Prodi later suggested that from a political point of view Mr. Rasmussen was correct, although there were no treaty provisions for joining and leaving the EMU (Miller 2002, 15). The government's appeasement strategy was a flop, 53.1 percent of the Danish voters rejected the euro against 46.9 percent voting "yes." Together with the booming Danish economy, the 2000 referendum put a lid on the domestic debate on the euro.

To the European audience, however, Denmark has since long been a quasi-euro member. The Danish Central Bank follows the ECB's "sound policy" strictly with the acceptance of great majority of the domestic audience (Marcussen 2005).[15] Indeed, the Danish krone has been tied to the D-mark at a fixed rate since 1987. Denmark has remained well within the constraints implied by the Stability and Growth Pact. Furthermore, Danish officials from the Foreign Ministry and the Ministry of Finance attempt to play an active part in the ECOFIN Council and hope to compensate for their "outsiderness" by being extra constructive. Danish diplomats are proud that President of the ECB, Jean-Claude Trichet, has argued that Denmark should count as a member of the eurozone in future statistics.[16] From a European perspective, there is not much national sovereignty in Danish euro-outsiderness.

Protecting National Orders and Borders

Although the discussion on whether to join the euro has cooled off in both the United Kingdom and Denmark, the debate on the opt-outs related to Justice and Home Affairs and Schengen has become heated during the last decade. United Kingdom and Danish ministers and officials are generally enthusiastic to cooperate with their European counterparts on these issues, but the domestic audience is hostile to handing over questions of national security to supranational institutions.

United Kingdom

The negative British stance toward the Schengen border free zone has been relatively stable since the 1980s where Margaret Thatcher refused to remove the border controls toward other member states. However, today the domestic audience is divided in their assessment of the Schengen cooperation on common borders. On the one hand, the House of Lords criticizes the government for being unable to provide evidence that British border control is the most effective way to control immigration and fight illegal immigration. Furthermore, it finds it "politically unwise" for the United Kingdom to isolate itself from the continuing development of EU-wide policies in such sensitive areas and argues that the United Kingdom has much to contribute regarding the preservation of civil liberties.[17] On the other hand, a significant majority of the domestic audience, led by Conservatives and other euro-skeptics, have "securitized" the British Schengen protocol, to the extent that it seems to constitute a guarantee of the survival of British nation (Wiener 1999). Hence, the Schengen protocol is likely to remain in place for many years.

The "un-European" Schengen exemption is presented differently to the European audience. The main argument put forward to justify the protocol is that it is only due to particular practical (not political) problems linked to the United Kingdom's status as an island country, and British diplomats and ministers make sure to underline that the protocols should not block further integration.[18] In day-to-day politics, there are no watertight shutters between British and EU policy in the development of common border policies. Despite the Schengen protocol, the United Kingdom has adapted its national legislation regarding for instance biometrics in passports to conform to EU standards. Furthermore, it has contributed in quite significant ways to the development of the EU security paradigm and sought to influence the development of the operational cooperation at the external borders.

On "visas, asylum, immigration and other policies related to the free movement of persons" (Title IV TEC), the United Kingdom has a very flexible protocol allowing it to opt-in on a case-by-case basis both before and after a measure has been adopted. Former Prime Minister Tony Blair has claimed that the opt-in possibility means that "[...] unless we opt in we are not affected by it and this actually gives us is the best of both worlds."[19] The act of opting in and out performatively enacts the sovereignty of the United Kingdom; it is because it is sovereign that it is able to perform the act of opting in and out as it pleases. The British government has chosen to opt into those areas that curtail the ability of migrants to enter the EU, but it has opted out of protective measures such as the Directive of family reunification and the Directive on the rights of long-term residents (see also Geddes 2005). Existing research argues that the British use of the opt-in possibility related to Title IV TEC is driven by the intent to shape EU policy in ways congenial to "domestic interests" (Ladrech 2004, 57). However, it is necessary to nuance the concept of "domestic interests." The domestic audience is split on this issue. Conservative members of the House of Commons often criticize the executive decisions to opt into new measures, claiming that the opt-in decisions represent a one-way transfer of sovereignty on immigration policy away from parliament to the supranational authorities in Brussels. Generally, the House of Lords is more positive toward harmonization of immigration policies (see also Givens and Luedkte 2004), and many of the opt-in/opt-out decisions have therefore not had the blessing of the Lords. The players (government and officials) react to this criticism of being at the same time too europhile and too Euroskeptic, by discursively confusing the ability to opt-in and right to independence. The following response from Tony Blair to the criticism of his choice to opt into a measure illustrates how decisions to opt in mix up two different understandings of sovereignty,

> But it is our complete choice as to whether to opt in; we might as well say that about any measure in Europe [...]. Obviously, once we opt in, that is presumably because we have decided that it is in our interests to do so. Only the Conservative party could say that a decision whether to opt in is somehow a negation of our sovereignty; surely, it is the expression of it.[20]

This choice of words is revealing in two ways. First, national sovereignty and integration have ceased to be oppositional terms in Blair's defense speech; it is by opting in that the United Kingdom secures not only its international sovereignty, but also its national sovereignty. Second, Blair claims to speak on behalf of a domestic audience, a "we," but in practice, the British government autonomously selects when it wants to participate in a given measure under Title IV TEC. "The people" need not be the foundational figure of sovereignty, in the case of the United Kingdom, the exemptions drift between different foundations, "government," "parliament," "people," "nation," and an abstract "we." Blair discursively invokes the sovereign people of the United Kingdom to justify decisions to opt-in and out, but it is a black hole, an artificial referent, parliamentary and popular protests against specific opt-in and opt-out decisions have not had any considerable effect on the government's decisions. In this way, international sovereignty as the right to enter into treaty agreements and the idea of national sovereignty are discursively muddled. Hence, while the decision to hand over monetary sovereignty has symbolically moved from government and parliament to "the people" qua the referendum guarantee, in Justice and Home Affairs authority and control resides strictly with the British government.

Denmark

While the British opt-out from Title IV TEC on asylum, immigration, and civil law provides its government with a favorable à la carte menu with surprisingly few domestic and legal restrictions, the Danish opt-outs are constructed to tie the hands of the players and does not provide Denmark with an opt-in possibility. One of the great paradoxes of the Danish JHA protocol is the striking discrepancy between the original motivation behind the Danish reluctance toward community competence within the area of asylum and immigration policy, and its current motivation to keep its opt-outs. In the beginning of the 1990s, Denmark, together with the Netherlands, was among the most liberal countries and feared that community competence within asylum and immigration policy would threaten the high level of protection given to asylum seekers in Denmark (Manners 2000, 98). But from the late 1990s, and in particular with the election of the Liberal-Conservative government in 2001, Danish asylum and refugee policy is stricter than that of the rest of the EU concerning rules on family reunification and requirements of attachment to Denmark.[21] To the right-wing politicians currently in power and the parts of the Danish domestic audience supporting them, Danish rules on asylum and immigration constitute important barriers to the perceived inflow of immigrants, asylum seekers, criminals, and terrorists. If the opt-outs are surrendered, these barriers will be removed according to the influential right-wing Danish People's Party,

> No supranational or international body should impose a particular refugee and immigration policy on Denmark. Who and how many we wish to let into our country are to be entirely the internal affairs of Denmark. The Danish People's Party will fight to ensure that refugee and immigration policy remains an area where Parliament is sovereign.[22]

This quote illustrates a domestic debate where the opt-out reaffirms the boundary between inside and the outside of the state and locates national sovereignty with parliament. Adapting to (and perhaps contributing to) this conception, Prime Minister Fogh Rasmussen has stressed that,

> A significant majority of the Danes wish to maintain the current Danish immigration policy. Therefore, they would also not support an abolition of the legal opt-out if there were a risk that it would undermine Danish immigration policy.[23]

However, serving the symbolic purpose of legitimizing Danish EU membership to the domestic audience, the exemption from cooperation on immigration, asylum and civil law is presented differently to the European audience. On a day-to-day basis, the opt-out has very little to do with grandiose symbols of national autonomy. Just as the United Kingdom, Denmark is far from a reluctant player in this important policy area despite its opt-out. Danish officials are extremely careful not to provoke the European audience and refer to the opt-outs as "temporary measures" or "minor technical problems" to allow for an engagement in policies covered by the opt-outs. A Danish official expresses a strategic concern for "the European cause" even in the areas covered by the protocol,

> We follow the unwavering principle that we participate in entirely the same manner as we would have done if we did not have an opt-out. This may also contribute to strengthen the impression that we are serious and

have an interest in the cause, which means that the other member states will not hold the opt-outs against us in the day-to-day management.[24]

The players do not only adapt informally, they also seek formal adaptation to the EU. As Denmark does not have an opt-in possibility, the Danish government has applied to the European Commission for intergovernmental parallel agreements associating Denmark with legislative measures under Title IV TEC (asylum, immigration, and civil law) where the Danish opt-out applies. This strategy is unknown to most of the public and while it is a legally defensible practice, one could argue that it represents a political bypassing of the protocol (Adler-Nissen, 2008b). Concretely, Denmark adjusts its domestic legislation via parallel agreements "[...] which are considered as being a vital interest to the country" (Vedsted-Hansen 2004, 67). The Danish government decides which measures represent "a vital interest." By practicing its right as an international sovereign to enter into parallel agreements with other entities, Denmark accepts to implement the same rules as the other member states, but it has formally declined the opportunity to influence the design of the rules in the first place. So far, Denmark has applied for six parallel agreements, but the Commission has only granted four.[25] According to the Commission, the following conditions apply if Denmark is to be granted a parallel agreement,

- Parallel agreements could only be of an exceptional and transitional nature.
- Such an interim solution should also only be accepted if the participation of Denmark is fully in the interest of the community and its citizens.
- The solution on a longer term is that Denmark gives up its protocol on Justice and Home Affairs.

The conditionality built into the parallel agreements function as a disciplining mechanism where Denmark promises one day to get rid of its disputed exemptions. To be granted parallel agreements, Danish officials must behave as representatives from applicant countries who argue that their country is making progress, that it is Europeanizing and moving closer to the European core (cf. Wæver 2000, 262–263).[26] By signing the parallel agreements, the players agree to the temporality of the exemptions and accept that Denmark eventually will have to give up authority on the areas where it has opted out. In this sense, the opt-out no longer guarantees autonomy, because it is transformed into a sort of delay-action device. During negotiations on parallel agreements,

Danish ministers and officials simultaneously articulate two different understandings of the situation; to the domestic audience, the opt-outs guarantee Danish sovereignty on Justice and Home Affairs as long as the population wish. On the European scene, however, the Danish political and administrative elites promise to work actively toward lifting the opt-outs "in a few years" and continuously assert that they are just waiting for the right moment to call a referendum.[27] Furthermore, as the decision to apply for parallel agreements is taken by government—not "the sovereign people"—the players must invent an alternative foundation for their decision to apply for parallel agreements. Danish Minister of Justice Lene Espersen recently argued to the Danish Parliament that the agreements were concluded to secure "[...] the common interest of the EU and Denmark."[28] In Espersen's exposition, the foundation of the sovereign choice to conclude parallel agreements is both domestic and European; it transgresses the boundary and nullifies the distinction between the national and the European sphere. In other words, while national protocols at the outset drew a clear division between national and EU competencies, the division is blurred in practice. In this sense, the players resemble a married man or woman having an affair. The danger in living a double life, however, is well known, one can easily make the mistake to disclose the "secret," or others who know of the "secret" may disclose it to the "wrong" audience.

Disclosing Duplicity

In a short-term perspective, the strategy of opting out was a smart move to convince reluctant domestic audiences that important elements of national sovereignty would be untouched by future European integration. In a longer time perspective, opt-outs handcuff the players and constrain their room of maneuver because they have to preserve two different ideals of the state. The players loose their grip on the two-dimensional sovereignty game when the domestic and European discourses on sovereignty and opt-outs openly clash. A disclosure of the duplicitous game may be triggered by pressure from the European sphere, the domestic sphere, or from the players themselves. When the EU makes its claims to supreme authority, criticizing the opt-outs for undermining solidarity, democracy, and legitimacy it draws on a constitutional ideology, which is closer to the national than international sovereignty discourse. However, when the British and Danish governments articulate opt-outs at home, they draw on the international law discourse, not the constitutional discourse, which has driven the European integration project forward. Figure 6.2 illustrates

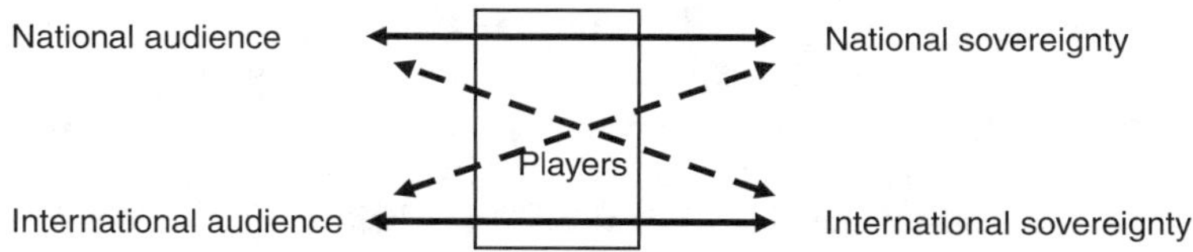

Figure 6.2   The entangled two-dimensional sovereignty game

when the two different conceptions of opt-outs collide resulting in conflicting claims to sovereignty.

Challenges from the International Audience

The most apparent threat to the "organized duplicity" is related to the structural pressure that the United Kingdom and Denmark, as all other member states, face to adapt to European rules, norms, and institutions—a pressure generally known as Europeanization. Because national opt-outs do not stop the European integration process, their consequences are also growing in sometimes unpredictable ways. In 1993 for instance, the Danish opt-out from Justice and Home Affairs was purely hypothetical, or symbolic, and had no concrete implications for Danish participation, but the opt-out is today excluding Denmark from an increasing number of legal measures.

The pressure from Europeanization shows its face directly to the domestic audience when a European "reality" intervenes in the domestic sphere. Then the players' monopoly of communication breaks down. Increasingly, the EU challenges the idea of opting out and the clear division between the national and the international sphere, which the opt-outs were meant to uphold, is disputed. When both the EU and the member states claim ultimate authority, there is a risk of "mutually assured destruction" (N. Walker 2003, 29). An example of such intervention is the recent ruling by the European Court of Justice (ECJ), which establishes that the European Community and not just the EU, has the power to require the member states to lay down criminal penalties for protecting the environment. This decision constituted a bombshell in the Danish EU debate, because despite the opt-out from supranational cooperation in Justice and Home Affairs (including criminal law), Denmark will be forced to apply to this.[29] Thus, the idea that the opt-outs protect Denmark's sovereignty was threatened. The Euroskeptics argued furiously that the ruling constituted a "breach of the Danish opt-out" and requested that the Danish government informed the EU that the ruling would not apply in Denmark.[30] As the ability of the opt-out to protect national sovereignty was questioned, the EU spokesperson from the major government party, Charlotte Antonsen, had to be creative in her response. She refrained from referring to the fear of harmonization of criminal law and argued instead that the original intention behind the opt-out from Justice and Home Affairs was *not* to protect Denmark against a common environmental policy, which had in fact always been a Danish priority in the EU. Defending the ruling, Ms. Antonsen said, "We have a clear interest that the other member states implement criminal penalties for harming the environment."[31] Instead of referring to the original meaning of the opt-out, the protection of national sovereignty, she referred to a Danish "we" with a "clear interest" in high environmental standards. Thus, she openly articulated the EU as an organization where states intervene in each other's domestic affairs. Hence, the international sovereignty is modified from a right to enter into treaties to the call for a common and legally binding political polity. However, Ms. Antonsen cleverly avoided the question of whether the opt-out was actually breached or not, instead, progress in environmental policy was used as a sign that the ECJ ruling is not undermining Danish sovereignty and the opt-out. This constitutes an innovative form of sovereignty production.

Challenges from the Domestic Audience

It is also possible to imagine that the domestic audience wants to be "fooled". What happens if the domestic audience becomes increasingly aware of, and or identifies with the European discourse? In the course of a couple of decades, the domestic discourse on sovereignty can go through a process of Europeanization. Important parts of the domestic audience, in particular parliamentarians and media, in the United Kingdom and Denmark are aware of the increasing problems posed by the opt-outs to the players on the European arena and some of them are less attached to particular symbols of national sovereignty. Originally, it might have been more comfortable for them not to address the ambiguity of opting out. The political and legal adjustments of the state vis-à-vis the European order only challenges the domestic "truth" about uncontested national and international sovereignty, if it is openly addressed. Today, however, it is difficult for the players to ignore the challenges from the national audience.

In the United Kingdom, it is well-known that the House of Lords is more pro-European than the Commons and is increasingly critical of the British strategy of opting out.[32] It is still a minority in the United Kingdom who openly call for a surrender of the British protocols, while in Denmark, the population and parliamentarians have become increasingly more pro-European and concerned about the exclusionary effects of the opt-outs. The Danish Parliament has urged the government to seek to participate and influence as much as possible on the areas where Denmark has opted out. Moreover, in 2007, it also requested an independent research investigation on the consequences of the Danish opt-outs to prepare for a new referendum to give up the protocols, with only the two anti-EU parties voting against the motion (see Danish Institute for International Studies 2008). In this sense, the "organized duplicity" has just as much to do with the handling of changing ideological schisms on the domestic scene as it represents a permanent tension between the state and the EU.

Challenges from the Players

As a last option, the players may also have an interest in disclosing the duplicity, as it were, to question the established domestic truth that the opt-outs should remain in place to legitimize continued EU membership. When UK or Danish governments and officials are excluded from an increasing number of policy measures that they would like to participate in, when they lose on the European scene, they may be appealed to present the European understanding of the opt-outs to move the domestic discourse and prepare for a referendum. This is what has happened in Denmark, where the prime minister in November 2007 announced a referendum to surrender the four opt-outs within his current four-year terms, arguing that the national protocols are outdated and detrimental to Danish influence. However, this discursive move necessarily brings a lot of uncertainty about motives and strategies into the domestic debate, as suggested by the Danish experience with a confusing debate before the euro referendum in 2000. Discussing the problems in relation to safeguarding state independence in the Union is risky business because it implies questioning the very rationale behind opting out: protecting national sovereignty. Hence, with the introduction of the European discourse on international sovereignty into the domestic arena, the very fundamental on which continued EU membership is justified is questioned. To make the argument that sovereignty is not threatened despite surrendering the opt-outs requires that the government presents a claim about the nature of the European integration process, that "we" are de facto dependent on each other, that "we" loose influence when "we" are not in the European core, and that "we" should be solitary and cannot stand alone. By addressing the EU as more than an intergovernmental organization and openly articulating the constitutional character of the European legal order, which goes beyond traditional international law, the original domestic meaning of the opt-outs as guarantees of national sovereignty is questioned. Such attempts of discursive modifications, which redefine what a state can claim absolute authority over, will immediately be contested by the Euroskeptic parts of the domestic audience, who will argue that national sovereignty can, and should, still be effectively claimed. Any referendum on opt-outs will therefore at the same time set the scene for a sovereign choice for the people and question the long-term viability of the sovereign nation-state, as we know it, in the context of European integration.

Conclusion

Representatives of the United Kingdom and Denmark have developed sophisticated means of "circumventing" the opt-outs to reduce their exclusionary effects, so the figure of an autonomous state is preserved at home despite its entanglement in the European integration process. On the European scene, the opt-outs change meaning from a principled stance against more integration to a more flexible position, which allows ministers and diplomats to pick and choose from the buffet of new EU initiatives.

This dynamic is accentuated differently in the United Kingdom and Denmark. In the United Kingdom, the government invented the opt-outs and the foundation of sovereign choices regarding the EU is traditionally linked to parliament and government, not the people. However, through the complex discursive battles, the possible surrender of the opt-outs is rendered a sovereign choice for the British people. In Denmark, the discursive change is almost the opposite, here the opt-outs were invented on the basis of a negative result of popular referendum, and they cannot be surrendered without hearing the people again. Meanwhile, the daily attempts to circumvent the opt-outs are justified with reference not to the people, but the government's understanding of "national interests."

State sovereignty is mediated before two different audiences and ideally, it has two different meanings. To the domestic audience, sovereignty is about ultimate authority and popular democracy and to the international audience it means state independence. However, it has become increasingly difficult for the state representatives to uphold the idea of two different spheres of sovereignty, the national and the international. As states integrate deeper into international organizations, the two conceptions of sovereignty get mixed up. This also implies that the internal and external images of the opt-outs compete openly. The problems with successfully claiming sovereignty through the instrument of protocols in the EU reveal that when international sovereignty is no longer only claimed in terms of right to independence, but also as a right to influence, national sovereignty is under pressure. In practice, opt-outs do not provide strong bulwarks against Europeanization and push governments to reconfigure the meaning of sovereignty both domestically and on the European scene. Although this dynamic does not fundamentally challenge the idea of a sovereign state, it indicates a changing and more taxing relationship between the international and the national order in the context of European integration. In this sense, Margot Wallström's provocative promotion of EU support for European films is illustrative of a deeper process of entanglement: the relation between the state and the EU is no longer as innocent as it used to be.

Notes

Thanks to Jens Bartelson, Chris Bickerton, Ulrik Pram Gad, Lene Hansen, Rutger Lindahl, Ian Manners, Daniel Naurin, Noel Parker, Maja Møller Sousa, Neil Walker, and Ole Wæver for valuable comments to previous versions of this chapter. The usual disclaimer applies.

1. Also in nondemocratic countries, the domestic speech-act of sovereignty needs an audience (Buzan, Wæver, and De Wilde 1998: 25).
2. The "Protocol on certain provisions relating to the United Kingdom of Great Britain and Northern Ireland," annexed to the Maastricht Treaty, spells out the details of the British opt-out.
3. In 1997, the United Kingdom decided to participate in the Social Chapter and the provisions of the protocol were inserted into the Treaty of Amsterdam.
4. Even then, parliamentary ratification was opposed by the opposition Labor and Liberal Democrat MPs and crucially by the "Maastricht Rebels" within the governing Conservative Party. The government of John Major came close to losing the confidence of the House, before the Parliament eventually ratified the Treaty (Gifford 2006: 862).
5. The document refers to itself as a national compromise, which can "unite [*sic*] the population on Denmark's participation in the continued EC." In the document, the "no" is carefully interpreted as a rejection of "United States of Europe," but not as a rejection of EC membership or European cooperation as such. With this interpretation, the agreement *invents* a united Danish people, which can then later be politically represented in the opt-outs and legitimize continued EU membership (<http://www.euo.dk/dokumenter/traktat/eu/nationalkompromis/> Adopted by all parties in Parliament except from the Progress Party, October 27, 1992, author's translation).

6. Speech by Prime Minister Anders Fogh Rasmussen at University of Copenhagen, "Visions for Denmark's active European policy." September 23, 2003, http://europa.eu/constitution/futurum/documents/speech/sp230903_2_en.pdf (accessed May 20, 2008)

7. Interview, February 28, 2006, Danish Ministry of Foreign Affairs.

8. Interviews, European Commission, December 2006; interviews, European Council Legal Service, May 2006.

9. Interviews, August 25, 2006, Danish Ministry of Refugees, Immigrants and Integration Affairs; Interviews, August 25, 2006 UK Home Office.

10. Hansard, 184/41, Cols. 470–9, January 24, 1991, quoted in *Manchester Guardian Weekly*, July 7, 1991, p. 6.

11. For an account of the five tests, see for instance Howarth (2007: 50).

12. Interviews, HM Treasury, April 17, 2007.

13. HM Treasury, *Seventh Report on Euro Preparations* November 2003, http://www.euro.gov.uk/publications/EPR7.pdf (accessed May 20, 2008)

14. Interviews, HM Treasury, April 17, 2007.

15. The left wing and the anti-European groups have criticized this policy not only for undermining sovereignty, but also for the economic logic behind it.

16. Interview, Danish UK Representation, September 5, 2007.

17. House of Lords 7th Report: Schengen and the United Kingdom's Border Controls', 1998/99.

18. Interview, Home Office, August 24, 2006.

19. *The Guardian*, October 26, 2004, <http://www.guardian.co.uk/guardianpolitics/story/0,1336027,00.html>

20. Prime Minister Tony Blair, House of Commons Daily Debate, November 8, 2004, <http://www.parliament.the-stationery-office.co.uk/pa/cm200304/cmhansrd/vo041108/debtext/41108-10.htm>

21. The combined attachment of the spouses/partners to Denmark must be greater than their attachment to any other country. This so-called attachment requirement is only one of a series of requirements.

22. Dansk Folkepartis valggrundlag til Europaparlamentet 2004, http://www.danskfolkeparti.dk/sw/frontend/show.asp?parent=18717&menu_parent=22669&layout=0 (accessed May 20, 2008).

23. Speech by Prime Minister Anders Fogh Rasmussen at University of Copenhagen, "Visions for Denmark's active European policy," September 23, 2003, np.

24. Interview, August 22, 2006, Danish Ministry of Refugees, Immigrants and Integration Affairs.

25. The Commission refused to grant Denmark parallel agreements with respect to the Regulation on insolvency proceedings and the Regulation on jurisdiction and the recognition and enforcement of judgments in matrimonial matters (Bruxelles II).

26. If Denmark is granted a parallel agreement, the government copies the EU measure in the form of Danish law that is then subsequently agreed on by Parliament. The domestic sub-audience understood here as the Parliament

is given a clear veto possibility, but it has never been used as the majority of MPs has supported the parallel agreements.

27. Interviews, February 28, 2006, Danish Ministry of Foreign Affairs.
28. Talepunkt til brug for samråd i Folketingets Europaudvalg den 9. februar 2007 om samrådsspørgsmål A—anmodning om redegørelse for EU's migrations- og indvandringspolitik, herunder Danmarks stilling på området set i lyset af det retlige forbehold, http://www.folketinget.dk/samling/20061/alm del/UUI/Bilag/142/352213.HTM (accessed May 20, 2008).
29. Judgment of September 13, 2005 of the Court of Justice in Case C-176/03 Commission of the European Communities v Council of the European Union.
30. "EU-straffe er forfatning ad bagdøren," http://www.arbejderen.dk/index. aspx?F_ID=28969&TS_ID=2&S_ID=17&C_ID=35 (accessed May 20, 2008).
31. "Domstol giver EU ret til at straffe," *Notat*, September 30, 2005.
32. Interviews, EU Select Committee, House of Lords, April 13, 2007.

7

Federalism, Confederalism, and Sovereignty Claims: Understanding the Democracy Game in the European Union

Andrew Glencross

> Sovereignty is about a claimed status but not about the problems these claims raise.
>
> Werner and de Wilde 2001, 296

Introduction: EU Democracy and the Tension between Federalism and Confederalism

It is commonly assumed that sovereignty is indivisible and hence that in any polity there has to be an institution able to claim ultimate political authority. By implication, indivisibility also means that confederation (a union of states) and federation (one state with more or less autonomous units) are mutually exclusive categories: "there can be nothing in between." (Onuf 1991, 432). Nevertheless, the European Union (EU) seems to be precisely the "in between order" (cf. Sørensen 1999; Wind 2001, 103) that undermines such peremptory statements about the nature of sovereignty. The complicated story of sovereignty within the EU is accompanied by an equally unusual and problematic system of democratic accountability. Whereas other chapters in this volume emphasize the way states play games with sovereignty for manifold ends, this contribution examines the manner in which EU member states' sovereignty claims constitute playing a game with democracy itself. Whilst EU democracy has often been seen as etiolated, this chapter argues that—unlike many democratizing proposals that seek to overcome or bury member state sovereignty claims—such claims should in fact be understood as an essential feature of the complex art of negotiating the relationship between integration and EU democracy.

It is important, for the purposes of the argument, to recognize that there is a fundamental tension between federal and confederal principles of organizing political authority (Hamilton, Jay, and Madison 2003). In a pure confederation, the unit of political representation is solely a collective one (a people, a state) and legal acts fall on states in their "corporate or collective capacities" (ibid., 67). Thus a confederal political order is "a contractual union of states" (Forsyth 1981, 3). Conversely, in a federal order, individuals are represented alongside territorial units for the purposes of decision making and legislation touches citizens directly (Hamilton, Jay, and Madison 2003). The representation of individuals thus circumscribes the autonomy of constituent units—it may also potentially alter their sovereign equality by giving more influence to the most populous units. The existence of federally guaranteed individual rights constitutes another major potential restriction on the sovereign capacities of units within a federal system. The EU's hybrid system of federalism and confederalism is thus characterized by the creation of an autonomous, constitutionalized legal order consisting of individual rights (Weiler 1999) beside a political order in which major decisions are taken by member states, often as (supposedly) equal participants.

This chapter rests on the supposition that the antagonism between these two, federal and confederal, principles is at the heart of the sovereignty game of integration and has important consequences for the functioning of democracy in Europe. The intention is less to make a point about the nature of sovereignty than to demonstrate the use to which sovereignty is put in the process of integration and to consider the consequences this has for democratic theory and practice. Interpreting the balance of confederalism and federalism as a sovereignty game, the argument traces the evolution of this central integrationist tension to show that the amalgamation of both principles is a very taxing game. This game is both ideological (based on national or supranational attachment) and rational (actors' preferences often depend on perceived interests). However, given that sovereignty is a claimed *status* that is most asserted precisely when that status is challenged (Werner and de Wilde 2001),[1] this chapter focuses in particular on the moments when member states have used sovereignty claims either to try to limit the supranational character of integration or to establish special rights for certain states.

The sovereignty game of integration has a profound impact on democracy since changes to a state's claimed status of sovereignty invariably affect democratic processes (Bartolini 2005; Bickerton, Cunliffe, and Gourevitch 2006). This is because state sovereignty and popular sovereignty in the democratic era are mutually constitutive and cannot be easily disentangled (N. Walker 2007). Thus, the mixture of confederalism and federalism in the EU system is the key to understanding the democracy game of European integration.

The purpose of this contribution is threefold, as reflected in the tripartite division of the chapter. The first objective is to describe and explain the sovereignty game of integration by reference to how sovereignty claims have produced the unusual mixture of federal and confederal principles of representation. The second goal is to show that this sovereignty game is also a democracy game and analyze accordingly the problematic consequences this second game has had on the member states and the EU alike. The third and final ambition is to explore how adequately various proposals regarding how to respond to these changes in the nature and practice of democracy deal with the problem of sovereignty claims.

Assertions of Sovereignty and the Combination of Confederalism and Federalism in the Sovereignty Game of Integration

European integration's impact on the Westphalian notion of the state is often understood in dichotomous terms (Jackson 1999). For some, the EU is no threat to state sovereignty (Moravcsik 1993; Keohane 2002); others regard the EU as the symbol of a fundamentally changed, post-sovereign order (MacCormick 1999; Weiler 1999). Typically, this polarized debate has recourse to some form of quantification of the extent to which sovereignty has been pooled (Donahue and Pollack 2001; McKay 2001) and tracing the motives for this common undertaking (Moravcsik 1998). However, such a debate does not necessarily tell us much about sovereignty since the arguments largely revolve around questions of substantial statehood as a capacity for certain actions (Sørensen 1999) rather than sovereignty as a claimed status. An alternative conceptual framework has tried to bypass these antinomies by using the notion of "interdependence sovereignty" (Krasner 1999) to explain the somewhat perplexing situation whereby states are losing individual control over certain transnational interactions while gaining a collective capacity to deal with them. Yet Jackson (1999) maintains that conceptualizing sovereignty as a resource that can be transferred, as Keohane (2002) does for instance, is a solecism.[2]

The intention here is to sidestep these controversies about the era of sovereignty in which we live. Instead, this section focuses on identifying assertions of sovereignty by member states as responses to the process of integration. These assertions are understood as essential to the maintenance of confederal principles within the hybrid system of political representation described earlier. The argument thus conceptualizes sovereignty not as a set of rights—easily identifiable, like the fasces carried by the Roman lictors—but as a claimed status that is then used "to legitimize certain rights, duties and competences" (Werner and de Wilde 2001, 297). Hence the analysis presents sovereignty claims as crucial instruments in constituting the EU political system.

As befits a complex concept like sovereignty, these assertions take various forms. However, not included within this category are instances of attempted legal resistance to EU supremacy (Goldstein 2001) or simple noncompliance (Falkner, Hartlapp, Leiber, and Treib 2004), because neither is part of the formal sovereignty game of delimiting the scope of the integration process and defining the status of member state sovereignty within this process. Rather, the term assertion refers here to those actions that either serve to establish a special status or rights for a certain state (or several) or else those that try to set boundaries to the scope of supranationalism, thereby protecting the sovereignty claims of all. Among the latter figure the remaining unanimity requirement in certain policy areas, the creation, in foreign policy as well as judicial and police cooperation, of a separate decision-making system with a separate legal basis attenuating the supervisory power of the European Court of Justice (ECJ), and the treaty-based prohibition of legal harmonization in certain policy areas. As regards the former type of sovereignty assertion, the measures include treaty protocols, opt-outs, and national referendums on EU matters, although this is not an exhaustive list. What follows is a brief description of these two types of sovereignty assertion and an explanation of how they have produced a dual system of political representation.

Sovereignty Assertions as Barriers to Supranationalism

As a hybrid polity the EU walks a tightrope between intergovernmentalism and supranationalism. From the outset, integration entrenched the "community method," incorporating the supranational principle, rather than the historically plausible alternative of a purely confederal institutional model (Parsons 2003). In fact, the first manifestation of a sovereignty assertion within the integration framework was an assault on the supranational principle itself: the "empty chair crisis" of 1965–66. Although de Gaulle's diplomatic struggle took the form of an institutional conflict—France's refusal to participate in meetings of the Council of Ministers, the senior legislative body representing states' interests—it was largely a debate over norms and expectations as de Gaulle refused to accept European Economic Community (EEC) competency except through unanimity.

Having briefly toyed with renegotiating the EEC Treaty, de Gaulle eventually "committed to the Community track but refused new progress along it" (ibid., 126) by forcing the "Luxembourg Compromise" on the other member states. Hence the solution was not to redesign institutions but to establish a new norm: "when very important issues are at stake, discussions must be continued until unanimous agreement is reached." Thus what was secured was not the sovereign status or prerogatives of a particular member state; unanimity preserves the formal equal status of all. Although informal, the Luxembourg compromise had long-lasting effects on integration (Garrett 1995). Yet supranationalism did not fall by the wayside. Subsequent battles between unanimity and qualified majority voting (QMV), however, gave rise to more formal attempts to use the confederal principle to limit the reach of supranationalism.

Several attempts to counterbalance the deepening of integration with a renewed commitment to intergovernmentalism are worthy of mention here. The first concerns the remnants of the Luxembourg compromise in what is now termed the first policy "pillar." In this pillar, where QMV has become the norm, treaty reform, the accession of new member states and taxation remain subject to unanimous decision making (Magnette 2005). The veto on treaty amendment, in particular, ensures that the EU appears a strictly voluntary association of sovereign states for the pursuit of mutual advantage (Boucher 2005, 103). Unanimous treaty amendment—in effect the process by which the units may alter the purposes for which they associate (ibid.)—is fully in keeping with international law. Under Article 40(4) of the Vienna Convention on the Law of Treaties (1969), states cannot be forced to become parties to amended multilateral treaties to which they have not consented (de Witte 2004b).

The confederal character of such an arrangement is pellucid. The EU treaty amendment procedure establishes a unity constituted by all states as equals—it is "a contract between equals to act henceforth as one" (Forysth 1981, 16)—rather than the federal alternative of a unity formed from a majority of citizens and/or a qualified majority of states (Trechsel 2005; Auer 2007). In this way, first pillar vetoes are part of the reason why member states can still successfully claim sovereign status and "enjoy the rights and powers related to that status" (Werner and de Wilde 2001, 304). Moreover, the unanimity requirement for admitting new members, which accords with the definition of sovereignty as the exclusive "ability to make authoritative political decisions" (Thompson 1995, 216), further underlines the equality of states. The corollary of having the authority to determine membership expansion is the member states' prerogative to determine their continued adherence to the EU. The EU Lisbon Treaty now outlines the terms for voluntary withdrawal (art. 35), which for some is definitive proof of member states' retention of sovereignty (Sørensen 1999; Boucher 2005).[3] Whatever the precise implication for state sovereignty, the right of withdrawal certainly means that there cannot be the same agonizing over whether the EU is a perpetual union as there was in the antebellum United States (Stampp 1978). In the pro- and anti-integration cleavage, this unambiguous confederal element—even if no mainstream party in Europe advocates quitting the union—thus serves to reassure the constituency of voters attached to the shibboleth of sovereignty.

The hybrid nature of representation was further complicated by the creation of the so-called second and third policy "pillars" at Maastricht, which added a new confederal element. Unanimous decision making in these sensitive policy areas, foreign policy and judicial and police cooperation respectively, was obviously in large part motivated by member states' understanding of sovereignty as both authority and control (Thompson 1995). However, the member states were not simply protecting their competences; they were also defending the right of states to represent their citizens. Thus what is especially interesting about this sovereignty game is the way in which both these intergovernmental pillars were insulated, to varying degrees, from the institutions of supranational representation, namely the Commission, the European Parliament, and the ECJ (Börzel 2005). In particular, by restricting the jurisdiction of the ECJ over these policy areas, the states ensured that legal acts bind states in their corporate or collective capacities and do not create rights for individuals. Even though the Lisbon Treaty abolishes the pillar system, the circumscription of ECJ jurisdiction is maintained. A precedent for such a move can be found in the Amsterdam Treaty, where elements of the former Justice and Home Affairs pillar were integrated into the first pillar although the procedures for legislating in this area did not follow orthodox community law (Hanf 2001). The insistence on unanimity, member state co-power of initiative and reduced ECJ jurisdiction, has resulted in what has been described as the creation of a new hybrid, "intergovernmentalised EC law" (ibid., 17). Indeed, this move has given rise to a new interinstitutional sovereignty game as the Commission and Council of Ministers clash over which legal regime relevant legislation should fall under.[4]

There were other attempts at Maastricht to delimit the potential expansion of supranationalism. One such was the introduction of the subsidiarity principle, which defined efficiency as the deciding principle for the level at which power will be exercised so that the EU can legislate "if and in so far as the objectives of the proposed action cannot be sufficiently achieved by the Member States and can therefore, by reason of the scale or effects of the proposed action, be better achieved by the Community" (art. 3b). This was supposed to "enhance further the democratic and efficient functioning of the institutions" (Preamble) by ensuring that political decisions "are taken as closely as possible to the citizen" (Preamble). Subsidiarity was pushed by the most adamantine champion of sovereignty, the United Kingdom, to establish that "member states are not prepared to accept an unlimited extension of Community competences" (Dehousse 1994, 125).

However, the subsidiarity principle has not established the boundaries of national and European competences respectively. This is because it employs the criterion of effectiveness for defining the applicable level of government action. This means that the ECJ is not called upon to rule on *Kompetenz-Kompetenz* directly, rather the court is to rule "on the compared efficiency of both [national and European] types of measure" (ibid., 110). Even at the time of introduction, a leading EU lawyer declared that it would prove a stillborn clause (ibid., 124) and time has proved this claim correct as the ECJ has only made two explicit subsidiarity rulings (Magnette 2005, 54). The initial failure of subsidiarity illustrates the difficulty of specifying exactly how sovereignty claims fit into the EU system. Yet the desire to allow states to use sovereignty claims to establish the division of competences continues. Hence the new role for national parliaments envisaged by the Reform Treaty, including both the "early warning" procedure (Protocol 2, art. 7) that forces a legislative draft to be reviewed if a third of national parliaments declare it to violate the subsidiarity principle and the attribution of veto power over unanimous Council of Ministers decisions to move to QMV in certain policy areas. Moreover a further declaration on the delimitation of competences for the first time specifies that in revising the treaties member states can choose to "reduce the competences conferred on the Union."

The second method of limiting the transfer of competences for the foreseeable future was the introduction into the amended treaty of Rome of specific clauses prohibiting harmonization in certain policy areas. In the fields of education (art. 126), vocational training (127), culture (128), and public health (129) (now 149–152 EC) the EU was only permitted to "adopt incentive measures, excluding any harmonization of the laws and regulations of the Member States." Moreover, the tension between diversity and uniformity has also given rise to the development of "flexibility" within the single market framework by adopting the principle of minimum standard harmonization (Barnard 2000). Minimal standards do not, in areas such as consumer protection (art. 153 (5) EC) or public health (art. 152 (4a) EC), prevent member states imposing higher national standards provided they meet certain justifiable conditions (Hanf 2001).

Sovereignty assertions as barriers to supranationalism, therefore, have played a key role in the construction of the political constitution of Europe. This sovereignty game has been played to limit the supranational ambitions of the European project by devising rules and procedures that protect the sovereignty claims of all states. However, there is another category of sovereignty assertion that needs to be explored: when individual states affirm their right to a special status thereby creating rules of their own making.

Sovereignty Assertions as a State's Right to a Special Status

This second type of sovereignty claim is perhaps most visible in various treaty protocols that mention the specific treatment reserved for certain states.[5] For instance, both Ireland (Protocol 17, Maastricht Treaty) and Malta (Protocol 7, Accession Treaty) are guaranteed the autonomy to legislate on abortion, although the EU has never tried to do so and lacks the necessary competences. However, protocols need not be merely symbolic statements destined to reassure states and their citizens about what the EU cannot do. Since entry into the EEC in 1972, Denmark has restricted nonresidents' right to buy second homes, especially in coastal areas. Its right to do so is a protocol privilege that goes directly against the single market's principle of free movement of capital. Other countries, with the exception of Malta, have not been permitted to restrict home ownership in this fashion.

The 2004 candidate countries—even though in areas with large prewar German populations foreign home ownership was controversial—were allowed to place merely transitional restrictions on EU nationals' ownership of real estate (Mihaljek 2005). Only tiny Malta was granted a permanent derogation, as already mentioned. Thus, when viewed from the perspective of sovereignty as "meta-political authority" (Thompson 1995, 214), the Danish state has kept its ability to treat foreign home ownership as a domestic political issue. Even though property speculation on the basis of capital inflows can have a serious effect on housing affordability for the local population, potentially causing other socio-economic problems, EU member states (with the two exceptions mentioned earlier) have effectively agreed to depoliticize this issue since they no longer individually wield authority in this area.

Akin to the above protocol guarantees are policy opt-outs. The latter are *ex ante* treaty agreements allowing member states not to participate in a new community policy. Opt-outs are a practical tool for enabling the inclusion of new political objectives within the treaty framework despite the opposition of certain states (Hanf 2001). Recalcitrant member states agree not to block treaty reform on condition that they will not be bound by these new arrangements. The first opt-outs were brokered at Maastricht. The United Kingdom opted out of the third stage of economic and monetary union, the single currency, as well as spurning the Protocol on Social Policy (Raepenbusch and Hanf 2001).[6] Denmark similarly refused to convert to the euro and also turned its back on defense cooperation in the nascent Common Foreign and Security Policy (Hansen 2002).[7] Later rounds of treaty amendment continued the opt-out trend favored by these same protagonists. The United Kingdom and Ireland (bundled together because of their Common Travel Area) opted out of the communitarization of visas, asylum, and immigration (Shaw 1998). Denmark did likewise but its opt-out is legally and practically different since, unlike the United Kingdom and Ireland, the country is part of the Schengen free travel area (ibid.; Adler-Nissen, this volume).

The opt-outs on the single currency were initially considered to be merely temporary derogations. However, more than a decade later, Denmark and the United Kingdom still remain beyond the euro pale while Sweden, not a member at the time of Maastricht, unilaterally refused to join (Lindahl and Naurin 2005). As concessions to confederalism, these assertions of sovereignty are practically, but above all symbolically, significant. In particular, they reveal certain countries' ability to define a special status for themselves within the EU. Arguably, certain nonmembers have likewise negotiated their relationship with the EU on the basis of identity-based sovereignty claims that privilege the symbolic value of staying outside the fold above having a say in a process of integration into which they are inexorably drawn. Thus nonmembership is nevertheless compatible with participation in Schengen (Iceland, Norway, and Switzerland), the adoption of single market legislation (Iceland, Norway, and Switzerland), and even financial solidarity (Switzerland awarded one billion francs to the 2004 accession states).

Intimately bound up with the euro opt-outs—as well as the ultimate opt-out of refusing membership, as occurred in the Norwegian and Swiss cases—is the phenomenon of the national referendum, which should be understood as an assertion of sovereignty. Whereas the other sovereignty assertions described here have been exercised by governments, acting in the name of a state, referendums are expressions of popular sovereignty even if they are often called at the discretion of the government of the day.[8]

Referendums have been held on enlargement, accession, continued membership, treaty reform, and the euro. Since this form of ratification is not prescribed by the EU, referendums in principle embody the autonomy of member states in choosing how to deal with the political challenge of integration. However, a government's decision to call a referendum can also be influenced by domestic political considerations far-removed from EU constitutional politics, which makes them unpredictable and hard to handle. Regardless of this dark side of referendums, their increasing use has made it much more difficult for governments to reject out of hand this mode of ratification for treaty revision. This can be seen both from the repeated calls in several member states for the Lissabou Treaty to be put to a popular vote and the care with which certain constitutional elements (the name itself but also the EU anthem and hymn) were jettisoned to allow governments to tell their citizens that these revisions were not substantive enough to warrant a referendum.

Paradoxically, although direct democracy at the national level symbolizes the confederal principle of collective representation, referendums can run counter to the other confederal principle of state equality. This is because votes in one member state may have important ramifications on others. Such a state of affairs is exactly what occurred in the aftermath of the French and Dutch popular rejections of the draft EU Constitution in 2005. Member states that ratified the EU Constitution—the outcome of a strictly confederal, that is, unanimous and equal, process—were prevented from putting into operation this new treaty as a result of popular sovereignty in two member states. This tension is set to increase in the future as the French constitution has been changed to ensure that there is an automatic referendum on any future enlargement (art. 88(5)).[9] Thus France will have a special—hence unequal—right to decide the fate of membership applications twice, firstly through government representation and secondly by the people directly.

The fact that national referendums on treaties have implications stretching beyond the borders of the member state in question has been used to argue that it is simply irresponsible to subject the constitutional future of the EU to national votes (Auer 2007). However, to deny states this authority would amount to a serious restriction of the confederal principle of representation as the only alternative is some kind of Europe-wide referendum based on either a majority of individuals or a double majority of states and citizens as happens in Switzerland. Furthermore, the critique of national referendums is also a denial of the national political community as a *pouvoir constituant* capable of changing the very form of government of a state (Yack 2001). It is precisely in this constituent capacity that the people redeem their right to self-government—implying that they are responsible to no third party—thereby constituting the basis for state legitimation in the modern era (Hont 1994). This explains why the federal alternative, a pan-European popular sovereignty, is so attractive. The formula sounds perfect: supranational legitimacy for a supranational project. Yet as the earlier discussion has shown, states have used sovereignty claims precisely to limit the supranational scope of the project and to ground—often on the basis of popular pressure—its legitimacy on confederal representation.

As revealed in the analysis earlier, the sovereignty game is something far more complex than a zero-sum game where sovereignty is imagined to be an indivisible capacity that is necessarily transferred from one institutional actor to another. If anything, the evolution of member states' claim to sovereign status as a result of integration has made their assertion of this claim *more rather than less relevant to EU politics*. Consequently, EU politics is now confronted with a "sovereignty surplus," characterized by multiple and overlapping sovereignty claims (N. Walker 2007). Yet it remains to be seen what the impact of the sovereignty game—the result of compounding systems of political representation—has had on democracy. This is a particularly pressing question given that democracy is traditionally associated with an ultimately exclusive model of sovereignty (ibid.).

Hence the next section of the chapter is devoted to understanding how exactly the EU hybrid polity's reworking of sovereignty challenges the concept and practice of democracy in Europe. Diagnoses of and remedies for the contemporary ailments of democracy caused by the sovereignty game of integration differ markedly but they seldom make reference to the principles of political representation structuring the EU polity. The fourth and final section reviews these assessments of and proposals for dealing with the consequences of integration from the perspective of how they address the problem of sovereignty claims. In this way, the ambition is to offer a new angle for interpreting the appropriateness of proposals for coming to terms with the effects of integration on democracy.

Sovereignty Games and Democracy in the EU

Federal, confederal, and compound forms of representation have long been thought to affect the nature of democracy (Hamilton, Jay, and Madison 2003). After all, the point of the American federal experiment was to make popular sovereignty compatible with liberty (Tocqueville 1994). In reality, the relationship also works the other way round as Carl Schmitt argued that "the federal foundation and federalism itself are destroyed by the democratic concept of the constituent power of the *whole* people" (1992, 55). According to Schmitt, the democratiza-tion of the United States in the nineteenth century resulted in "a federal state without a federal foundation" (ibid.). Similarly, cultural factors are also part of the representation and democracy equation.[10] It has been shown, for instance, that in federal Austria and Germany, a common linguistic and cultural community results in a nationwide demos that discusses politics from a centralized rather than fragmented perspective (Erk 2003; 2004). However, given the dual nature of the EU as both a commonwealth in itself and a union of commonwealths, the effect of the above sovereignty games is Janus-like, affecting both EU democracy and member-state democracy. Hence the strategic relationship between sovereignty, integration, and democracy will be examined from this dual perspective, albeit briefly since this section is intended as a prelude to a discussion of the reform proposals that have arisen from the changed context of European democracy.

Sovereignty Games and EU Democracy

A common complaint regarding the EU polity is its complexity, aptly illustrated by the up to thirty different steps of the current codecision procedure. In fact, the problem of complexity is the defining characteris-tic of pluralist democracies when compared with parliamentary models of democracy (Coultrap 1999). EU pluralism is precisely the result of adopt-ing the dual system of representation as an alternative to an uncompli-cated supranational majoritarian system that would ride roughshod over state sovereignty claims. The result is a vertical and horizontal separation of powers that promotes consensus through mutual checks and balances as well as continual institutional dialogue. This plural regime, however, is distinctly out of kilter with many citizens' notions of politics on the basis of the operation of parliamentary democracy (Schmidt 2004). In fact, the alien nature of the EU's consensus-based model of democracy has been used as a justification for shielding it from referendum votes in which citizens cannot appreciate properly the merits of the system (Dehousse 2006; Moravcsik 2006).

Regardless of the more subjective issue of whether the EU system is beyond the ken of most ordinary citizens, political scientists have iden-tified a host of other problems resulting from Europe's peculiar dual representation that vexes democracy. Notable among these is the lack of transparent decision making arising from the closed meetings of the Council of Ministers—secrecy being the cloak behind which diplomatic maneuverings between states try to reach consensus positions (Hayes-Renshaw and Wallace 2006, 342). In addition, the low salience of many problems of regulatory policy within the compass of EU authority in tandem with the opaqueness and technocratic element of decision making favors the access of corporate interest groups to the detriment of civil society (Streeck and Schmitter 1991).

Moreover, the treaty bargains struck over the size of each member state's cohort of representatives in the European Parliament have produced a serious imbalance of representation, with the small countries well over-represented in terms of citizens per Member of the European Parliament (MEP) (Rodden 2002). Of course, federal systems almost universally contain some form of unequal representation to prevent simple majoritarianism (Dahl 2001, 47). However, the peculiarity of the EU is that, besides the evident antimajoritarian devices of unanimity and QMV in the Council of Ministers, the institution supposed to embody the principle of popular sovereignty, the European Parliament, is also seriously malapportioned. Owing precisely to the need to respect the status of member states, small countries have obtained a highly generous overrepresentation of MEPs per capita—so much so that the EU's directly elected legislature is the world's second most malapportioned lower house (Rodden 2002, 155).

Yet the most important democratic consequence of the sovereignty game of integration for the EU has been the hollowness of European public participation, debate, and accountability (Schmidt 2004). The abstruse, consensus-building model of politics dominated by national executives rather than European political parties has combined with a variety of other factors, including public indifference to hamper electoral contestation of leadership and policy (Follesdal and Hix 2005). The low salience of the business of the European Parliament is not surprising given that the member states have tried to prevent this supranational body from diminishing the importance of the confederal principle of representation. This effort has also drawn succor from national parties' disinclination to politicize the integration cleavage within the domestic arena (Mair 2005), a cleavage that is in any case not isomorphic with the traditional left/right dimension of European politics (Bartolini 2005). The net result, therefore, is a polity that, unlike European nation-states, is not based on government by the people through active popular participation nor does it follow the logic of a government of the people through elected representatives and neither is it really government for the people because its effectiveness is easy to call into question (Schmidt 2004, 977).

Sovereignty Games and Democracy in the Member States

Since the impact of the sovereignty game of integration on democracy in the EU's member states is an equally familiar part of the EU studies literature only a brief exposition is necessary. Domestic politics has been adversely affected by more than simply the growth of supranationalism, which challenges claims to domestic autonomy. The way in which the sovereignty game of integration is played—national governments are key actors in this process—has also proved significant, with the need to maintain a complex hybrid polity with the problems this has posed for democracy.

First, there has been the augmentation in the discretionary power of national executives as a result of their participation in transnational governance structures that are more isolated from the gaze of national parliamentary scrutiny (Anderson and Burns 1996; Raunio 1999).

Second, the creation of a new institutional level for policy-making has also allowed executives to "venue shop" to find a more favorable arena for implementing their preferences (Guiraudon 2000). Venue shopping, alongside the secrecy of the Council of Ministers, also profits governments by facilitating the blame avoidance potential that exists where there is a two-level game of international bargaining (Vaubel 1994; Rotte and Zimmerman 1998). Both these changes in national democratic practices, therefore, relate to the powers member states derive from the confederal element of the EU.

Third, and perhaps most important, the sovereignty game has profoundly affected democracy by altering member states' ability to define the political, what Thompson (1995) calls "meta-political authority." As described earlier, integration has in many policy areas diminished states' capacity to define an issue as a political problem requiring a domestic solution. This is a recurrent trend in everyday EU politics. It is well illustrated by the recent conflict between the Commission and Austria as a result of the latter's attempt to restrict the number of German students studying in its medical and dental faculties because Austria does not use a *numerus clausus* (i.e., restricted, grade-based) entry system. In this example, following a 2005 ECJ ruling,[11] (a similar problem has arisen in Belgium following an influx of French students), the Austrian government stands accused of breaching the principle of free movement of students, meaning that it is unable to define—and thus settle—a question of education policy as a domestic affair (Anderson and Glencross 2007).

Moreover, since member states are locked in to the sovereignty game it appears impossible for them to redefine an issue as one of domestic politics, even in the case of policy failure. Thus despite the dubious record of the Common Fisheries Policy in terms of stock conservation (Payne 2000), member states cannot try to remedy this failure on their own by opting out *ex post*, as shown by the *Factortame* case (MacCormick 1999). Hence national governments' ability to respond to policy problems or public concerns is now far more constrained than according to the simple domestic model of *lex posterior derogat legi priori* (a later law overrules an earlier law).

Since these changes in national democracy have also coincided with the democratic woes of the EU system as a whole, the net result has been the "depoliticization" of European public life (Mair 2005, 2007; Schmidt 2006). Indeed, it appears that the thinness of EU democratic life has had a deleterious effect on national politics (Mair 2007, 8). Besides the circumscription of states' metapolitical authority and their ability to respond to their citizens' concerns, the European project has seen the growing use of nonmajoritarian institutions "from which politics and parties are deliberately excluded" (Mair 2005, 12). Given this reconfiguration of European democracy, it is no surprise that manifold proposals have been put forward to come to terms with the impact of the sovereignty game on democracy. In particular, given that the causality behind this relationship seems to stem from the EU level downward, the mooted reforms invariably have EU democracy as their starting point. The following section analyzes the arguments that dominate this debate by looking at whether their attempts to respond to the democracy game consider how the sovereignty game has reconfigured democracy.

Reconciling Integration with Democracy: The Problematic Role of Sovereignty Claims

Participants in the debate about how to reconcile European integration with democracy can be separated into two main camps. Whereas some propose a more or less radical restructuring of the EU to breathe new democratic life into its institutions, others believe it is more germane to use this opportunity to reconsider the nature of contemporary democratic practices. It would be **histrionic** to say that there is an enormous gulf between these two visions of the state of democracy in Europe. Nevertheless, there is a clear line of separation demarcating those who fret not about the health of EU democracy, like Coultrap (1999), Moravcsik (2006), and Majone (2006) and those who recommend immediate action to improve its democratic legitimacy (Schmitter 2000; Hix 2007). However, on closer scrutiny, both these perspectives seem problematic when it comes to appreciating the crucial role of sovereignty claims in the construction of the EU. Changing the democracy game of the EU polity will significantly affect the sovereignty game—just as the latter has reconfigured the former. Hence proposals for reforming the EU in the name of democracy, if they are to be convincing, have to take seriously the sovereignty game. In particular, if the intention is to find an alternative to sovereignty claims because they have proved problematic for democracy, these proposals have to give a convincing account of what will replace or abolish the instrumental use of sovereignty claims.

Democratizing the EU: Overcoming Sovereignty Claims through Supranationalism?

Democratizing the EU is synonymous with increasing the importance of supranational representation at the expense of confederalism. Hence the usual suggestions are threefold: beef up the powers of the European Parliament (Andersen and Burns 1996), turn the Council of Ministers into an upper house alone (Habermas 2001), and find new ways of engendering the transnational representation of citizens, either through pan-European referendums (Auer 2007) or the promotion of supranational citizen associations (Schmitter 2000). In every case, the intention is to reduce the veto power of the member states thereby interfering with their claims to sovereign status as embodied by unanimity in the Council of Ministers or the right to reject treaty change, including via referendum. The inevitable result of these proposals, therefore, is the reduction of the autonomy of the member states by curtailing their confederal capacity to reject EU treaty amendment or negotiate consensus compromises by wielding the veto threat.

Other institutional reforms seek to enhance supranational representation for the sake of greater efficiency, which, it is thought, will in turn lead to greater output legitimacy. This is the case for the establishment of the new president of the European Council, the highest political body comprising heads of state or governments of the member states meeting four times a year, and the eventual abolition of the one state one commissioner rule contained in the Reform Treaty. In fact, both these reforms would constitute a new departure in the sovereignty game as they clearly go against the principle of state equality that is fundamental in confederal representation. By abolishing the rotating European Council presidency and the automatic award of a commissioner, the sovereignty claims of small countries—sometimes the only asset they have left (Werner and de Wilde 2001, 304)—will no longer prove so useful or satisfying.

When viewed from a certain angle, of course, the notion of state equality appears dubious. The contrast, for instance, between the fallout from the French "no" to the EU Constitution that the EU political elite has still barely digested and previous referendum rejections that led immediately to new votes is striking. However, reform of the presidency and the college of commissioners means that the confederal principle of state equality founded on states' sovereignty claims would be greatly attenuated. In particular, substantial and very visible changes to state equality, such as the loss of a commissioner, will greatly affect the element of majesty that underlies successful sovereignty claims (Onuf 1991). The importance of this aspect of sovereignty should not be underestimated, especially insofar as the majesty stemming from equal treatment sustains the state's relationship with what has been called the domestic audience for sovereignty claims (Werner and de Wilde 2001, 290). Hence the majesty stemming from state equality is not simply a question of respect from other states; it is also a feature of self-respect. In a reconfigured EU, nation-state majesty would, in all likelihood, have to be maintained or reinvented—which explains why the TEC fudged this matter.

All the above proposals for democratic EU reform thus represent an attempt to transform its hybrid nature of political representation by diluting the principle of confederalism that tries to uphold both member state equality and liberty. This suggests that the often-asserted claim that the equation between federalism and centralization so feared by the United Kingdom is "an ahistorical reading" (Dehousse 2005, 116) is misleading. The attenuation of the confederal principle of representation may not automatically equate to a more overweening center, but it would produce a concentration of political representation around that center. Furthermore, by breaking down confederalism's antimajoritarian bulwarks, such as vetoes and unanimous treaty revision, member states would find serious obstacles to sovereignty assertions, whether to limit supranationalism for all or to individually assert special claims.

In other words, the instrumental uses to which sovereignty claims could be put would simply diminish once it became harder to use them in practice. Such proposals rest on blatantly blithe assumptions, namely that not only will institutional arrangements render sovereignty claims unproblematic but that member states will accept such reforms in the first place. Yet the troubling feature of these proposals is less the latter assumption than the former, which fails to recognize the dynamic use to which sovereignty claims have been put in the course of integration as discussed earlier. By recognizing this feature of integration, it is possible to draw an entirely different conclusion than the prescription that sovereignty claims are simply a bother that have to be overcome. Given that sovereignty claims arise most when the claimed status of sovereignty is challenged (Werner and de Wilde 2001), it seems likely that further successful integration—at least according to the official motto of "united in diversity"—would require a new way of instrumentalizing sovereignty. Here is not the place to put forward detailed proposals on this subject.

But it is relatively easy to single out new ways of articulating sovereignty claims perhaps consisting of a revamped subsidiarity system on the basis of the criterion of diversity rather than effectiveness, a reconfigured interinstitutional relationship allowing the Council of Ministers greater scope for amending legislation proposed by the Commission and the ability to reassess ECJ rulings (both tabled by the UK government at the Amsterdam IGC), or even a version of the American constitutional doctrine of nullification (Tipton 1969) operating via national parliaments or direct democracy.

The analysis of the reciprocal relationship between democracy and the sovereignty game of integration revealed the ongoing problem of incorporating the autonomy and equality of states within a democratic, partly supranational polity. Nevertheless, some of the literature on the EU's democratic deficit assumes—explicitly (Moravcsik 2006) or implicitly (Coultrap 1999; Follesdal and Hix 2005; Hix 2007)—the relative stability of the EU constitutional settlement. When this is the case, rather than requiring a democratization of the EU, the impact of the sovereignty game of integration on democracy is thought to demand above all a new understanding of democratic governance and how best it functions. Yet the question still remains as to what this means for sovereignty claims.

Democratic Governance: Can Sovereignty Claims be Buried?

Two strands of thought can be distinguished within the literature on democratic governance in the EU. The first tries to dispel fears about the hollowness of EU democracy; the second believes that within the existing system a dose of "limited democratic politics" (Hix 2007), on the basis of the left-right dimension, needs to be injected to reconnect the polity with its citizens. Common to both is once again a sidelining of the problem of sovereignty claims within the delicate and, as seen earlier, highly contested system of EU competences and institutions.

Essentially, the first school is that of pluralist democracy. According to this model, whatever the alien nature of the mixed system in comparison with parliamentary regimes, the EU remains democratically legitimate thanks to its highly institutionalized checks and balances (Coultrap 1999; Majone 2006). Nonmajoritarian institutions, it is insisted, are potentially just as legitimate as majoritarian ones. However, what matters in this case is institutional design and the nature of the objectives to be pursued (Majone 2005). Hence if the EU is to be faulted it is not for its democratic deficit but for unsound institutional design and inappropriate policy objectives (ibid.). Paradoxically, the solution mooted for both these short-comings is precisely a new constitutional settlement that would strengthen the confederal principle at the expense of the supranational, "community method" (ibid.). So it seems that after first dismissing the link between the sovereignty game of integration and the problem of democratic legitimacy, sovereignty claims reappear. Not for the sake of legitimacy but to make the system function better in terms of outputs. This only goes to show that there is good reason to believe that sovereignty claims, rather than having to be buried, can be used to tackle the problematic democratic consequences of the sovereignty game of integration.

The second way of understanding democratic governance is to assume that the current integration status quo is too entrenched to be reformed substantively, yet still amenable to the injection of left-right politics over policy choice (Follesdal and Hix 2005; Hix 2006, 2007). This politicization approach believes that a minimal majoritarian element is possible thanks to the QMV-elected president of the Commission, which allows a more partisan college (Hix 2006, 19). What is surprising about this argument, as Bartolini (2006) points out, is the fact that the left/right cleavage is bound to raise fundamental, if not disquieting, questions about the constitution of the EU system itself, notably its competences and decision-making rules. Indeed, the cleavage over integration itself within member states has become more noticeable. Research on the recent referendums in the four countries that submitted the EU Constitution to a popular vote, which produced two ratifications and two rejections, emphasizes the essential "first order," that is, European element, of the results (Glencross and Trechsel 2007). Thus it is not at all clear why a limited democratic politics of left-right policy choices in a polity that has little redistributive capacity should be a priority over the debate regarding the future shape of integration.

Attempts to reconcile integration with democracy, whether from the supranational perspective or the governance approach, thus stumble precisely over the question of sovereignty claims. This is because neither treats member states' assertions of sovereignty as an integral part of how to respond to the intermeshed sovereignty and democracy games. Yet the uncanny feature of democratic legitimacy in the EU is the fact that this compound polity also rests on a compounded legitimacy: it "depends on both EU and national levels" (Schmidt 2004, 982). Since sovereignty claims are aimed at both external and internal audiences, they seem uniquely capable of finding if not a solution then at least a modus vivendi for democracy and sovereignty games played out at two levels. As presented in section one, the current EU system demonstrates the creative use to which sovereignty assertions have been used in the construction of this hybrid polity. It is therefore odd to discover that such an instrument does not play a more prominent—as well as innovative—role in attempts to reconfigure the EU system.

Conclusions

By examining the contested principles of representation structuring the EU polity, this chapter tried to shed some new light on the strategic relationship between sovereignty, integration, and democracy. European integration poses manifold challenges to sovereignty and democracy. The result is a certain "deficit anxiety,"[12] prompting attempts to show that democracy can be reconciled with what is often called "post-sovereignty" but that is perhaps better captured by N. Walker's notion of a "sovereignty surplus" (2007, 5). No such guarantees or reassurances were offered here. Rather, the chapter demonstrated how the problem of reconciling sovereignty claims with democracy has become marginalized when it comes to finding solutions to the adverse effects of integration on democracy in Europe.

Current proposals to overcome or bury member states' sovereignty were shown to suffer from serious shortcomings. As a result, the analysis suggests that member state assertions of sovereignty ought to be considered as a means of negotiating the relationship between integration, sovereignty, and democracy. However, the recent experience of the Lissabou Treaty points to a continued failure to take sovereignty claims seriously. Most egregiously, the treaty was pruned of the rhetoric of its constitutional forebearer so as to give member states a ready excuse not to ratify it by referendum—despite retaining the vast majority of the institutional and decision making changes contained in the EU Constitution. Obviously, this state of affairs is the product of member state collusion. Still under the shock of the referendum rejections of the EU Constitution in France and the Netherlands, Europe's political elite has opted to elide the sovereignty issue. Disingenuously, these elites portray the Lissabou Treaty as a tidying-up exercise without sovereignty implications, thereby rendering referendums redundant.

In this way the whole gamut of sovereignty claims—as barrier to supranationalism, as a state's right to a special status, and as expression of popular sovereignty through referendums—has for the moment been buried. Yet the experience of integration is one of a welter of contestation and renegotiation over the rules of the game of integration politics, interspersed only briefly with moments of calm. With several important changes scheduled for future implementation, such as the eventual abolition of the one commissioner per country rule or the move toward a new system of QMV, and with the detail of others—notably the United Kingdom opt-out from the Charter of Fundamental Rights—unspecified, there are many looming complication. Perhaps it will be necessary for this new political settlement to be called into question before a collective epiphany about the role of sovereignty claims in the EU system is possible. Whatever the timing, this awakening will probably consist of the realization that the continuation of integration in a way acceptable to states and their citizens requires the juxtaposition of contradictory principles of representation that results from the use of sovereignty claims.

Notes

1. Jackson (1999, 433) goes further in claiming that sovereignty is "an institution which is periodically renovated to respond to new historical circumstances."
2. MacCormick (1999), famously, has taken a more nuanced view by likening sovereignty to virginity, viz. something that is lost but not gained by another party.
3. The absence of a specific withdrawal clause did not prevent Greenland, which joined as part of the Kingdom of Denmark but obtained home rule in 1979, from seceding from the EEC in 1985 with the consent of the European Council. Witte (2004a) argues that a right of withdrawal under the EEC treaty can be implied from state practice in the EEC treaty given that the United Kingdom called a referendum in 1975 on continued membership of the European Communities.
4. Such a conflict arose over the question of harmonizing criminal sanctions in the field of environmental protection. The commission argued this should occur under the Community regime whilst the Council of Ministers sought to implement legislation as an EU framework decision. The ECJ ruled in favor of the Commission in Case C-176/03 *Commission v Council.*
5. For reasons of conceptual clarity I do not dwell on the German Constitutional Court's notorious decision on the constitutional validity of the Maastricht Treaty. This seems to represent an assertion of sovereignty to limit supranationalism but articulated in the name of an individual state, thereby blurring the conceptual framework adopted in this section.
6. The United Kingdom subsequently signed up to the Social Protocol in 1997 following a change of government (Shaw 1998, 68).
7. Denmark also obtained a specific guarantee that EU citizenship would not jeopardize Danish sovereignty on deciding matters of citizenship. In addition, Denmark was also exempted from supranational cooperation on asylum, immigration, and judicial cooperation.
8. Ireland, following a Supreme Court decision on the Single European Act, is the only member state constitutionally obliged to hold a referendum on EU treaty revision.

9. The European precedent for holding a national vote on enlargement was France's 1972 vote on EEC expansion.

10. Schmitt probably overstates the importance of democratization as the post civil war era was notable for the construction of a national sense of political community (Greenfeld 1992). In fact, the relationship between democratization and nationalism is highly complex, as Yack (2001) has argued very powerfully that popular sovereignty as a modern phenomenon unintentionally fostered the assumption that political organization supposed a national community.

11. C-147/03 *Commission v Austria* [2005] ECR I-5969.

12. I credit this expression to Cormac Mac Amhlaigh of the European University Institute.

Part III

Horizontal Sovereignty Games

8

Sovereignty beyond Borders: Sovereignty, Self-Defense, and the Disciplining of States

Tanja E. Aalberts and Wouter G. Werner

Originally, the right to self-defense was included in the UN Charter as a limited and temporary exception to the prohibition on the use of force. In that way, it underscored the fundamental transformation in the reading of sovereignty and war that emerged in the twentieth century. Where in the *Jus Publicum Europaeum* sovereignty entailed the right to determine the ways to fight a public enemy, including war, the UN Charter linked sovereignty to the protection against acts of aggression. Paradoxically, the attempts to outlaw the use of force resulted in the creation of several new discursive spaces to legitimize the use of force: armed force could (and should) now be justified in terms of exceptions, as exceptional measures aimed at restoring normalcy. This discursive practice already started in the late 1940s but gained new momentum after the 9/11 attacks. This chapter focuses on the recent attempts to further stretch the limits of self-defense and to link this right to large-scale reconstructions of domestic societies through the alleged connection between state failure and terrorism.

> The terrors of lawlessness must be responded to...if need be, by the terrors of the law
>
> —*Lorimer 1883, 93*

> Does this morality [that the strong are best at proving they're right] teach us, as is often believed, that force "trumps" law? Or else, something

quite different, that the very concept of law, that juridical reason itself,
includes a priori a possible recourse to constraint or coercion and, thus,
to a certain violence?

—Derrida 2005, xi

Introduction

This chapter examines how the concept of sovereignty is linked to justifications of foreign intervention, especially when the use of force is involved.
At first sight, this might seem counterintuitive. In many writings, the concept of sovereignty is understood as the logical corollary of the principle
of nonintervention. Already in the sixteenth to eighteenth century natural
law school, the principle of nonintervention was understood as an a priori,
a dictate of reason without which a community of sovereign, independent
states would be impossible (see Winfield 1922; Vincent 1974). In similar
fashion, Vattel argued that "it clearly follows the liberty and independence
of Nations that each has the right to govern itself as it thinks proper, and
that no one of them has the least right to interfere in the government of
another…" (Vattel 1758, Book II, iv, para 54). In the post-1945 international legal order, the link between sovereignty and nonintervention
became even closer, tight up as it was with the prohibition on the use of
force as a peremptory norm of international relations.[1]

Yet, international practice shows many examples where states have
sought to justify foreign interventions in terms of the protection of sovereignty, that is, as a matter of self-defense.[2] To understand these argumen-
tative practices, it is necessary to take a closer look at state sovereignty as
a fundamental principle of international law and politics. This will be discussed in the first section of this chapter. It will be argued that sovereignty
is to be understood as an "interpretive concept." In this way, it is possible
to understand both the evolution of sovereignty and the way in which
its function has remained stable in the last few centuries. Subsequently,
the next section will explicate the function of sovereignty as an ordering
principle, that established a link between rights and freedoms on the one
hand and responsibility on the other. In turn, it will be argued that this
sovereignty/responsibility link enables the disciplining of the primary
subjects of international law. The third section will take a closer look at
this disciplinary potential via the relation between sovereignty and the
use of force. It will set out how sovereignty evolved from a concept that left
states free to determine their public enemies and the ways to fight them,
to a concept that forced states to rely on exceptionalism to justify their
foreign interventions. This practice, as will be demonstrated in the final

section, has been furthered in the recent "war on terror," by stretching the principle of self-defense on the one hand and the link between terrorism and state failure on the other hand. Thus sovereignty has become bound up with large-scale interventions and attempts to recreate and discipline former enemy states.

Sovereignty as an Interpretive Concept

To be able to understand the resilience of state sovereignty—that is, its combined endurance and flexibility—it is necessary to prevent two fallacies. The first is the "descriptivistic fallacy," the idea that sovereignty must necessarily represent a corresponding state of affairs in empirical reality (the signified). The second is the "normativistic fallacy": the idea that the meaning of sovereignty, as a normative concept, merely represents a bundle of rights, duties, and competencies. Although the descriptivistic and normativistic fallacy are fundamentally different, they share the idea that, to make sense of "sovereignty," it must represent something else (either a state of affairs or a bundle of rights, duties, and competencies). This chapter takes a different perspective, emphasizing not primarily what sovereignty *represents*, but rather what it *presents*, what it brings about (for this argument see also Werner 2001).

To capture its constitutive function, we understand sovereignty as an *interpretive concept*. The term "interpretive concept" was coined by Ronald Dworkin in his critique of positivist legal theories and his attempts to make sense of US constitutional practice (Dworkin 1986, 45–86). An interpretive concept is a normative institution that (1) ascribes social status and (2) contains a set of norms of conduct. Characteristic of an interpretive concept, moreover, is that the members of a society do not treat the rules of the institution as a taboo that cannot be questioned or changed. On the contrary, the members of the society take a so called "interpretive attitude" toward the institution; an attitude that has two components (Dworkin 1986, 47):

- The first is that the members act on the believe that the institution "does not simply exist but as value, that it serves some interest or purpose or enforces some principle—in short, that is has some point—that can be stated independently of just describing the rules that make up the practice"
- The second is that the rules of the institution, what the institution requires, "are not necessarily or exclusively what they have always been taken to be but are instead sensitive to its point, so that the

strict rules must be understood or applied or modified or qualified or limited by that point."

From this conceptualization of institutions as interpretive concepts follows that they are dynamic concepts too: agents consider the institution in the context of its point or purpose and restructure the rules of the institution in the light of that function. This means that—as has been the case with sovereignty—an institution can survive fundamental changes in a society. An example of this is the survival of the concept of state sovereignty in international society despite the fundamental transformation from dynastical legitimacy to self-determination as one of the guiding principles of international legitimacy.

Whereas an interpretive concept is an intersubjective institution, shared by members of a community, it is not necessary that they all agree on the application of such a concept to an individual case. They might very well disagree on what the institution requires in a particular situation—in fact, that is what an interpretive concept is about. As long as the "international community" (implicitly or explicitly) agrees on the most general and abstract propositions about the institution, they share a background that makes genuine disagreement on the requirements and scope of an institution meaningful. In this context, it is helpful to recall Dworkin's distinction between "concept" and "conception." To illustrate the distinction between concepts and conceptions, Dworkin uses the example of the institution of courtesy in an imaginary community (Dworkin 1986, 90–96). In this community, people share the concept of courtesy and agree, at the most general level, that courtesy stands for "respect." However, there are major differences of opinion about the correct interpretation of what respect requires in different circumstances (does it mean showing respect to people of a higher rank or does it require a more egalitarian interpretation, does it require a different treatment of man and women or does it require an equal treatment of both? etc.). There are, in other words, different *conceptions* of the institution or concept of courtesy. The parallels between Dworkins's example and the concept of sovereignty are clear: there is, at the most general level, agreement that sovereignty stands for "freedom," "equality," and "independence."[3] However, what these abstract notions consist of in practice is less unambiguous. That is to say, from the status of sovereignty itself no "given, determinate, normative implications" follow (Koskenniemi 1991, 408). This leads to competing conceptions of sovereignty and disputes where both parties appeal to the sovereignty principle to support their respective claims. It also enables the aforementioned practice of justifying intervention practices on the basis of sovereignty.[4]

To decide which of the competing conceptions of sovereignty is legally correct in a concrete case, it is necessary to rely on specific rules and principles valid under international law at the time of the dispute. This does not mean, however, that sovereignty is thereby reduced to these rules and principles. It remains relevant as a general concept (or institution in Dworkinian sense) that structures legal and political discourse and that, in turn, is kept alive by the enduring disputes about its proper meaning. The current discussion hence is akin to insights from the linguistic turn in both legal thought and International Relations theory, inspired by Wittgensteinian conceptions of language games, notably in their rejection of a given referent (signified), and the ensuing move from a correspondence notion to the constitutive role of language. Taking an "interpretive" stance to sovereignty, such post-positivist approaches focus on its changing meaning and historical contingency instead.[5] However, by addressing in more detail the function of institutions, Dworkin's notion of the "interpretive concept" enables us to scrutinize what sovereignty does beyond its, by now widely accepted, disposition as a social construct or discursive fact. Thus, our perspective moves beyond the contingency notion by elaborating meaning in relation to the *dual* function of institutions, and by distinguishing two uses of sovereignty (as *status* and as *rights/duties*) to analyse its resilience. To understand how it operates as a general concept it is necessary to further elaborate the "point" of sovereignty within the legal order.

Sovereignty as a Way of Organizing Responsibility

Within the framework of international law, the concept of state sovereignty is used in at least two interrelated ways, running parallel to Dworkin's interpretive concept. First, sovereignty is used to describe the status of a political community (the status of "sovereign" or "independent" statehood). Second, the concept of sovereignty is used to endow states with certain fundamental rights, powers, and duties (their sovereign rights), establishing norms of conduct. State sovereignty in international life, therefore, performs functions that are akin to those performed by the concept of individual liberty in the national context. Both the individual liberty and the state sovereignty argument take as their starting point the existence of independent ("free" or "sovereign") agents who are equal by "nature," endowed with a minimum core of fundamental rights and whose freely expressed consent forms the basis order and society.[6] As Koskenniemi has summarized this analogy between individual liberalism and state sovereignty: "Both characterize the social world in descriptive and normative terms. They describe social life in terms of the activities of individual agents ('legal subjects', citizens, states) and set down the basic conditions within which the relations between these agents should be conducted" (Koskenniemi 1989, 192).

The notions of state sovereignty and individual liberty are easily misunderstood as being purely individualistic and antisocial. The institution of sovereignty is then construed as a variant of "possessive individualism" (Ruggie 1983), whereas sovereign states have been presented as essentially outside international society (Patomäki 2002). This reading of sovereignty can be found within the traditional body of International Relations writings, as well as political discourse, on sovereignty. Conceiving of sovereignty notably in terms of "freedoms, rights, immunities," that is, autonomy and independence from outside interference, this basically takes an individualistic stance on sovereignty, whilst concomitantly linking it to notions of power and control. This is reflected most clearly in light of the debates on globalization, regional integration, and the erosion of sovereignty.[7] It also materializes in the discussion of international law as impinging sovereignty by limiting the freedom of maneuver—in particular through the development of the human rights regime that is central to the intervention debate. In other words, sovereignty and sovereign statehood are presented as given entities, which exist independent from their international environment, in a vacuum. Any international development (including integration, globalization, and international law) then necessary reduces this freedom and hence erode sovereignty as a zero-sum game (the more globalized, Europeanized and/or "legalized," the less sovereignty is left).

Such readings of sovereignty, however, fail to grasp one of the essential features of the (legal) institution of sovereignty: that is, the specific way it orders international life by linking freedom and responsibility. Through the notion of sovereignty, international law not only presents states as free and equal, but also creates subjects (legal persons) that, by virtue of their privileged status, are held to respect an extensive set of obligations. The freedom and equality of states exists within an (international) normative order that dictates the scope and content of this room to maneuver (Shaw 2003, 190). Within this order "sovereignty" hence entails not only the capacity to make legal claims on the basis of possessed rights, but also the possibility of being held accountable for one's acts.

From its inception in modern international law, the idea of the state as a sovereign legal person has been linked to attempts to civilize power. Thus, when the term "international legal personality" was coined, the aim was not to create a normatively free sphere in which states could operate. On the contrary: the concept of international legal personality was advocated as a way to recognize the new power configurations in Europe, to bring the newly arising powers within an overarching normative structure. Through the assignment of a specific, privileged status, the normative order constituted its own sovereign subjects and presented them as the principal bearers of international responsibility.[8] As Nijman has argued: "...the concept of international legal personality functioned to legitimise the participation of the German Princes in international life, but by *the same legal move* established their *responsibility* to conform to the justice-based rules of the law of nations" (Nijman 2004, 499, emphasis added).

The elements of recognition, legitimation, and responsibility also come together in the very term "international legal personality." Etymologically speaking, "personality" does not stem from the idea of a self-contained, free individual, but from the term *persona*—that signified a theatrical mask in classical antiquity plays (Nijman 2004, chapter 6). The mask of sovereignty is best understood as a way of presentation in a play that (re) defines one's identity and role. Just like in a play, it does not make much sense to "unmask" the actor to see what "really" goes on: the reality is given, or rather: constituted within the play itself. In that sense, it is not so much the states that play sovereignty games, it is the sovereignty play that constitutes those who are in the game, and are granted a "voice" in the first place.[9] Thus it is the game itself that creates the conditions of possibility of sovereign "being" at all (Aalberts 2004).[10]

The relation between sovereignty and responsibility is not just a theoretical invention. In international legal and diplomatic practice, the ability and willingness to live up to international obligations has long been recognized as one of the core elements of what it is to be a sovereign state. In the *Island of Palmas* case (1928), for example, arbiter Huber argued that territorial sovereignty not only gives states the right to exercise jurisdiction over their territories, but it also puts them under an obligation to respect the rights of other states:

> Territorial sovereignty...involves the exclusive right to display the activities of a State. This right has as a corollary a duty: the obligation to protect within the territory the rights of other States, in particular their right to integrity and inviolability in peace and war, together with the rights which each State may claim for its nationals in foreign territory. Without manifesting its territorial sovereignty in a manner corresponding to the circumstances, the State cannot fulfil this duty.[11]

The logic underpinning the *Island of Palmas* case is echoed in the modern criteria for statehood. According to the 1933 Montevideo Convention the existence of a "government" is one of the criteria for statehood in modern international law.[12] Under customary international law, this criterion is usually interpreted in terms of "effective and independent government," precisely in light of the obligations of statehood under international law (Crawford 2006). In similar fashion, the 1949 Draft Declaration on Rights and Duties of States reconfirms the relation between sovereignty and responsibility by emphasizing the need for self-discipline and the obligations that come with sovereign statehood. The Declaration contains 10 articles defining duties, whereas only 4 formulate rights that are related to the status of sovereign statehood.[13] One of the core articles lays down that "Every State has the duty to carry out in good faith its obligations arising from treaties and other sources of international law."[14] By extension it can be conceived as rights as obligations, as has been explicitly formulated by the International Law Commission: "If it is the prerogative of sovereignty to be able to assert its rights, the counterpart of that prerogative is the duty to discharge its obligations."[15] This reverses the widespread conception of sovereignty as legitimizing a sphere of freedom to sovereignty as a specific way of organizing international responsibility. More specifically, as a normative institution it assigns a social status (legal personality as sovereigns), and contains norms of conduct (sovereign rights and duties) with the function ("point") to hold agents accountable. Sovereignty then entails a task to fulfill, rather than a freedom to indulge.

In international relations practice, one can detect a political translation of this logic in the *Responsibility to Protect* report by the International Commission of Intervention and State Sovereignty (ICISS). As a rejoinder to the sovereignty/intervention dilemma formulated in the Secretary General's Millennium Report, the report reformulates sovereignty. By the example of the UN Charter, it pinpoints both the agency and the responsibility that follow from a sovereign status: "There is no transfer or dilution of state sovereignty. But there is a necessary recharacterization involved: from *sovereignty as control* [*sic*] to *sovereignty as responsibility* in both internal functions and external duties" (ICISS 2001). Moreover, the report also testifies a shift from sovereign duties in relation to the rights of fellow-sovereigns (such as their territorial integrity and the rights of their nationals, as formulated in the *Island of Palmas case*), toward duties as concomitant to sovereignty rights in relation to one's own population, which in addition are increasingly conceived as international responsibilities.[16]

The intrinsic relation between sovereignty and responsibility has important implications for the topic of this chapter. It implies that international law can be used to identify irresponsible states and accordingly to legitimize measures aimed at disciplining such states. If the obligations of states are primarily limited to the protection of narrowly defined interests of fellow sovereigns, such disciplining acts have a fairly limited character as well. However, if international law is deployed for the protection of universal values and the interests of the international community as a whole, irresponsible behavior calls for a much stronger response. As will be set out in the next sections, this logic has been mobilized in the recent "war on terror" to legitimize interventionist strategies against the most irresponsible sovereigns: the rogue states and the failed states.

Stretching Sovereign Space:
The Fluid Limits on the Use of Force

In *Jus Publicum Europaeum*, the right to use force was considered to be an attribute of state sovereignty; a right that is *inherent* to the concept of sovereignty (see Schmitt 1974; Grewe 2000). This not only meant that the determination of the ways to fight a public enemy was left to the state, but also that acquisition of territory by means of conquest constituted a valid title to territory in international law (Brownlie 1991, 14–51; see also Malanczuk 1993).

With the decline of the *Jus Publicum Europaeum*, the relation between sovereignty and the use of force changed drastically. As was set out in the introduction, in the course of the twentieth century, sovereignty became linked up with a more radical prohibition of intervention, including the prohibition on the use of force as a peremptory norm of international law. This further materialized in article 2(4) of the UN Charter, which also formulated the only exceptions to this rule: "threats to international peace and security" (art. 39 and 42) and "self defense" against armed attacks (art. 51) and/or imminent threats.[17] Documents like the Charter or the 1970 Resolution 2625 (reflecting customary law) not only formulate the prohibition on the use of force, but also stress that the basis of this norm is the principle of sovereign equality. GA Resolution 2625 explicitly states that the inviolability of the territorial integrity and the political independence (and thus the right to be free from outside armed intervention) is included in the notion of state sovereignty.[18] In light of the foregoing, it is noteworthy that rather than formulated as a negative right, the Resolution also refers to inter alia "the obligation not to intervene" and the "duty of States to refrain from . . . any form of coercion aimed against the political independence or the territorial integrity of any State." Thus parallel to the 1949 Draft Declaration on Rights and Duties, the resolution emphasizes negative rights in terms of positive duties. Moreover, an explicit link is made between equality as a matter of status as well as a right and duty: "All States enjoy sovereign equality. They have equal rights and duties and are equal members of the international community."

As exception to the egalitarian foundation of the UN, the Security Council was established to replace traditional war by collective enforcement mechanisms in the name of community values such as international peace and security, and the fight against aggression. Strictly speaking, such a collectivization implies the elimination of the traditional concept of war as an armed struggle between equal states (and thus equal enemies). However, the prohibition on the use of force did not imply a decline in the actual use of force in (international) society. Although "war" was officially banned from post-1945 international legal discourse, in practice the use of force remained. As was predicted by critics like Carl Schmitt, the prohibition on the use of force would not do away with enmity and war, but rather lead to new discursive possibilities to legitimize the use of force. The notion of war as a matter between formally equal enemies was thus replaced by the idea that force was used against a law-breaker or a threat against international peace and security. As a consequence, it would become difficult to distinguish between a *justus hostis* and criminals or elements that need to be dealt with in the name of humanity (Schmitt 1974, 112–183).

In this context, it is important to recall that the cold war environment of the East-West rivalries generally precluded the operation of the collective security arrangements in post-1945 practice. This meant that states, when resorting to the use of force, had to rely on the only legal justification left: individual self-defense. While the right of self-defense was originally incorporated in the Charter as a limited and temporary measure ("…until the Security Council has taken measures…"), in international practice it turned out to be the major justification invoked by states using force against other states. This was also the practice in cases where humanitarian emergencies took place, such as with the intervention in Pakistan in 1971 and the interventions in Cambodia and Uganda in 1978 (Wheeler 2000). In this context, Neff has spoken of the "self-defense revolution": "…the full emergence of self-defence to the front and centre of the international stage, as a kind of all-purpose justification for unilateral resorts to armed force" (Neff 2005, 315). Post-1945 self-defense has been stretched as to include the rescue of nationals abroad, the anticipatory use of force, and actions against serious foreign subversion. In effect, it meant that self-defense moved to the center of a neo just war doctrine, whose core consists of the protection of state sovereignty against armed intervention, with the use of force as an exceptional mechanism to ensure the sovereignty of states. This trend of the deployment of the right to self-defense as an all-purpose justification for the use of force is buttressed by the framing of the recent "war on terror."

Shortly after the 9/11 attacks, the Security Council affirmed the right of self-defense.[19] Although the Security Council only referred to the right to self-defense in general terms (*"Recognizing* the inherent right of individual or collective self-defense in accordance with the Charter..."), in light of the above the symbolic meaning of this recognition immediately after the 9/11 attacks was clear and compelling. Equally clear was the support from the NATO member states, who for the first time in the history of the alliance invoked article 5 of the NATO Charter (defining an attack to one member as an attack to the whole alliance). On September 12, NATO decided that, if it is determined that the attack against the United States was directed from abroad, it shall be regarded as an action covered by the right to collective self-defense.[20] After the member states were convinced, the 9/11 attacks were conducted by Al-Qaeda, they accepted the applicability of article 5 of the NATO Charter.[21]

The effects of accepting such a collective and/or individual right to self-defense in response to terrorist attacks are far-reaching. Self-defense now not only covers immediate responses to attacks by identifiable actors, but also open-ended operations against an amorphous enemy. The invocation of "self-defense" in response to attacks by terrorist networks raises questions as to the boundaries of the right to self-defense in at least three respects: temporal, spatial, and qua object. The temporal limits of self-defense are put into question, because it can become unclear when the attack that triggered the right of self-defense took place. The right of self-defense against terrorist attacks can follow from a "consistent pattern of violent terrorist action" against a state (see also Cassesse 1989). It is difficult to tell when such a consistent pattern exists and it is possible that a state can conclude that, in hindsight, it had already been at war with a terrorist organization for a considerable time.[22] Moreover, it is indeterminate when the war on terrorism will stop. The war on terrorism is, after all, not only a self-defense operation designed to do away with a specific attack, but an open-ended operation that will only end when "every terrorist group of global reach has been found, stopped and defeated."[23] Such a sustained operation knows no spatial limits either. Terrorists are, after all, spread out throughout the world and could, as both the 9/11 attacks and the 7/7 London bombings have shown, even hide in the homeland. Thus, after the 9/11 attacks, the United States (and their allies) not only emphasized the need to deal with states harboring terrorists, but also engaged in extraterritorial operations such as targeted killing of suspected Al-Qaeda members abroad. Finally, as the war against Afghanistan has shown, the object of self-defense is broadened considerably. Here, a self-defense operation was used to realize a regime change (the Security Council expressed its "strong support for the efforts of the Afghan people to establish a new and transitional administration leading to the formation of a government"),[24] and thus went beyond an operation aimed at repelling an armed attack. The operation rather aimed at incapacitating the enemy in very broad terms, that is, to take away "safe havens" for terrorists. This was emphasized in Resolution 1368 through the notion of state responsibility: "… *stresses* that those responsible for aiding, supporting or harbouring the perpetrators, organizers and sponsors of these [terrorist] acts will be held accountable."[25] Whereas the claim regarding the extension of self-defense and state responsibility for harboring terrorism was already formulated in the so-called Shultz Doctrine in the 1980s,[26] in light of the "war on terrorism" self-defense arguments are more explicitly linked to the struggle for a world without rogue regimes and failed states, that is, to restore normalcy; and more widely accepted as such by the international community at large.[27]

Sovereign Equality as a Ground for Making Distinctions

From the preceding section, it can be inferred that the "war on terror" is on the basis of a specific reading of sovereignty: the notion of sovereign equality, which underpins both the right to self-defense and to nonintervention, is used to make a distinction between different types of states. Decent or responsible states are set apart from irresponsible states; from unwilling, rogue states and unable, failed states. The net result is that the right to self-defense, while formally still equally applicable to all states, is applied in a discriminatory fashion. What was at stake in the war against Afghanistan, for example, was not just the protection of one state (the United States) against a formally equal state (Afghanistan). The widespread support for the US-led coalition cannot be isolated from the way in which Afghanistan had been branded as an irresponsible, undisciplined state since the 1990s. In a series of UN Security Council Resolutions, Afghanistan was condemned for the manifold ways in which it violated fundamental norms of international law and put under scrutiny of UN sanctions committees.[28] Especially if such an "irresponsible state" confronts a hegemonic state with special legal powers (as a permanent membership of the Security Council), the boundaries of the prohibition of intervention become more fluid. As Simpson has argued,

> [C]ertain States, pre-designated as outlaws [i.e. Afghanistan under the Taliban regime, Iraq and Libya], lack the immunities available to other

States in warding off the possibility of armed intervention. So regardless of any evidence showing links between, say, Pakistan or Saudi Arabia and the attacks on Western interests, it is improbable that these [reputed lawful] States find themselves on the peripheries and subject to attack in the near future (...). The distinction is not simply one of politics. The breaches of international law committed by [Afghanistan] contribute to outlaw status and the outlaw status determines the legality of the measures taken against these states.... (Simpson 2004, 340)

Whereas Simpson emphasizes that this sets the irresponsible states outside the legal order (as literally outlaws), we want to emphasize that the disciplinary element is provided by the sovereignty status within the legal order itself. The state in question is not disciplined because it is outside the law, but exactly because it is constituted and regulated by law; because it wears the legal persona of sovereignty. The link between sovereignty and responsibility is thus used to justify intervention in states that lack the discipline to grasp the relation between freedom and self-constraint. In this sense, the term "outlaw" is a bit of a misnomer, insofar as it lays emphasis on exclusion, ignoring the more nuanced inclusion/exclusion logic at play. Discipline is not exercised through exclusive membership rules and gatekeeping, but through the subsequent imposition of a norm of appropriate and responsible being for all equal members included in the international society (Aalberts 2006). Thus, irresponsible states, be they rogue or failed states, are outlaws within the law of nations.[29]

Indeed, the relation between sovereignty and responsibility, coupled to conceptions of outlawry also figures prominently in the discourse of failed states within the "war on terrorism." To be sure, state failure (in rudimentary terms being states lacking empirical capacities of effective control and monopoly of force) is not a new phenomenon. As a political issue it has been on the agenda since the end of the cold war, but as an empirical phenomenon it arguably dates at least back to the Concert of Europe (Grovogui 2002).[30] Moreover, nineteenth-century international lawyers already distinguished between "civilized," "barbarian," and "savage" communities, thus foreshadowing the discourse on failed states (Koskenniemi 2002). There are, however, at least two essential differences between nineteenth-century discourses on "civilization" and post-cold war discourse on "failed states." First, the notion of "tribes" or "uncivilized societies" that were excluded from international society is now replaced by the notion of equal, sovereign states that fail to perform their duties. Thus the logic of difference and exclusion that characterized the nineteenth-century international society is now integrated into the sovereignty discourse. Disciplining measures, therefore, must be justified within the sovereignty discourse, too.

In this context, it is important to note that the breakdown of governmental authority within a state does not automatically imply that such a state ceases to exist as an international legal person. Although effective government is one of the criteria relevant for the emergence of statehood,[31] its endurance is on the basis of the *presentation* (not *representation*) of an entity as state—thus taking transient eruptions in case of civil war, foreign occupation, collapse of central government, or even government in exile into account in accordance with the principle of continuity: "[T]emporary absence [of government] (*which may last for years*) [...] does not affect the identity [i.e., international personality] of the State concerned" (Fastenrath 1995, 670, emphasis added). In these situations the concept of state sovereignty is used to uphold the status quo and to prevent the termination of one of the members of international society. Metaphorically speaking, the failed state is like a mask, a sovereign *persona*, without an actor that effectively performs the corresponding role. However, given the relation between state sovereignty and responsibility, especially if it comes to fundamental obligations of states, state failure constitutes a major problem for international law (Thürer 1996; Wallace-Bruce 2000; Kreijen 2004; Koskenmäki 2004). It is, therefore, not surprising to find that failed states are presented as legal anomalies or even "impossibilities" (Herdegen 1996, 77). It is through the newly imputed link with terrorism that allegedly renders them a dangerous political anomaly, too. This constitutes the second difference with nineteenth-century discourse. In light of their potentiality as breeding ground for terrorism,[32] failed states have gained renewed prominence as a security issue in the "war on terrorism."

In the recent war on terror, at least two routes have been followed to deal with the anomaly of state failure. The first follows the logic of the law of state responsibility by linking the question of responsibility to the question who exercises control over (unlawful) conduct. Article 9 of the Articles on the Responsibility of states for internationally wrongful acts, for example, provides that in cases where governmental authority is absent or default, the conduct of a person or group shall be considered an act of a state if the person or group is in fact exercising elements of the governmental authority.[33] This provision echoes the rationale of article 8, which holds that the conduct of a person or group shall be regarded an act of a state if that person or group is in fact acting under instructions of or under the direction or control of the state concerned. In the legal justifications offered for the attack on Afghanistan, this logic played an important role. It was argued that the relations between the Taliban and Al-Qaeda were so close that it was difficult to tell who was acting under whose instruction, control, or direction. On the basis of a relatively liberal reading of the test of "control,"[34] it was argued that the 9/11 attacks could be attributed to the (failed) state of Afghanistan, thus legitimizing acts of self-defense against this state.[35] Such acts, as we set out in the previous section, were not limited to repelling an immediate attack, but covered attempts at a whole-scale reconstruction of the state and society in question.

The second route goes beyond the confines of positive international law. It is on the basis of the argument that, since failed states are incapable of meeting their duties as sovereigns, it is the responsibility of the international community to step in and take action. In this context, it is not always clear who may take such action on behalf of the international community. While the UN Security Council has a clear legal mandate, some states who claim to represent the international community can offer only more shaky legal and moral foundations for their actions. In this context, an interesting merger of self-defense and humanitarian intervention is taking place. Whereas the notion of "secondary responsibility" in the Responsibility to Protect report related to human rights, and arguably testifies a move beyond Hobbesian international politics in the post-cold war period, with the "war on terror" it is conceived in terms of high politics of security again—this time mixed with a muscular humanitarianism (Orford 1999; see also Orford 2003). Failed states, in other words, are portrayed as dangerous to citizens, fellow sovereigns, and the international community and/or humanity at large alike. Moreover, assistance or harboring terrorism is conceived not only as an "internationally wrongful act" in itself, but in particular in relation to the right to territorial integrity of fellow-sovereigns.

This move also clarifies how in political discourse failing states and "rogues" are increasingly coupled, whereas allegedly they occupy extreme positions on a scale of statehood—lacking effective control in the one case, displaying an abundance of control in the other: "From one perspective, totalitarian regimes and failed or failing states are at opposite ends of the spectrum. But there are similarities: one is unable to avoid subverting international law; the other is only too willing to flout it"[36]—that is, neither is living up to its international responsibilities of the international community. Both then are designated as outlaws (or even criminal elements within the international order), forfeiting by extension in both cases their sovereign rights within the community:[37] "Whether the dangers to international order come from totalitarianism or chaos, all countries have the right to respond."[38] Accordingly, one can detect three shifts relating to state failure as a political issue: from a humanitarian to a security issue, from a domestic to an international responsibility, and from a multilateral to a unilateral issue (a matter of individual self-defense).

As an illustration to this shift of the sovereignty game within political discourse, and in particular our argument regarding the link between sovereignty and responsibility, it is worthwhile to quote a US governmental official, Richard Haass (Director Policy Planning of the State Department) at length:

What you're seeing from this Administration is the emergence of a new principle or body of ideas—I'm not sure it constitutes a doctrine—about what you might call the limits of sovereignty. Sovereignty entails obligations. One is not to massacre your own people. Another is not to support terrorism in any way. If a government fails to meet these obligations, then it forfeits some of the *normal* advantages of sovereignty, including the right to be left alone inside your own territory. Other governments, including the United States, gain the right to intervene. In the case of terrorism, this can even lead to a right of preventive, or peremptory, self-defense. You essentially can act in anticipation if you have grounds to think it's a question of when, and not if, you're going to be attacked.[39]

A similar emphasis on rights and responsibilities as structuring the international order is central to Blair's "doctrine of the international community," which was first formulated in the 1990s but also became a prominent wager in the "war on terrorism." Explaining its principles, then Foreign Secretary Jack Straw is even more explicit: "The rights of members of the global community depend exclusively on their readiness to meet their global responsibilities"—and this means, according to the Blair administration, that the principle of noninterference requires qualification in certain respects.[40] Whilst taking a more multilateral route than the Bush administration, it still remains unclear who has the authority to speak and act on behalf of the international community. In an imprecise way it appears to be linked to responsible behavior again. Thus the relationship of sovereignty and responsibility is turned around in political discourse—it is not just that sovereignty via legal personality relates to state responsibility and legal accountability, but vice versa that "responsible" behavior identifies the "true sovereigns," whereas irresponsible behavior requires a qualification of that sovereign status. Responsibility subsequently easily slips from a legal-procedural matter into a political-substantive issue. Whereas Blair makes a reservation regarding regime change in 1999, three years later Jack Straw is more obtrusive in his definition of modern global community, linking terrorism with state failure with the lack of democracy, and subsequently with a call for early intervention.[41] Taking it a step further, some have indeed defended regime change in the context of (the broadening of) the right to self-defense: "A war of self-defense may be fought in an offensive mode to the last bunker of the enemy dictator, with a view to the total collapse of the belligerent state (including, as a by-product, a regime change)" (Dinstein 2003, 20).[42]

In this way, the concept of sovereignty thus underpins an exceptional right of self-defense that goes well beyond a limited, temporary right to ward off an armed attack. Through the linkage between sovereignty and responsibility, it becomes possible to use an egalitarian principle par excellence as a basis for making distinctions between states. Within the sovereignty game, the right to sovereign equality then translates into a duty to be "equally sovereign" in terms of performing the same rights and duties in a similarly responsible manner (i.e., to be sovereign of a certain kind and/or certain manner). It is the (self-assigned) task of responsible sovereigns to take action against irresponsible states and restore normalcy. Such action might require the stretching of legal boundaries, or paradoxically, even require the violation of international norms to protect them.

Notes

1. See also *Case Concerning Military and Paramilitary Activities in and against Nicaragua* (Nicaragua v. United States of America), Merits, ICJ Rep. 1986.
2. For concrete examples see sections below.
3. For key formulations of sovereignty in abstracto, see the *Austro German Customs Union Case*, Separate opinion Judge Anzilotti, PCIJ Series A/B, no. 41, 1931; and *Island of Palmas Case*, Permanent Court of Arbitration, 2 RIAA 829, 1928.
4. For a poststructuralist analysis of the sovereignty/intervention boundary arguing that intervention practices participate in the stabilization of the meaning of sovereignty, see Weber (1995).
5. See, *inter alia*, Bartelson (1995), Biersteker and Weber (1996b), Werner and De Wilde (2001).
6. This most famously transpires from Vattel's (naturalist) formulation: "Since men are by nature equal, and their individual rights and obligations the same, as coming equally from nature, Nations…are by nature equal and hold from nature the same obligations and the same rights…A dwarf is as much man as a giant is; a small republic is no less a sovereign State than the most powerful Kingdom" (Vattel 1758, Book I, para 18).
7. Key representative in this debate is Krasner (1999).
8. G.W. Leibniz is the main advocate of the theory of international legal personality, which he linked to a notion of relative sovereignty. This paragraph builds on its excellent treatment by Nijman (2004).

9. Most likely the word "persona" stems from the Latin *per sonare* (literally "to sound through"); the construction of the mask was invented to strengthen the sound of the player's voices.

10. In other words, the game should not be mistaken for merely regulating international affairs of preexisting state entities, which would reduce the institution to norms of conduct only. Such a reading in fact transpires from Nijman's elaboration of the mask metaphor. She expands the mask as a camouflage or conceal of states' internal structures from their international personality of sovereign statehood within the Westphalian model (Nijman 2004, 448). This runs parallel to Robert Jackson's (1990) quasi-statehood thesis. Rendering sovereignty and law mere regulative principles, such a reading however overlooks the point regarding the constitutive nature of sovereignty as status or identity, as defined within the game itself (Aalberts 2004).

11. *Island of Palmas case* (Netherlands v. United States), RIAA II 829, 1928.

12. 165 LNTS 19, 1936. See also Grant (1999).

13. Yearbook of the United Nations, 1948–1949, p. 948.

14. Article 13, Yearbook of the United Nations, 1948–1949, p. 948.

15. Yearbook of the International Law Commission, 1973, II, p. 177. See also the award in the *Spanish Zones of Morocco Claims Case* (Britain v. Spain), 2 RIAA 615, 1925, p. 641 ("[R]esponsibility is the necessary corollary of a right. All rights of an international character involve international responsibility") and the separate opinion of judge Séfériadès in the *Lighthouses in Crete and Samos Case* (France v. Greece), PCIJ Series A/B no. 62, 1937, p. 45.

16. This in turn runs parallel to the development of *erga omnes* obligations within the international legal order. Although not crystallized as an established rule with particular consequences yet, genocide, slavery, and racial discrimination and the use of force are recognized as examples (*Barcelona Traction Case* [Belgium v. Spain], ICJ Rep. 1970, para 34).

17. Article 51 of the UN Charter reads as follows: "Nothing in the present Charter shall impair the *inherent* right of individual or collective self-defense if an armed attack occurs against a Member of the United Nations, *until* the Security Council has taken measures necessary to maintain international peace and security. Measures taken by Members in the exercise of this right of self-defence shall be immediately reported to the Security Council and shall not in any way affect the authority and responsibility of the Security Council under the present Charter to take at any time such action as it deems necessary in order to maintain or restore international peace and security" (emphasis added). The broadening of the use of force in response to armed attacks to their preemption in case of imminent threats derives from the *Caroline Case* (1837).

18. Declaration on Principles of International Law Concerning Friendly Relations and Co-operation among States in Accordance with the Charter of the United Nations, GA Resolution 2625 (XXV), October 24, 1970

19. Resolution 1368 of September 12, 2001, S/Res/1368 (2001). This was reaffirmed in Resolution 1373 of September 28, 2001, S/Res/1373 (2001).

20. Press release PR/CP (2001)124, available at www.nato.int/docu/pr/2001/ p01–124e.htm (accessed on April 19, 2007).

21. Note, however, that the United States argued that such multilateral support the war on terrorism was welcome, but not strictly necessary. Colin Powell made this position clear when he stated that "At the moment, notwithstanding all of the coalition building we have been doing, President Bush retains the authority to take whatever actions he believes are appropriate in accordance with the needs for self-defense of the United States and of the American people. We will be going to the UN for additional support…but, at the moment, should the President decide that there are more actions he has to take, he will make a judgment as to whether he needs UN authority or whether he can just rely on the authority inherent in the right of self-defence…." Secretary Colin Powell, Remarks with His Excellency Brian Cowen, Minister of Foreign Affairs of Ireland, September 26, 2001 available at http://www.yale.edu/lawweb/avalon/sept_11/powell_brief19.htm

22. See Bob Woodward and Thomas E. Ricks, Washington Post Staff Writers, Wednesday, October 3, 2001, "CIA Trained Pakistanis to Nab Terrorist But Military Coup Put an End to 1999 Plot," available at http://home.pacbell.net/ reichar/operation.html: In the aftermath of last month's attacks on the United States, which the Bush administration has tied to bin Laden, Clinton officials said their decision not to take stronger and riskier action has taken on added relevance. "I wish we'd recognized it then," that the United States was at war with bin Laden, said a senior Defense official, "and started the campaign then that we've started now. That's my main regret. In hindsight, we were at war."

23. President George W. Bush, Address to a Joint Session of Congress and the American People, September 20, 2001, available at www.whitehouse.gov/ news/releases/2001/09/20010920–8.html (accessed on April 19, 2007).

24. Resolution 1378, November 14, 2001, S/Res/1378(2001).

25. Resolution 1368, September 12, 2001, S/Res/1368(2001). In the follow-up resolution, this was reaffirmed with reference to the aforementioned 1970 GA Resolution 2625(XXV) and the Security Council Resolution on terrorism of August 13, 1998, S/Res/1189(1998), namely the principle that "Every State has *the duty to refrain* from organizing, instigating, assisting or participating in terrorist acts in another State or acquiescing in organized activities within its territory directed towards the commission of such acts" (emphasis added). Subsequently, the Security Council invoked Chapter VII for the authorization of the use of force.

26. US Secretary of State George Shultz argued in 1986 that "[T]he Charter's restrictions on the use or threat of force in international relations include a specific exception for the right of self-defense. It is absurd to argue that international law prohibits us from capturing terrorists in international waters or airspace; from attacking them on the soil of other nations, even for the purpose of rescuing hostages; or from using force against states that support, train, and harbour terrorists or guerrillas." Israel and Apartheid South Africa were US allies in this stance, whereas the majority of the international

community was less supportive (George Schultz, " Low-Intensity Warfare: The Challenge of Ambiguity," Address to the National Defense University, Washington DC, January 15, 1986; quoted in Byers 2002, 406).

27. See for a similar "diagnosis" of the war on terror Lippens (2004).

28. See in particular Security Council Resolutions S/Res/1193(1998), S/Res/1214 (1998), S/Res/1267(1999), and S/Res/1333 (2000).

29. This inclusion/exclusion logic is very prominent in Ferdinand Téson's (1992) liberal theory of international law, which parallels illiberal states to criminal individuals in domestic society. This means in his perspective that, as criminal elements within and to the international order, illiberal states do not benefit from the full range of membership rights but are still bound by its elementary principles.

30. For an early discussion of anarchy/statehood, see also Baty (1934).

31. See also *Western Sahara Advisory Opinion*, ICJ Reports 1975.

32. See for instance T. Dempsey, Counterterrorism in African Failed States: Challenges and Potential Solutions, Strategic Studies Institute, April 2006.

33. Articles on Responsibility of States for Internationally Wrongful Acts, as formulated by the International Law Commission, and adopted by the General Assembly [GA/A/Res/56/83, January 28, 2002].

34. This is not the place to discuss the different interpretations given to the term "control" in the area of state responsibility. Suffice it to say that the International Court of Justice took a relatively strict position in the *Nicaragua* case, holding that control meant "effective control," that is: directing or enforcing the acts in question (*Military and Paramilitary Activities in and against Nicaragua* Nicaragua v. United States of America, Judgment of June 27, 1986, para 115). In the *Tadic* case, the ICTY took more qualified position. While reiterating the principle of control, it stated that the degree of control may vary. The Tribunal argued that it was sufficient to have "overall control," that is: a role in the organizing, coordinating, or planning of the acts in question (ICTY, *Prosecutor v. Dusko Tadic*, Judgment of July 15, 1999). In the justification of the attack on Afghanistan, the United States and its allies choose to rely on the more flexible interpretation of the ICTY.

35. It should be noted that before the "war on terror," the Taliban had only be recognized as the legal government of Afghanistan by Pakistan, United Arab Emirates, and Saudi Arabia. The latter two cut diplomatic ties with the Taliban on September 21st and 25th, 2001 respectively. Despite the international nonrecognition, as the de facto regime of Afghanistan the Taliban was addressed by the Security Council for international obligations since the late 1990s; see for instance S/Res/1267 (1999) and supra fn28.

36. J. Straw, "Principles of a Modern Global Community," April 10, 2002, available at www.britemb.org.il/news/straw100502.html, emphasis added (accessed on April 23, 2007).

37. Again, the parallels to the Standard of Civilization transpire, as Lorimer declared that intolerant anarchies cease to be fully equal sovereigns (quoted by Simpson 2004, 239).

38. Straw, April 10, 2002 (supra fn37). For the qualification of the noninterference principle, see also T. Blair, "Doctrine of the International Community," Economic Club Chicago, April 24, 1999, available at www.number-10.gov.uk/output/page 1297.asp (accessed on April 23, 2007).
39. Richard Haass, quoted by Nicholas Lemann, "The Next World Order," *The New Yorker*, April 1, 2002, p. 45–46 (emphasis added).
40. Straw, April 10, 2002 (supra fn37) and Blair, April 24, 1999 (supra fn39).
41. Straw, April 10, 2002 (supra fn37). See also his speech on "Failed and Failing States," European Research Institute, Birmingham, September 6, 2002, available at www.eri.bham.ac.uk/events/jstraw060902.pdf (accessed on April 27, 2007).
42. In the updated National Strategy for Combating Terrorism, the US administration also explicitly links the defensive combat against terrorism to regime change operations. Recognizing "that we are at war and that protecting and defending the Homeland, the American people, and their livelihoods remains our first and most solemn obligation," the US administration explicitly puts the stakes on effective democracy as a counter to all the sources of terrorism attacking principles of liberty and human dignity (available at http://www.whitehouse.gov/nsc/nsct/2006/). In the words of Secretary Condoleezza Rice: "Attempting to draw neat, clean lines between our security interests and our democratic ideals does not reflect the reality of today's world" (Op-Ed in *The Washington Post*, December 11, 2005).

9

Securing Sovereignty by Governing Security through Markets

Anna Leander

On September 16, 2007 the employees of the US security firm Blackwater became involved in a shooting incidence in the Nisour Square in Baghdad. They were escorting a US State Department delegation, which according to the firm, came under attack. According to bystanders, the Blackwater employees opened fire unprovoked, shooting in all directions and seemingly at anyone moving, including those trying to flee or help those wounded. Seventeen Iraqi civilians died in the incidence and at least twice as many were wounded. President Al-Maliki immediately came out to "revoke Blackwater's license" for operating in Iraq and Iraqi authorities engaged the process of ending contractor impunity in their country. However, it soon became clear that there was no license to revoke and that the Iraqi government may not have the authority to deny Blackwater the right to operate in Iraq, let alone decide the fate of private contractors more generally. On their part, the US authorities promised to open their own investigation and expressed regret at the civilian casualties but did not end their contracts with Blackwater in Iraq or elsewhere.[1] The incapacity of the Iraqi government to impose its authority and right to control the use of force on its territory, to hold Blackwater and/or its employees accountable for the incidence, made Jeremy Scahill[2] conclude that "nothing gives a more clear indication to the Iraqis that they don't have a sovereign government" (2007b). Scahill is right in pointing to the limitations of the Iraqi government's role as the ultimate authority deciding on laws on

Iraqi territory. However, it does not follow that the Mansour incidence is illustrative of the extent to which the private markets for force have undermined sovereignty generally.

The Blackwater incidence usefully highlights the complex ways in which sovereignty has been *both* transformed and secured through the extensive privatization of the use of force. This chapter discusses this dual process of transformation and securing. It does so departing from the notion of a sovereignty game introduced by the editors that it gives a Foucauldian twist. Sovereignty in this chapter is thought of as specific form of governance, organizing politics around a central authority and working through a hierarchical and unitary system of law (Foucault 2004, 92–113; Dean 1999, 103–110). In this context, the sovereignty game is a rather specific game: it is a game organized around states' claims to ultimate authority in politics. However, at the same time both sovereignty and the sovereignty game are highly variable. Politics can be (and has been) ordered around states in very many different ways. The question at the heart of this chapter is how sovereignty and the sovereignty game are rearticulated as other forms of governance develop. The answer departs from Foucault's hunch that ordering principles for politics do not replace each other but coexist historically.[3] The aim is to give substance to this hunch by looking at how the coexistence of neoliberal[4] and sovereign forms of governance functions in the field of security. The chapter does this by looking at how visible and widely agreed upon changes have combined with dissimulated and denied ones to produce both profound alterations and continuity in the sovereignty game. It begins with a discussion of the rules of the sovereignty game in security and then proceeds to look at its players.[5]

The Rules of the Game

To talk about the "rules of the game" when it comes to sovereignty in the field of security—or anywhere for that matter—is a bit misleading. It suggests an inexistent precision. As Stephen Krasner has rightly insisted and repeated in all his publications: "the rules of sovereignty were not explicitly formulated in one organic package by any political leader or theorist" (2001a, 249). Rather the "rules of sovereignty" are a perennial object of struggle and disagreements. However, anything does not go in the sovereignty game. At any given time those engaged in the game have an understanding of what is generally admissible or not in the game. This is why it makes sense to talk about sovereignty as an exercise in "organized hypocrisy" (Krasner 1999). Hypocrisy is only possible because there are (vague, malleable, evolving, and contested) rules to be hypocritical about. The current privatization of the use of force has profoundly reshaped these rules while ensuring that the sovereignty game in the field of security can be continued.

Visible Change: Governing Security through Markets

The presence of private actors is no novelty for the sovereignty game in the security field. On the contrary, throughout the modern era states have relied on private actors when skills or men have been short in supply, or when they have had to "do dirty work" from which the state wanted to distance itself. The novelty is that markets in military services, where private actors operate independently of states, have again become acceptable. Since the end of the cold war, states have fostered markets and tried to govern security through them. They have introduced "neoliberal" government techniques in the security sector. Decentralization, state-withdrawal, quasi-markets, and the responsibilization of individuals increasingly stand in the center of security governance. This creation of markets is a substantial change in the rules of the sovereignty game. From the mid-nineteenth century onward, the game was premised on the state monopoly on the legitimate use of force (Thomson 1994; Leander 2006, chap. 4) and on the outlawing mercenaries[6] (Percy 2007). It is now premised on the existence of markets. Lest we want to move into a brave new world lingo where monopoly and market are equivalents we need to acknowledge that this is a change. This section underscores its broad and general nature.

That markets have become central in the US context is news to no one as there has been a highly public and politicized discussion around the trend. Extensive outsourcing has resulted in a situation where contractors have become indispensable to the armed forces. They provide essential logistical backup. Contractors take over "noncore tasks"—such as cooking, construction of barracks, or coordination of transports—that are nonetheless vital (Rasor and Bauman 2007). But also undisputedly central tasks are outsourced. This is true of intelligence (Tigner 2007; Fainaru and Klein 2007) and of an array of tasks linked to the technological "revolution in military affairs". Contractors operate unmanned (aerial, surface, or sub/surface marine) vehicles that are used in combat and intelligence gathering (Zamparelli 1999; Guillory 2001; Heaton 2005). But perhaps most important for the United States, outsourcing makes the permanent "overstretching of the armed forces" politically viable. The market is the alternative to a draft. The Pentagon official estimate is that the Armed

Forces employ some 20,000–30,000 contractors in Iraq for 160,000 troops (Fainaru 2007c). However, this underestimates the extent to which outsourcing eases the burden on the armed forces. A Department of Defense survey estimated that some 180,000 contractors work in Iraq (Singer 2007, 2).[7] Many of them work for US public agencies, filling functions the public armed forces would formerly have filled themselves. The armed forces are also increasingly dependent on the international market for filling their own ranks. They hire internationally sometimes offering citizenship and/or Green Cards in exchange (Madigan 2007).

The extent to which neoliberal forms of governance are significant outside the United States is likely to be less well known. In the European Union (EU), the introduction of neoliberal governance forms in the security sector may have been slower and more discrete, but should not be underestimated. Markets govern the defense industry: "the leading European defence companies no longer operate as passive executors of government instructions.[...] As corporations seeking to survive in dynamic markets, they cannot wait until groups of politicians and military committees have deliberated over a 'Grand Plan'. In some respects, the organizational structures of European defence, and the associated attitudes, are out of line with the new corporate realities of the defence business" (Lovering 1998, 227). Similarly, just as in the United States, the outsourcing of intelligence, the revolution in military affairs, and the reliance on "dual use" and "off the shelf" technologies is placing contractors in the battlefield (Assemblée Nationale 2003). The United Kingdom created a "sponsored reserves" status for these contractors: "sponsored" by the firms who pay their salary but "reserves" within the ranks of the armed forces (Krahmann 2005). Last but not least, also the EU has a booming, private security sector whose marketization has been encouraged by the commission.[8] Part of this sector holds a strong position on the international market. The most prominent firms are UK based, including firms such as Aegis or Erinys that hold major contracts in Iraq.[9] But the Scandinavian countries, France and Germany also have significant private security sectors (Kaldor 1998).

Finally, in the developing world outsourcing and privatization have become central government strategies. To some extent, this is so because it makes defense spending invisible and/or more legitimate to outside creditors (Rufin 1993). But relying on markets is also necessary to fill gaps in the training and equipment of public armed forces (Howe 2001). Moreover, the market provides what allied public armed forces and states are (no longer) willing to provide. Cubic, for example, trains the Georgean armed forces, DynCorp the Columbian, and MPRI has had a central role in providing military assistance and training in various frameworks in

Africa (Bigwood 2001; Singer 2003; Paton Walsh 2004; MPRI). Third, states can reduce their defense costs by making individuals, firms, and organizations (including NGOs) who can afford to pay for their own security do so. This leads to arrangements where those who need protection hire private security providers or alternatively pay the public armed forces, or do both at the same time. Characteristically, in Sierra Leone Koidu Holdings (a mining company) pays for a contingent of public officers from the operational support division (OSD), works with the international PSC SecuricorGray and has an in-house local security division (Abrahamsen and Williams 2006b, 9–10). Fourth, many states turn their armed forces into commercial ventures renting them out for multilateral operations or using them for publicly sanctioned looting (Wulf 2005). Finally, outsourcing the control over the use of force to local "private" power holders (or warlords) may be a way of upholding sovereignty at the central level. It is a strategy of state survival. Powerholders inside the state "mimick" warlord strategies to boost their sovereign status (Reno 1998; see also Bayart, Ellis and Hibou 1997; Chevrier 2004).

As this shows, governing security through markets has become widespread throughout the world. The significance of this development for sovereignty is often minimized. In part because it is argued that even if there is a market, states retain the "monopoly on the legitimate use of force" and in part because it is suggested that the market is not really a market but a political creation and the firms not really private but the extension of the state. Although both claims have some merit, they severely understate the significance of the changes that have taken place.

Dissimulated Change: De facto *Privatizing the Legitimate Use of Force*

The claim that security is increasingly governed through markets is unlikely to provoke much dissent. The same cannot be said of the claim that this alters the monopoly on the legitimate use of force. Rather, states governing security through markets may face "trade-offs" (Avant 2005) and "new complexities" (Singer 2003). They may be losing control. They do not relinquish the right to define the *legitimate* use of force. This is true on the formal level no doubt. Legal systems (national and international) continue to be premised on that assumption. But as this section outlines, this version underestimates the real degree of autonomy of the private contractors and hence masks the real degree of change in the rules of the sovereignty game.

When a market for military services is created, private actors have to be handled a direct right to decide on the use of force for rather obvious reasons. Private actors—the firms who take on contracts and their employees—have to decide when and how to use force in the context they are employed. The private security guard has to decide when to use force, as illustrated in Nisour. The intelligence contractor has a legitimate right to interpret information and sometimes to decide whether it should be acted upon. For example, in Colombia the US firm AirScan directed the Colombian air force to drop a cluster bomb on a village of civilians (Miller 2003). The remote controller of an Unmanned Aerial Vehicles (UAV) is using force. Just as when public armed forces use force, rules (sometimes) guide the decisions of these private actors. Sometimes (but only sometimes) there will be some form of "rules of engagement" outlining under what kind of conditions what kinds of force may be used by the private actors. Often they are as vague as those specified by the Coalition Provisional authority for contractors in Iraq starting by declaring (in capital letters) that "nothing in these rules limits your inherent right to take action necessary to defend yourself" (Fainaru 2007d). But even when they exist and are more firm, rules must be interpreted. The creation of markets turns private actors into legitimate interpreters of rules on par with public security professionals.

More controversially, firms are not only interpreters of public rules but also coauthors—and sometimes sole authors—of the rules regulating the use of force. This is the case when the rules for how, when, and against whom force can be used are specified in a contract, as they often are. The centrality of contracts is linked to the contextual and varied nature of contractor activity that defies one size fits all formulations. For example, the rules specifying how a firm guarding oil installations in Ecuador (Engström 2007) may use force are bound to vary substantially from the rules specified in the contract covering the use of UAVs in Afghanistan (Heaton 2005, 164). But the context does not dictate the rules regulating the use of force. Firms formulate and negotiate their contracts and the "rules of engagement" specified in these. Private security firms assess security needs and suggest ways they might be filled. This is what they do when they are hired as consultants and when they advertise themselves. It is therefore not surprising that even when firms work in the same context, for similar institutions, their rules of engagement vary considerably. In Iraq, the rules of firms working in U.S state agencies may vary from "contract to contract, from company to company and even from team to team" (Fainaru 2007b). Firms are in other words coauthors of the rules rather than simply accepting terms imposed by their clients (who may just as well be private as public by the way). Even more strongly, the task of formulating the rules is sometimes itself outsourced. The practice of security firms formulating (and evaluating) their own contracts has attracted substantial critical attention (Markusen 2003; Singer 2003). And even more generally, the formulation of overarching rules influencing the use of force in a given area is sometimes also outsourced to private firms. MPRI, for example, has considerable responsibilities for writing military doctrine and defining military training both in the United States and abroad (Leander 2005b; MPRI). Private firms in other words participate in the spelling out of the general rules for the legitimate use of force.

Finally, firms have a say over the legitimate use of force because they can decide whom they will work for. It is inherent in markets that buyers and sellers have a high degree of freedom when it comes to buying and selling. If they do not, we are in a command economy. This is also true in the market for force. There are rules (formal such as export controls and informal such as the normative pressure not to work for enemies of ones home government) that restrict this freedom. There may also be cartel like arrangements shaping the sale of security services in given areas. But ultimately the decision of whether to sell is left up to the firm. Concretely translated, private firms operating in a market for force can chose whether to work for a client. They can in other words weigh—often decisively—on the decision of what kind of force will be used by whom. That is, private actors legitimately control what kind of force is used in what types of situations by whom.

The privatization of the legitimate use of force is most clearly expressed in the confusion and tension surfacing whenever the formal hierarchical sovereign law system crosses the multiple, decentered, and largely informal one of the private sector. Essentially the tension and confusion concern who has the last word in deciding what specific norm applies in the given context. This confusion is sometimes resolved at gunpoint. Civil wars are examples of this: the fight is (very often) about whether the established public authority should give up its ultimate say to a private one (Holsti 1996). But also in mundane everyday occurrences involving private and public security professionals in conflict situations the conflict is sometimes dealt with at gunpoint. For example, following an accident between a SUV full of contractors and the US armed forces in Iraq, the contractors imposed their view of the situation on the soldiers by disarming them and laying them on the ground while they disentangled their SUV (Nordland, Hosenball, and Kaplow 2007). Informal pragmatic ad hoc arrangements are another way of dealing with the tension. In Nigeria, for example, Private Security Companies manage security in the oil area by coordinating a combination of private and public security professionals. Ultimately the hierarchy between public and private norm setters hinges on "informal arrangements and their [the PSC] capacity to develop well-integrated procedures, joint training, and close operations coordination" (Abrahamsen and Williams 2006a, 11). However, and finally, a very central way of dealing with the tensions and confusions that arise when the sovereign system crosses the neoliberal one may be denial and/or suppression. Indeed, both firms and state officials go to considerable lengths to deny that there is a tension. That firms work only for "legitimate clients" and only against states when these are ostensibly illegitimate (i.e., to stop "the next Rwanda") are evergreens in the business rhetoric. Similarly, armed forces, defense, and police administrators have a repertoire that invariably integrates the claim that governing through markets—at least in the version practiced by them—is a new (and more effective) means of achieving public ends.

Sticking to the claim that the basic rule of the sovereignty game, the state monopoly on the legitimate use of force, is intact in these conditions becomes a formalistic statement. What we have in the field of security is not fundamentally different from the situations in other areas: public and private authorities coexist in partially overlapping, competing, and contradictory ways. Interesting and complex tensions are the consequence as the state system based on hierarchical relations among legal norms de facto coexists with a multifacetted, pluricentric complex system of private rules defying both unity and hierarchy (Fischer-Lescano and Teubner 2004). This said, the illusion that the rules of the sovereignty game remain intact, that states retain a monopoly on the legitimate use of force is of considerable practical significance: it masks part of the fundamental change in the rules of the sovereignty game brought about by privatization. By the same token it effectively blocs broader political discussions about this change and its desirability. It is a form of "symbolic power" (Bourdieu 1992). The change in rules of the game can pass unnoticed and be presented as a mere variation on existing themes.

Securing the Sovereignty Game in Security

Securing the continued centrality of sovereignty in the field of security is about more than dissimulating change and preempting public debate. The centrality of sovereign practices in security has also been positively bolstered and confirmed by the introduction of markets. The transformation of governance processes in security—the shift toward neoliberal governance techniques where outsourcing, privatization, responsibilization, decentralization, and state withdrawal are central—makes security governance congruent with governance in other spheres. Since these changes are framed as changes in (rather than contra) sovereignty, they have helped legitimate and perpetuate the sovereignty game.

Today it is easy to forget the extent to which the sovereignty game in security was under pressure in the wake of the cold war. The question at the time was if the world was headed toward Gorbachev's "new world order" where security and particularly military relations would have a far less central place. In sociology, authors talked about the post-military society (Shaw 1991). In international relations, attention was increasingly directed toward globalization and the retreat of the state while security discussions focused on the necessary transformation (and slimming) of existing state-based defense institutions (Clark 1999). The consequence was that these were under very real pressure to justify their own existence and had to scramble with decreasing budgets expressing their low ranking on the list of public priorities (Schméder 1998; Bigo 2000). At the end of the cold war, the future prospects of the sovereignty game in security seemed dim on most accounts. This is no longer the case, for reasons closely tied to the transformations at the heart of this chapter: the introduction of governance through markets justified and normalized the sovereignty game. The end of the cold war caused the crisis of the sovereignty game and triggered the processes that ensured its continuation.

It did so by making the governance of security congruent with governance in other fields. The end of the cold war signaled an end to the politically motivated strict state control over anything military related. Managing the military, the police, and the security through markets became imaginable. The "neoliberal revolution" with the accompanying new public management could be extended also to the defense sector (Brauer 1998; Bislev, Hansen, and Salskov-Iversen 2002; Minow 2003). Market competition and "post-Fordism" could be introduced. The state could withdraw. Firms were asked to fend for themselves, dispensing with subsidies and controls (Kaldor 1998). Citizens were increasingly expected to take responsibility for their own security. At the same time, the decreasing willingness to pay for armed forces put pressure on armed forces and states to draw on the rapidly developing markets. As a consequences of these shifts in governance forms, the security field no longer appeared as an anachronistic field, the only one still governed by old style, top-down state bureaucracies. As in other fields, the expertise and knowledge of a wide range of autonomous private actors could now be integrated in the policy process. A language of market and effectiveness could make sense of the activities in the field. The security field could be governed by the same neoliberal techniques as other fields of society.

The extent to which this helped justify activity in the field is perhaps best seen in the willingness of security professionals, administrators, and policy-makers linked to defense establishments to embrace reforms. Indeed, the new public management reforms had the effect of increasing resources. This is not primarily linked to private firms and markets being cheaper and more effective and hence improving the use of existing resources. The call is still out on whether privatization in the security field actually leads to any efficiency and financial gains. Impressive potential gains from privatization coexist with an actual history of enormous waste and ineffectiveness.[10] The point rather is that for officials governance through markets increases the resources available. Partly for banal accountancy reasons: governing through various forms of markets, subcontracting, and outsourcing activities diverts spending from main budgets. It makes the actual resources used in a field less visible and more difficult to scrutinize. But partly, the reason to embrace New Public Management in security is the political and social context: privatization and market creation have become policy-making priorities. Money spent to buy services and equipment in markets is *de facto* judged by different (more generous) criteria than money on public services. The reliance on private markets and firms is justified in and of itself (Markusen 2003).

The creation of private markets of security profoundly alters the rules of the sovereignty game: it ends the monopoly on the legitimate use of force on which this game rested. However, at the same time it secures the game. Sovereign governance forms in security are shown to be perfectly compatible with neoliberal forms of governance and hence to be similar to sovereign forms of governance in other spheres. At the same time a formalistic attachment to the ultimate say of the state in matters of legitimate use of force masks the change that is entailed. The rules of the sovereignty game on this account have undergone profound change that has served to consolidate the centrality of sovereign practices.

The Players in the Game

Governing security through markets is also having profound effects on the players in the sovereignty game in security. Private actors are increasingly present sometimes ostensibly on par with states. As the modern sovereignty game is played by states, one might have expected such challenges to their centrality to make the game meaningless and/or unimportant. Yet, nothing of the sort has happened. The reason is partly that the enmeshment of the private and the public spheres has made the public private and the private public, hence obscuring the growing centrality and presence of private actors. In addition to this, when private actors have been ostensibly visible, they have mostly not been taken to challenge the sovereignty. Rather, their presence has been interpreted as illustrating the need to differentiate among states who can manage markets and states still having to learn. This combination of enmeshment and unequal status of sovereign players has distracted attention away from conflicts and tensions that might have arisen between public and private actors. It has concentrated conflicts around divisions within states and divisions between northern and southern states. Both forms of conflicts are compatible with a sovereign ordering of politics and can be read as confirming its continued centrality.

Dissimulated Change: The Enmeshment of Public and Private

In the stylized world of political and legal thought, the private-public, inside-outside, and state-market realms are distinct spheres with clear dividing lines. However, the world of political practice looks rather different. The spheres are largely continuous realms as indicated by the omnipresent reference to "blurred" lines. But the reference to blurred lines assumes distinct realms whose dividing lines can blur. In the security field, governance through markets is making this situation increasingly rare. At all levels and in all kinds of functions, there are many people who are in both spheres at the same time. It is therefore more accurate to think of the spheres as enmeshed. This enmeshment is important for the stabilization of the sovereignty game as it bolsters the impression that public actors continue to rule unchallenged by private market actors. By dissimulating the change in the nature of the public actors, it ensures the continuity of the sovereignty game.

The security professionals working in the rapidly expanding market are mostly members of the armed forces and the police. Everyone is an ex-something (Singer 2003). Those with special skills, from elite troops of one kind or another, have been particularly sought after as the 15,000 or so false Navy SEALs testify (Lee Lanning 2002, 176). Blackwater pays six times more than the US armed forces for military qualifications at an equivalent level. But it is not the only American firm to pay more than the public armed forces or the police or is the situation unique to the United States. Also in Nigeria, Russia, or Columbia, working for a private security company is an attractive way of complementing a low salary or pension, in addition to being an opportunity to get interesting work.[11] These professionals very often keep their jobs also in the public sector hence embodying the continuity between public and private spheres. Since the market is increasingly "global," the security companies for whom professionals work may well take them abroad.

Hence, an unknown number of security professionals form Africa, Latin America, and Asia have worked on contracts in Iraq embodying the continuity between the national and the outside.[12] Finally, private actors on the battlefield embody the continuity between the state and the market spheres. In Iraq, in the Democratic Republic of the Congo, and in Afghanistan the private security professionals engaged in a conflict are often undistinguishable from soldiers, for many civilians, for those on the opposing side and for military field commanders who integrate them into their understanding of the battlefield situation (Verkuil 2007, 27).

Also on the management side, the number of people whose existence is simultaneously on both sides of the public-private line is rapidly growing. Many managers work in both the public and the private sectors at the same time. Firms are often set up and organized by people with a past in the public. Sometimes they formally continue to work in the public taking a leave while running their private firm. When this is not the case, they maintain close contacts to the public administration and often see themselves as merely continuing their (public) job from "the other side of the table." To add to this, private security sector firms routinely hire high-ranking policy-makers on their boards. Cheney epitomizes this trend (Didion 2006). But Cheney is no unique example. Many firms have board members who are *at the same time* active policy-makers. This is more than a revolving-door policy. It is a simultaneous presence. It may be worth underlining that it is not a US specific phenomenon but one visible across different contexts and continents (Joly 2003; War on Want 2006; Akeh 2007). At least as significant as the presence of public officials in the private, but far less noticed, is the presence of the private in the public. The markets have entered public administrations and become integral parts of these. The Pentagon counts the contractors in to the total US war effort. But it is not the only place where markets are represented inside states. Public officials have come to rely on market actors, work for them and believe in the fact that "with contractors you get more bang for the buck" (Whelan 2003). In many contexts, they also depend on the market for financing their own activities. For example, in Ecuador, the private security sector indirectly finances the public armed forces: they have to rent the police force for any operation involving the use of weapons (Engström 2007).

This presence of the public in the private and the private in the public is really a matter of enmeshment. It does not signal the swallowing up or cooptation of one sphere by the other. To reduce the private firms to extensions of public policy is to misunderstand them. They may work for public agencies and authorities but their existence is not reducible to this.

They also have an existence as market actors striving to make money and capture market shares. This is why Eric Prince (the CEO) of Blackwater insists in his congressional hearing that "we are a private company and the key word is private" (2007). It is also important to realize that it is because they are private and autonomous that the private firms are valued by public administrations. Their independent expertise is often what is sought. It would be equally mistaken to reduce the public to the private, suggesting for example that policy-makers working in the private sphere are only private actors, following firm interests and somehow shred their "public" identity and values even if they continue to hold public office. Whether they are security professionals or policy-makers they retain also a public identity. This is the reason enmeshment is an adequate term for the situation: it captures the extent to which what is happening is neither a blurring of lines between distinct spheres nor simply a matter of cooptation or corruption of one by the other but a growing presence of the two spheres inside each other.

Although this enmeshment signals real change both in who matters for security and in the nature of the public, it stabilizes the sovereignty game in the field of security. It obscures the extent to which states now share their central role in security with private market actors, that is the degree to which the actors of the security game have changed. It also obscures the extent to which the nature of the public itself has been altered and become enmeshed with market the private. Enmeshment lends credibility to the stretching of the category of the public that comes to cover also the activities of private firms. It is in other words essential for reducing the visibility of private actors in the security field.

Visible Change: From Equality to Empire

There are many situations where the centrality of private actors in the security field is difficult to ignore. Yet, the sovereignty game seems largely unaffected by this visible emergence of private actors. It proceeds as if public actors were still the uncontested key actors. This is intriguing. The drift away from the equal treatment of the players in the sovereignty game is the magic at work. By defining states that cannot prevent private actors from being visible as "failed" and by denying them the status as full sovereign players, the emergence of private actors can be treated as a marginal phenomenon to be handled by the ever more intrusive "capacity building" policies of fully sovereign states.

Enmeshment only works if the role of private activity can credibly be understood as something falling within the category of things undertaken by the public. This is not the case when private actors are too sharply separated from and/or defined by contrast to the state. Illustrations of this include security provision by "war lords" or "big men" (Derlugian 2005). More mundanely it includes the many situations where vigilantes (Buur 2006), hunters' associations (Bassett 2003), or (reinvented) tribal protection systems (Heald 2007; Nolte 2007) are central for the provision of security. These private actors are often authorized and encouraged by states and can hence be read as expressing new forms of sovereign authority. But it is not an authority that can easily be presented as "public" in the sense of being part of the state or drawn into an enmeshed public—private continuity. Enmeshment also fails when states are "privatized," when public officials act ostensibly mainly for private gain and are seen as doing precisely that. This is the case for example when heads of states use their own "private" armies as commercial ventures for the exploitation of private resources (UN 2001) or when members of the public armed forces act purely for personal gain as is the reputation of Nigeria's mobile (armed) police units going under the nickname "kill and go" (Abrahamsen and Williams 2006a, 3). These situations have in common that there is no public category that could credibly mask the presence and role of private actors.

There is good reason to think that the emergence of situations where private actors have a visible place in the security field has much to do with the neoliberalization of security governance.[13] However, states, not markets, are usually held responsible for the visibility of private security actors. They are differentiated according to whether they can handle the private market development. On this account, it is because certain states do not have the "capacity" to deal with their internal security situation that private actors are emerging as central in the security field. Echoing the focus on "capacity building" in other areas and its dominance in the thinking of most relevant (state, multilateral, and nongovernmental) institutions, building capacity to control security becomes essential. At the same time, the security sector is overtaking other fields as the conventional assumption that development would create security is being replaced by the inverse assumption: that security is a precondition for development (Buur, Jensen, and Stepputat 2007; Duffield 2007). Development aid is consequently channeled from traditional development areas (infrastructure, health, and education) into the security where it is used to facilitate capacity building in the security sector. Hence the rapidly growing interest in security sector reform.

For the sovereignty game, the responsibilization of states translates into a differentiation among the sovereign players. States are no longer just states. They are states with qualifiers such as quasi, failed, weak, or rogue underlining their incapacity to control private actors and the market for force on their territories. These qualifiers have a bearing on the practical meaning of the sovereign status. Some states find themselves in an uphill struggle trying to defend their status as sovereign players even if private actors are indeed visible (e.g., Columbia, Georgia, Sudan). Others, deemed too failed or rogue to deserve to be recognized as sovereign states, may find their position and role as sovereigns players eliminated altogether as for example when a consortium of international donors and institutions take on the management of sections of the Chadian economy through their control over the Chad-Cameroon pipeline, when Ethiopia restores order in Somalia or when international supervisors are allocated to the key ministries in Monrovia. This relativization of the sovereign status is intensely contested. However, the trend is there. The qualifiers have made their way into the language policy-making communities, the media and academia alike. The same is true of the idea that in cases of extensive human rights violations and/or threats to international stability "major states or regional or international organizations could assume some form of de facto trusteeship" (Krasner 2004a, 119; also Ehrenreich Brooks 2005). The idea that differentiated sovereignty justifies outside tutorship is not "new" on a broader historical scale (as Krasner has repeatedly pointed out). It has analogies in the eighteenth and nineteenth centuries. However, viewed from the vantage point of twentieth century decolonialization struggles (and achievements) it is a remarkable reversal to imperial argumentation (Bishai 2004).

The visible, resisted, and contested move from an egalitarian to an imperial understanding of the status of sovereign players has helped securing the central role of states in the game. It has normalized the idea that if and when private actors do play an ostensibly central role in the security field, this does not challenge the centrality of states in general. It merely underlines the need to distinguish among the players in the sovereignty game and to support (or impose) capacity building in weaker states. The shift from an egalitarian to an imperial discourse on the nature of sovereignty has made it plausible both to acknowledge the presence of private actors in the security field and to deny their significance for the sovereignty game.

Securing the Centrality of Sovereign States as Players

The enmeshment of public and private and the shift from an egalitarian to an imperial discourse have helped secure the sovereignty game by obscuring the extent to which there is change in the nature of the key players (they are no longer clearly public) and in their roles (they are no longer formally equal). However, the two processes have also played an important role in another way: they have prevented conflicts and tensions that stem from the emergence of the market to become crystallized around the public-private divide. By doing so, they have bolstered the impression that the market alters nothing fundamental about the public-private divide and that markets are therefore perfectly compatible with sovereignty. It has confirmed the compatibility of neoliberalism and sovereignty in the security sphere.

A direct consequence of placing the private in the public and the public in the private is that conflicts and disagreements stemming from the rise of markets are not structured as conflicts opposing private and public actors. Instead conflicts are structured around divisions within the public and within the private. In the United States, for example, the issue of security privatization has to some extent opposed Democrats and Republicans. Although the Clinton administration endorsed the general outsourcing and market creating policies, the key opponents (including in particular Senator Jan Schakowsky[14]) have been Democrats and key proponents (including Cheney and Rumsfeld) have been Republicans. But divisions along party lines are too rough. The divisions run between public administrations and—on a more detailed level—between individuals; often in rather unexpected ways. The investigation in the wake of the Nisour incident clearly illustrates this. In Iraq, the State Department had sided in with Blackwater against other authorities and in particular the Justice Department (Committee on Oversight and Government Reform 2007). Similarly, the inspector general had obstructed the work of his office and refused to collaborate with the Department of Justice in investigations involving security contractors (Waxman 2007). Conflicts and tensions resulting from the creation of markets in security in other words do not pit private market actors against public state actors. They create new divisions within states. Conflicts are opposing different parts of states and public bureaucracies. They are not state versus market conflicts. For the sovereignty game this matters: it confirms that what is at stake is not some fundamental reshuffling of authority but merely more of the good old struggle over what the aim of public policy should be and how it can best be achieved; a struggle reflecting diverging expert views. This is something the sovereignty game has always lived with.

Similarly, the way qualifiers to statehood and sovereignty have developed and been used has minimized the extent to which conflicts surrounding the emergence of markets come to be structured along the private—public divide. The flat responsibilization of (failed, rogue, weak, etc.) states and governments for their failure to keep private actors invisible is a direct denial of the role that the market or market actors may have played in the process. But more than this, the qualifiers direct attention to the North-South divide, and away from the division between the public and the private. The states with qualifiers are overwhelmingly southern and those using the qualifiers to differentiate sovereign status and justify interventions are overwhelmingly northern. Consequently, and colonial pasts helping, the conflicts surrounding the introduction of qualifiers readily turn into North-South conflicts. In the confrontation over qualified sovereign status, the image of a self-sacrificing, humanitarian, civilizing North contributing to the development in the South confronts that of the destructive, exploiting, self-interested North sapping the independence and development prospects of the South. The point here is not to adjudicate which of these images is more truthful. Rather, the purpose is to underscore the extent to which this North-South framing casts the dispute in terms that can be used to confirm the centrality of states in the sovereignty game; the conflict is ultimately about diverging sovereign interests.

The conflict has been transformed from one where public actors might have opposed the creation of markets into one where sovereign states with differing and sometimes radically opposed interests confront each other. The confrontation is turned into a clash of sovereignties. A classical picture of what the sovereignty game is all about. The same trick is worked by the enmeshment of actors: it turns the conflict into one taking place *within* states, opposing divergent different understandings of how best to promote the public good, a classical conflict in sovereign forms of politics. Conflicts that might have arisen as private actors have taken on a central role in security and could have been thought to challenge the key role of public actors magically disappear. They are transformed into conflicts that do not challenge sovereignty as the main ordering principle in the field. If anything, the continuation of intense conflict over what policies to pursue at home and over clashing sovereignties abroad confirms sovereignty's continued significance.

Conclusion: Securing Sovereignty

This chapter has argued that the governance of security through markets has been the source both of substantial changes in the sovereignty game and of the securing of this game. Market governance has altered the basic rule of sovereignty game in security by watering down the state monopoly on legitimate force to inexistence. Private actors have both control and legitimate authority over the use of force. Market governance has also altered the nature and the status of the players in the sovereignty game as the public and private have become increasingly enmeshed and sovereignty increasingly differentiated. However, at the same time governance through markets has secured sovereignty. It has aligned the sovereignty game in security with neoliberal governance forms. It has normalized security. But more than this the effects of market governance on the nature of the public-private divide has fostered misrecognition of the changes under way. Consequently the sovereignty game in security, recast in governmental terms, is well secured, probably at least as secure as it would have been if market governance had not been introduced.

That profound change in the sovereignty game may be compatible with (perhaps even necessary for) its continuity is not a foregone conclusion. Scholars who think of sovereignty as a specific set of principles would certainly find it difficult to agree. Thomson, for example, suggests that if practices changed so much that states could "shirk responsibility for non-state violence internationally, by simply claiming that the latter is a purely private undertaking" and if there was an "end to or at least significant erosion of the state's monopoly on the authority to deploy violence beyond its borders" we would be shifting away from sovereignty to something else (Thomson 1994, 153). This chapter has suggested that both things are occurring but that we have not moved away from sovereignty to something else. The reason is that sovereignty (and the sovereignty game) is not attached to a specific set of rules but one way of organizing political thinking and practice. This mode may well coexist (as I have here argued it does) with other forms of governance such as the neoliberal or the disciplinary. This will cause clashes and tensions. It will not "end" the sovereignty game. The game ends when political practice and thinking ceases to be organized around states; when the king's head is finally cut in political theory and practice as Foucault phrased it. Governing through markets has not led this to happen. If anything the opposite is true.

But for how long is sovereignty secure? Is the market working like a time bomb that will eventually explode the sovereign system and lead to the dissolution of state authority (as suggested e.g., by von Trotha 2000)? Or will the tensions between the governance through markets and governance through states eventually become so strong that states will have to rein in the market and reassert political control (as suggested by Verkuil 2007)? Obviously, there can be no definitive answer. However, three observations drawn from this chapter may be worth keeping in mind when contemplating the question. First, the sovereignty game is surprisingly resilient and malleable. It is a grid of practice and interpretation that is difficult to escape. Second, (however) neoliberal forms of governance are so profoundly anchored in contemporary political practice and thinking that they pass largely uncontested, not to say unreflected. Third, (this said) how the two coexist is neither strictly fixed nor agreed upon. It is constantly struggled over. We are therefore likely to see market governance and sovereignty continue to coexist, create tensions but also reinforce each other in surprising ways expressing the constant struggles of those concerned by the developments.

Notes

This chapter has benefited from the generous and constructive comments of the editors of this volume. Moreover, Stefano Guzzini and the participants in the COSTA24 seminar on the private construction of threats (Basel October 20, 2007), in my fellow-seminar at the Hansewissenschaftskolleg (October 17, 2007), and in the DIIS "markets for peace" workshop (December 6–7, 2007) made helpful comments. Even if they would all still have many objections to this version of the chapter, I hope that they recognize their role in sharpening its argument that obviously remains my responsibility.

1. At the time of writing (November 2007) it seems the state department will end Blackwater's Iraq contract after considerable pressure but the process is still ongoing and whether there will be any general consequences for Blackwater (preventing it from working on other state contracts) remains unclear.
2. Jeremy Scahill is the author of a book on Blackwater (2007a) that launched much of the media attention the company has received and an active media commentator
3. "There is no historical replacement of historical form [...] There is in fact a triangle: sovereignty, discipline and governmentality" (Foucault 2004: 111).
4. The Foucauldian neoliberal governance form is one where governance is done through state withdrawal, the creation of quasi-markets, decentralization, responsibilization, and empowerment of individuals (Foucault 2004; Hindess 2004; Rose and Miller 1992; Leander and van Munster 2007). It is concretely expressed government techniques in what goes under the general heading "new public management."
5. There is also profound change in the stakes of the game: technical security is more central both in the security field and in other fields. This point is not elaborated in this chapter. I have written about it elsewhere including in (Leander 2005b, 2007).
6. Today the term mercenary is usually replaced by words coming with less negative connotations such as contractors, private military firms, or private security firms. This masks the similarities between these actors and traditional mercenaries.
7. The figures remain uncertain even for contractors employed by firms working for public US agencies and even more so for other firms. They are particularly unreliable for "third country nationals," "local" employees, and subcontractors working for the main contractor. Judging from the controversies that have involved South African, Korean, Pilipino, Ugandan, Tanzanian,

Peruvian, Fijian, Columbian, and Nepalese (just to mention some) security contractors their numbers could be rather extensive.

8. In a succession of controversial cases, the commission has pushed for the opening of the market. See ECJ (2006) and the references therein as well as Dorn and Levi (2007).

9. In its discussions of regulation, the UK government has repeatedly made very clear that the sector is to be nurtured and developed nationally and internationally (Zedner 2006; Foreign and Commonwealth Office 2002).

10. There is no proof that outsourcing is efficient but considerable indications that it is not: Markusen (2003), GAO (2007), Waxman (2007), Rasor and Bauman (2007), and Verkuil (2007). These indications are bolstered by the resistance of the business against actual measures designed to enhance cost savings in the sector. In 2001, for example, DynCorp blocked a bill that would have forced federal agencies to justify private contracts on cost-saving grounds (War on Want 2006: 19).

11. Security professionals' motives are complex and varied but interest in working actively often figures at least as centrally as earning a good salary (Sapone 1999; Fainaru 2007a).

12. This practice is most visible when scandals erupt around illegal recruitments or breaches of contract by international firms. The OHCHR working group on mercenaries has made an effort to report on some of the scandals in a more systematic fashion (UN 2007).

13. The pressure on budgets, the forced dissolution of "neo patrimonial" systems and the opening up of markets weakens state institutions in the security field and forces those who want protection to look for it outside the state, in new arrangements. At the same time it pushes security professionals to engage in the market (Clapham 1996; Duffield 2001; Hibou 2004; Leander 2005a).

14. Jan Schakowski has a longstanding engagement with the issue of security contracting and has proposed a series of bills to curb contracting practices, including the recent SOS (stop outsourcing security) the fate of which remains as uncertain as that of her earlier initiatives.

10

The Refugee, the Sovereign, and the Sea: European Union Interdiction Policies

Thomas Gammeltoft-Hansen

Scene: Tarifa beach in Spain on 2 September 2000; in the forefront a young couple with a picnic basket sunbathing, in the background the body of a dead migrant washed ashore after an unsuccessful attempt to cross the treacherous Strait of Gibraltar from North Africa.

When photographer Javier Balauz had his picture published in newspapers across the world, it created public outrage over the "indifference of the West."[1] Today, hardly a week goes by without reports of migrants dying following attempts to cross the Mediterranean or West African Sea to reach Europe. The humanitarian tragedy is perhaps the starkest evidence of the difficult situation the European Union (EU) is experiencing in relation to its southern shores.

On the one hand, it speaks of the growing pressure of immigration by destitute and desperate people willing to risk their lives in an unseaworthy dingy in the attempt to reach the Canary Islands, Malta, Spain, or Italy. It is estimated that between 100,000 and 120,000 irregular migrants try to cross the Mediterranean each year (ICMPD 2004, 8). New routes are constantly established and human smuggling has grown to be one of the most lucrative forms of international crime.

On the other hand, the tragedies may also be seen as a result of the ongoing expansion of Europe's migration control. Following the eastward expansion it has become both more difficult and less lucrative to reach the EU over land, and the bulk of African and many Asian migrants thus turn to the maritime routes. Simultaneously, advanced radar systems, deployment of NATO ships and airplanes, and a number of joint member state naval missions has made it impossible for migrants to take the easy corridors, forcing them instead to venture longer and more dangerous crossings. In what seems to be a self-sustaining dynamic, every new route prompts new control initiatives and vice versa.[2]

The result has been a radical expansion of the Mediterranean basin and parts of the Atlantic Ocean outside West Africa as a venue for migration control. Most recently, the EU's border agency, Frontex, has been coordinating a number of missions between member states in response to what is often referred to as the "tides" or "waves" of migrants "flooding" the European shores (Pugh 2004, 54). The objective of these initiatives is primarily preventive: to intercept migrants before they reach EU territory or territorial waters. As the sovereign ability to control migration flows at the borders is coming under pressure, the geographical locus is shifted outward, toward the sea and toward cooperation with third states.

The refugee occupies a special position in this development. Traditionally, the refugee is the exception to the sovereign right of states to enforce migration control. Under international refugee law states in principle oblige themselves to allow entrance for any person presenting an asylum claim at their borders or within their territories, until the validity of that claim has been examined. In a time where concerns over both asylum and immigration have risen across Europe, states have been keen to come up with policy innovations to somehow rid themselves of these obligations.

Moving migration control outside the territory, to the high seas or inside foreign territorial waters, has been presented as one such innovation and raises important questions of international law. Although the international human rights and refugee law is normally referred in order to harness restrictive asylum policies within the EU, the applicability of these norms to actions performed by member states outside the Union has been the subject of considerable debate and contention.

Taking as its starting point the tricky conceptualization of sovereignty within international legal discourse, the present chapter argues that the current opaqueness as to the geographical reach of a state's responsibilities is rooted in the inability of the present refugee regime to truly free itself of the territorial principles of the Westphalian state system. Rather the question of extraterritorial responsibility is caught in a "late sovereign order," in which questions of jurisdiction may be interpreted both territorially and universally. This interpretive breadth creates a field of contestation, in which states may rely on different sovereignty claims when acting in the extraterritorial context to reconquer their loss of sovereign control by *de facto* or *de jure* relinquishing themselves of some of the human rights obligations otherwise owed to asylum-seekers and refugees.

There is no generally accepted definition of interception. United Nations High Commissioner for Refugees (UNHCR) has proposed that

> interception is defined as encompassing all measures applied by a State, outside its national territory, in order to prevent, interrupt or stop the movement of persons without the required documentation crossing international borders by land, air or sea, and making their way to the country of prospective destination.[3]

This includes a wide number of instances, ranging from the control performed at visa consulates to the privatization of control by sanctioning carriers for letting undocumented migrants board their planes. This chapter will confine itself to the discussion of interception at sea, which is also referred to as interdiction. In particular, the chapter focuses on the Mediterranean and the sea between the West African coast and the Canary Islands as the maritime areas where the EU is currently concentrating its efforts to curb migration toward Europe.

The Refugee in the Late Sovereign Order

To understand the particular issue of the refugee in international law, it is necessary first to consider the basic structure of state sovereignty as it has developed in modern international legal discourse. Within international law, the concept of sovereignty can be described as a double-bladed sword referring to two rather distinct descriptive frames (Spiermann 1995, 124–126). On the one hand, it refers to the state as a *national* sovereign, the principle of self-containment and territorial exclusivity. In this sense international law is conceived as a residual system, concerned with establishing the principles necessary for the coexistence of states, for example, nonintervention. The need for international law only arises when states need to settle disputes outside the realm of national law; within its territory each state holds absolute jurisdiction (Spiermann 2005, 79–83).

The basic principle of national sovereignty and independence can be illustrated by the following passage by the Permanent Court of International Justice from the 1927 *SS Lotus* Case:

> The rules of law binding upon States…emanate from their own free will…. Restrictions upon the independence of States cannot therefore be presumed.

> Now the first and foremost restriction imposed by international law upon a State is that—failing the existence of a permissive rule to the contrary—it may not exercise its power in any form in the territory of another State.[4]

While the second sentence is often cited as a general presumption for the sovereign freedom of states against international law, the last sentence is perhaps equally important to understand how the principle of sovereign independence is vested within a Westphalian framework. In principle, sovereign power is to be exercised within a "sovereign nation cage," horizontally covering the territory and the territorial sea and vertically extending from the "Von Kármán line" 50,550 miles above sea level down to the subsoil of national territory ending at the center of the earth (Palan 2003, 97). However, outside the realm of these sovereign cages, such as when disputes arise on the high seas, the international law of coexistence becomes accordingly vague (Spiermann 2005, 88).

On the other hand, the state has been conceived as an *international* sovereign, retaining the power to enter into binding agreements with other sovereign states. This is the field of treaty law that has grown substantially over the last half century. Sovereignty in this sense is not exercised on the basis of territorial principles or perpetuating authority, but rather on the sovereign capacity of states to commit themselves within the international law of cooperation and thereby submit themselves as legal subjects under international law (Spiermann 2005, 92–94). On the face of it this may appear to infringe on the conceptualization of the state as a national sovereign; human rights treaties impose a range of obligations for the sovereign state within its territory, not just vis-à-vis aliens, but also toward its own citizens. However, it conversely establishes an extension of other states' sovereign sphere to the extent that their legal interests may transgress territorial borders on a range of new issues (Werner 2004).

This extension has been articulated by Judge Huber in the 1928 Las Palmas case:

> Territorial sovereignty…involves the exclusive right to display the activities of a State. This right has as a corollary a duty: the obligation to protect within the territory the rights of other States, in particular their rights to integrity and inviolability in peace and war, together with the rights which each State may claim for its nationals in foreign territory.[5]

Through the development of the international human rights regime, this obligation toward aliens of other states could be said to have developed to include all persons, regardless of nationality. Further, while the earlier remark refers to customary norms of interstate relations, the principle is of no less relevance under treaty law or obligations *erga omnes* (Werner 2004).[6]

How an issue is framed within this double structure is crucial, as the different conceptualizations of state sovereignty will point to different legal norms taking precedence. This in turn creates a field in which different sovereignity claims have been relied on to advance opposing arguments. While some scholars have emphasized the notion of international sovereignty as a mere appendix to the primacy of national sovereignty, others have argued that the present era is one in which the international law of cooperation is becoming increasingly dominant (Friedmann 1964, 88).

In the following, I shall suggest that while both conceptualizations are of continued relevance and must be seen as necessary complements in the functioning of international law, it is remarkable how the proliferation of treaty and human rights law cannot escape the territorial foundations flowing from the conceptualization of sovereignty within a Westphalian frame of territorial exclusivity. Borrowing a vocabulary developed by Neil Walker, the present configuration of sovereignty claims in respect to refugees may perhaps best be described within the framework of *late sovereignty*.

According to Neil Walker, the conceptual duality of the term sovereignty sketched out above is key to understand its present value in articulating and framing existing power relations in the transitional stage between a Westphalian and a post-Westphalian order (N. Walker 2003, 19–23). In the former order claims to authority are made strictly within a statist structure, whereas in the latter sovereign power is increasingly asserted along *functional* boundaries crosscutting the territorial division of the Westphalian map. (ibid., 22). The latter may be observed not only in the emergence of functionally limited polities, such as the EU, coexisting within the same territorial space as its constituent national sovereign member states, but also in the growing emergence of cooperative legal frameworks between EU or member states and third countries effectively extending sovereign functions beyond EU borders.

Yet, despite these functional assertions of power, the Westphalian order is not rejected in favor of a new framework for sovereignty, rather the territorial or national conceptualization of sovereignty is adapted to understand the new order (ibid., 19). This means, first, that the international law of cooperation continues to draw in large parts on the basic principles of national sovereignty in its justification and implementation. Second, and related, the growing cooperation effectively extending sovereign power beyond the territory has not been matched unequivocally by a similar deterritorialization of correlate sovereign responsibilities. Instead a discursive field is opened in which questions of jurisdiction and state responsibility seems to oscillate between these two poles—the territorial and the universal (Werner 2004). In other words, in the establishment of functional polities such as the EU and in assertion of state power beyond the territory, sovereignty becomes an interpretive frame that may be used to legitimize both. In the late sovereign order of globalization and increased international governance on the one hand, and enduring Westphalian norms of territorial exclusivity on the other, concrete interpretations within the sovereignty frame become increasingly contested.

The Refugee in International Law

In the case of the refugee these traits are evident both in the constitution of the refugee within international law and in the current policies of extraterritorialization pursued by European states. As one scholar notes:

> The refugee in international law occupies a legal space characterized, on the one hand, by the principle of State sovereignty and related principles of territorial supremacy and self-preservation; and, on the other hand, by competing humanitarian principles deriving from general international law...and from treaty. (Goodwin-Gill 1996, v)

As part and parcel of the broader human rights regime, most scholars would probably argue that international refugee law belongs to the international law of cooperation. Refugees are the exception to states' legitimate pursuit of migration control, and treaty law, such as the 1951 Refugee Convention, entails an obligation for state parties to extend a number of rights and benefits to all individuals falling within the definition.

Yet, the link to principles of state sovereignty and territorial supremacy in the codification of this area of law are indeed striking. Despite the appearance of universality, this regime is in the true sense of the word *international*. Refugee protection is not guaranteed in a global homogenous space, but materializes as a patchwork of commitments undertaken by individual states, tied together by multilateral treaty agreements (Palan 2003, 87).

This concerns first the mechanism of responsibility assignment. At the core of the refugee regime is the obligation not to send back, or *refouler*, a refugee to a place in which he or she risks persecution.[7] This obligation kicks in when an asylum-seeker or a refugee is present within the territory or jurisdiction of the state in question. While in principle this obliges the state to undertake a refugee status determination process, as soon as an asylum claim is launched within its territory or at its borders, the Refugee Convention contains no explicit mention of how and where the asylum procedures should be carried out (Fitzpatrick 1996, 229; Goodwin-Gill 1996, 178; Barnes 2004).[8]

Second, beyond the *non-refoulement* prohibition, rights under the 1951 Refugee Convention are not granted *en bloc* but rather according to a principle of territorial approximation, meaning that more rights are acquired as the refugee obtains a higher "level of attachment" to the host state. This incremental approach reflects a concern of the drafters not to extend the full scope of rights in situations where refugees may arrive spontaneously in large numbers (Hathaway 2005, 157). Thus, in particular the social and economic rights may only be claimed, when a refugee is "lawfully staying" or "durably resident" within the territory of the host state. Conversely, a refugee outside the territory of a state, but within its jurisdiction is only entitled to a very basic set of rights centered on the *non-refoulement* obligation.[9]

Last, the rights flowing from international refugee instruments are crucially dependent on individual states for their implementation. Unlike interstate conflicts under the law of coexistence, obligations under refugee and human rights treaties are as a rule owed toward a collective of state parties and do not therefore necessarily invoke the direct interest of other states. This has left the Refugee Convention with no international courts and no effective enforcement mechanisms (Goodwin-Gill 1996, 218). Thus, the mechanisms to ensure the implementation of refugee rights are left to intergovernmental organizations, such as the UNHCR, that are highly dependent on financial and political support from the very states they are supposed to supervise, and often, more importantly, the national courts of each state, which, depending on the respective constitutional traditions, may be able to exert a smaller or larger influence and to varying degrees draw on international instruments in national adjudication.

Together these traits paint a rather chequered picture of a refugee rights regime that, despite the language of universality, is still firmly vested within the Westphalian structures of national sovereignty. The above may also account for the recent surge to *externalize* or *extraterritorialize* both the regulation of migration control and the provision of refugee protection. In a world where states' ability to control flows of people across their borders is already challenged, moving migration control outside the borders is perceived as a strategy to prevent triggering refugee responsibilities and/or shift them to third states.

Extraterritorial Jurisdiction and
the Commercialization of Sovereignty

In the late sovereign order, this quest for extraterritorialization brings forth two aspects of the way that the interplay between different conceptualizations of sovereignty structures state responses to refugees—one being the legal debate over extraterritorial jurisdiction and the other the political dynamic of commercialization of sovereignty.

The first concerns state jurisdiction as the sphere in which a state may legitimately exercise its sovereign functions. The overall point of departure within human rights and refugee law is that states are bound by human rights in relation to all persons within their jurisdiction (Kessing 2007).[10] The question is how jurisdiction is established when moving outside the "sovereign nation cage." Within international law extraterritorial jurisdiction has been conceived of in two ways—as a property flowing from a state's effective control over a defined *territory*, or as a relationship between a state's exercise of authority or control over an *individual*. The first clearly derives from the principle of national sovereignty, extending jurisdiction to all geographical areas where a state exercises *de facto* sovereign control, such as in the case of, for example, military occupation.[11] The second is primarily reflected in more recent case law dealing with cases where state agents act inside another state, whether unlawfully or following agreement between those states, and seems to reflect an expansive interpretation not to "allow a State party to perpetrate violations of the Convention on the territory of another State, which it could not perpetrate on its own territory."[12]

It is important to underline, however, that in both these conceptualizations, *extra*territorial jurisdiction is conceived of as *extra*ordinary.[13] Despite the proliferation of extraterritorial state functions in a globalized world, the territorial jurisdictional competence remains the point of departure in international law. In practice international courts have thus applied rather high tests to establish extraterritorial jurisdiction for the purpose of human rights responsibilities. In the *Bankovic* case, involving the NATO air bombings of a radio station in Serbia during the Kosovo conflict, the European Court of Human Rights held that a sufficient degree of effective control over Serbian territory had not been asserted.[14] Similarly, establishing personal jurisdiction has generally been limited to cases involving full control over an individual, such as in the case of abduction or detention, rather than in relation to particular functions of state sovereignty, such as preventing onward passage for an asylum-seeker.[15]

The notion of extraterritorial jurisdiction has thus been interpreted very differently among states and seems to create a disparity where, under a strict reading, states can avoid incurring legal responsibilities for acts committed extraterritorially in situations where neither territorial nor personal jurisdiction can be established. This has lead some authors to argue that the kind of interception operations we see in the Mediterranean, the extraterritorial detention of combatants or the outsourcing of otherwise domestic sovereign functions take place in a "legal vacuum" or "legal black hole" (Wilde 2005, 15f). While these terms may be ill-chosen, as these actions are more often than not governed by elaborate cooperative legal arrangements between states, it may be more correct to argue that the interpretive breadth in establishing jurisdiction extraterritorially or assigning responsibilities in cases involving competing jurisdictions easily defers human rights obligations to the basic modus operandi of territorial responsibility assignment.

A second feature of the late sovereign order is the growing "commercialization of sovereignty" as a political strategy in the late sovereign order. This term has originally been derived to describe the emergence of tax havens and offshore economies. According to Ronen Palan commercialization of sovereignty or "jurisdiction shopping" within this field emerges as a result of the inability of international law to bridge the gulf between national sovereignty and the internationalization of trade and capital (Palan 2002, 164). In other words, the dual conceptualization of sovereignty creates the structural conditions for states to try to attract international capital by exploiting existing differences between national sovereign regulations or intentionally relaxing regulation in particular areas of their territory (Palan 2003, 157).

Considering refugees and migration control, this commercialization is possible exactly because of the territorial principles of the refugee regime in regards to the distribution of responsibilities and the standards of protection owed. Thus, examples of such bartering of sovereign authority are numerous in the attempt to relocate refugee protection or asylum processing to less-developed countries where fewer and less costly rights are owed, both in Europe and elsewhere.[16] In the context of migration control, a similar trend of "jurisdiction shopping" emerges as EU's neighbors and developing countries, either for economic benefit or under threats of sanctions, provide a legal platform in the form of their land and sea geography, thereby enabling EU states to operate migration control while simultaneously shifting the primary responsibility for refugees to those countries within whose territorial jurisdiction control is operated.

Both the varying interpretations of extraterritorial jurisdiction and the commercialization of sovereignty effectively constitute sovereignty games, in which states, or in this case the EU, may seek to horizontally dislocate responsibilities owed under international law and thereby reassert their sovereign power in areas of regulation that are otherwise marred by legal constraints flowing from either national liberal traditions or international human rights. In this sense changing the playing field for exercising sovereign power away from the national territory becomes a strategy for states in the late sovereign order to avoid obligations owed, *de facto* or *de jure*. As a result, the refugee is left to the unmitigated power of the sovereign executive when exercising migration control or to use the terminology of Giorgio Agamben, the migrant encountered on the high seas is effectively reduced to an "illegal body" to be controlled, to "naked life" (Agamben 1998a, 100f; Noll 2003).

EU Interdiction Policies

In the following, it will be sought illustrated how these sovereignty games operate in the context of the recent interdiction policies developed by the EU and member states. The first two sections will discuss extraterritorial jurisdiction claims for interdiction taking place on the high seas and within the territorial waters of a foreign state, respectively. The third will focus on the interplay of different international legal regimes, specifically how jurisdiction claims and asylum responsibilities are shifted by redefining operations from "migration control" to "search and rescue at sea."

Interdiction on the High Seas

Moving migration control to the high seas is not a new phenomenon. With the rise of boat refugees in the 1970s and 1980s, high sea interdiction practices quickly became the favored response of coastal states concerned with mass influx. Outside Europe, the more famous examples include the United States' interception of Haitians and Cubans from the early 1980s up until today and more recently the Australian "Pacific Solution," which was developed following the "Tampa" incident in 2001.[17] Similarly, in Southern Europe interdiction schemes on the high seas have been operated by Italy, France, Greece, and Spain in the Adriatic Sea, the Mediterranean, and around the Canary Islands (Lutterbeck 2006).

Under the Frontex auspices, the EU has also been looking to expand interdiction operations. Of the operational missions already carried out two involve interdiction outside territorial waters. One was the Nautilus Operation taking place in October 2006, during which the high sea was patrolled to prevent migration from Libya reaching Malta, Sicily, or Lampedusa. Although this mission was originally conceived to incorporate Libya, thus allowing for EU vessels to patrol within Libyan territorial waters, it was nonetheless hailed as a success claiming to completely prevent migrants from arriving in Malta during the time of operation.[18] The second operation was the HERA II set to curb the migration flow toward the Canary Islands. Involving planes, helicopters, and navy ships, this operation intercepted 14,572 persons on the high seas and Spanish territorial sea and 3,887 in the territorial waters of Senegal, Mauritania, and Cape Verde during its five months operation from August 2006.[19] This mission has been succeeded by HERA III operating interdictions in the same area.

To which extent are states undertaking such interdiction operations on the high seas bound by international law not to return those intercepted claiming asylum or fearing torture or other inhumane treatment? So far courts and governments have varied greatly in their interpretation of the jurisdictional implications in such situations. Both the Australian and US interdiction policies have been on the basis of an exclusively territorial understanding of jurisdiction and thus the *non-refoulement* obligation. Testing the US interdiction and subsequent return of Haitians in *Sale v. Haitian Centers Council*,[20] the US Supreme Court supported this interpretation arguing that:

> ...a treaty cannot impose uncontemplated extraterritorial obligations on those who ratify it through no more than its general humanitarian intent. Because the text of Article 33 [of the 1951 Refugee Convention, setting out the *non-refoulement* principle] cannot reasonably be read to say anything at all about a nation's actions toward aliens outside its own territory, it does not prohibit such actions.[21]

A similar interpretation may have inspired Australia when, following the Tampa incident, the 2001 Migration Amendment Act excised parts of both Australian sea and land territory, most notably Christmas Island and the Ashmore Reef, from the "asylum zone" (Pugh 2004, 60). Likewise, for asylum purposes US sovereign territory only extends to the high water mark and not government vessels or offshore bases, such as that on Guantanamo (ibid.). Both cases can be seen as a radicalization of the strictly territorial understanding of jurisdiction, arguing that states are even at liberty to withdraw their territorial jurisdiction, so that even though an asylum-seeker is *de facto* present within the territory or territorial sea, she is not recognized as *de jure* present.

However, both the *Sale* verdict and the Australian excision practices have been widely criticized. International lawyers and human rights organizations have argued that the *Sale* case builds on an erroneous and incomplete reading of both the Refugee Convention and extraterritorial jurisdictional principles and represents a "policy decision" that did not alter the United States' international obligations.[22]

Perhaps more important, the US and Australian interpretations have not gained much currency in Europe, where in particular the European Court of Human Rights has taken a more expansive reading of extraterritorial jurisdiction in situations such as those involving interdiction in international waters. In *Xhavara,* the court thus held that Italy was exercising jurisdiction within the meaning of the European Convention on Human Rights, when a boat with immigrants sunk following collision with an Italian navy vessel trying to board it under an agreement between the two countries.[23] Second, the European Court of Human Rights has rejected the ability of states to excise parts of their territory for migration purposes. In *Amuur v. France,* aliens held within French airport transit zones were found to be within French jurisdiction and territory for all purposes of the Convention, despite any French legislation to differentiate regulation of these zones from the rest of their territory.[24] In line with this interpretation it is worth noting that migrants intercepted by European ships on the high seas under the HERA mission according to the authorities all are taken to the Canary Islands, where they have the possibility to launch an asylum application.

To the extent that European interdiction policies on the high seas constitute a sovereignty game, it is thus more likely a question of reasserting state power *de facto* than *de jure.* As noted earlier, the international refugee and human rights regimes are intimately dependent on national institutions—courts, appeal mechanisms, NGOs, and press—to ensure that individuals are actually able to access international rights. The reach of these institutions seldom extends beyond the physical territory of the state and even more unlikely to uninhabited geographical areas such as the high seas. Both UNHCR and Amnesty International have raised concerns that asylum-seekers may not be able to exercise basic rights or formalize asylum claims when interdicted at sea or held at closed island detention centers such as those in Lampedusa and the Canary Islands; the very remoteness of these places is an impediment for national and international rights organizations to access asylum-seekers and monitor state actions (Gil-Bazo 2006, 579).[25]

This has been a particular concern when interdiction policies leave the state unchecked in receiving asylum claims, which raises concerns that authorities may downplay the number of asylum-seekers in mixed migration flows. From 1981 to 1990, the period before declaring that *non-refoulement* only applied on the territory, the United States interdicted and returned more than 21,000 Haitians. Yet, despite the grave human rights situation in Haiti during this period, the Coast Guard found only six claims strong enough to warrant a full asylum procedure (Legomsky 2006, 679). On the Canary Islands, authorities have been keen to emphasize that the vast majority of those intercepted were "illegal immigrants." Despite the increase in migration pressure over the last years, both the total number of asylum claims launched and the recognition rates have gone down, which has led Amnesty International to suggest that asylum claims are deliberately overheard and discouraged.[26] Whether this is true or not, it does suggest that moving migration from the land to the sea entails a possibility for states to carry out control further away from the eyes of those institutions that normally constitute the checks and balances in the exercise of executive power.

Interdiction in Foreign Territorial Waters

A particular aspect of European interdiction policies as developed in the Frontex context has been increased cooperation with North and West African States and consequently the expansion of geographical scope from the high seas into the territorial waters and land territory of third states. As argued in the following text, within the theoretical framework set out earlier, this could be seen as a more advanced strategy for interdicting states to relieve themselves of international human rights responsibilities when conducting migration control. Rather than argue for the strict territorial application of, for example, the *non-refoulement* principle, which has proved untenable in the European context, the territorial jurisdiction of another state may be invoked to shift the primary responsibility for any protection-seekers to that state.

As part of the HERA II mission, bilateral arrangements were made that allowed the Spanish, Finnish, Italian, and Portuguese ships and airplanes to patrol and intercept vessels bound for the Canary Islands, not just on the high seas but also inside Cape Verde, Senegalese, and Mauritanian territorial sea, contiguous zone or air space.[27] Thus, any vessel intercepted within this 24-mile zone of these states is turned back, either to its port of departure or to a port within the territorial waters in which interdiction occurred. During the 4 months of operation 3,665 persons were intercepted within these zones and returned. Cooperation with the Senegalese authorities further extended to bringing Senegalese immigration officers on board European ships, and Frontex argued that these officers were formally in charge of rejecting migrants' passage to international waters. The operation was hailed by Frontex as a great success and cooperation with West and North African states has been extended for the continuation, HERA III. Similarly, arrangements with Libya have been sought as part of the Nautilus operation in the Eastern Mediterranean to be able to operate inside its territorial waters. Although this has not materialized, negotiations are ongoing.[28]

So, from the viewpoint of international law what does it matter that interdiction is carried out inside foreign waters rather than on the high seas? The most obvious consequence would be to exclude all asylum-seekers fleeing directly from their country of origin to invoke the 1951 Refugee Convention. Article 1 of this Convention clearly stipulates that the *ratione personae* only extends to individuals "outside the country of his nationality" and an asylum-seeker would thus have to exit the territorial sea to benefit from, fro example, the *non-refoulement* principle enshrined in article 33. While this is obviously of concern, it should be noted that, for example, the prohibition against *refoulement* to torture or other inhumane treatment enshrined in article 3 of the European Convention on Human Rights (ECHR) does not have this limitation.

Second, and of primary concern to the present chapter, it may be asked whether asserting extraterritorial jurisdiction is effected by moving interdiction from the high sea to the territorial sea of a third state. On first look, one could make an argument answering in the negative. Flowing from the international law of cooperation, the International Law Commission has argued that "[i]nternational life provides abundant examples of activities carried on in the territory of a State by agents of another State... [t]here is nothing abnormal in this."[29] Following this reasoning, one should be able to assert a principle similar to that of state actions carried out on the high seas, namely that since the basic function of human rights is to regulate the exercise of public power, it should not matter where this power is exercised (Lawson 2004, 86).

Some case law seems to support this interpretation, both under the International Covenant on Civil and Political Rights (ICCPR) and the ECHR. In *López Burgos*,[30] the Human Rights Committee held that the arrest and subsequent mistreatment of Mr. Burgos by Uruguayan Security Forces in Argentina did bring him within Uruguayan jurisdiction. Similarly, in the context of the ECHR, *Öcalan*[31], involving the arrest and forcible return of PKK leader Öcalan in Kenya, did establish Turkish jurisdiction in respect to the applicant.

In these cases the reasoning built on the premise that the defending states had effective personal control of the applicants and that it would be "unconscionable... to permit a State party to perpetrate violations of the Covenant on the territory of another State, which violations it could not perpetrate within its own territory."[32] On first look this appears to support a rather expansive interpretation of a state's extraterritorial jurisdiction in cases involving not territorial control but a personal or more incidental link between the acting state and an individual.

Other case law does, however, emphasize a rather high test for the level of control that a state needs to assert vis-à-vis an individual to establish extraterritorial jurisdiction in the personal understanding. To several lawyers, the Grand Chamber ruling of the European Court of Human Rights in *Bankovic*[33] came as a surprise. Many had expected that the NATO smart bombs killing the relatives of the applicants would be enough to establish such a level of control (Coomans and Kamminga 2004; Loucaides 2006). Yet, the Court emphasized the extraordinary character of extraterritorial personal jurisdiction arguing that:

> Article 1 of the Convention must be considered to reflect this ordinary and essentially territorial notion of jurisdiction, other bases of jurisdiction being exceptional and requiring special justification of each case.[34]

The court found that in the present case such justification was not met in establishing a personal relationship and then went on to conclude that since the actions had occurred outside the "legal space" of the convention (Serbia [FRY] was not a party of the ECHR at the time) and effective control of the territory was not established, the acting states could not be made responsible under the convention.[35]

As regards actions taking place on the territory of a state not party to the convention, the court thus seems to make a distinction between the extraterritorial responsibilities of states in cases where "full control" is exercised over an individual, such as in the case of arrest of physical detention and state actions that merely result in violations of human rights on foreign soil or territorial waters, even when these violations are so important that they infringe the right of life (art. 2).

Under such a reading it becomes harder to establish jurisdiction when a state is operating interdiction inside foreign territorial waters. Does turning back a ship entail effective control in the personal sense? The argument could be made in cases where EU ships physically board ships or detain those on board, but it is more doubtful whether merely denying onward passage or escorting vessels back is sufficient to meet the test of extraterritorial personal jurisdiction.

Failing this, interdiction in foreign waters moves back to the question of who exercises effective control over the territory in question. Although case law does support the possibility of shared extraterritorial jurisdiction,[36] this has normally required a high degree of structural and military involvement over a defined geographical space.[37] While one could presumably argue that under the traditional international legal doctrine a ship exercising government functions on the high seas or foreign territorial sea is to be considered "floating territory" (Ross 1961, 172), the presence of Senegalese immigration officers on board Frontex ships is clearly a move to underline that not only is this Senegalese jurisdiction, but the actual denial of onward passage is also conducted by Senegalese authorities.[38]

Without going into arguments *pro et contra ad infinitum*, it should be clear that the case for asserting EU member state responsibility when operating interdiction in foreign territorial waters is at best substantially weaker than when operating on the high seas. From the case law earlier, one may venture the following interpretation: Where on the high seas and in situations where responsibility could not meaningfully be attributed to the state on whose territory actions are committed (such as following unlawful extraterritorial arrests) both the European Court of Human Rights and the Human Rights Committee have been keen to avoid "human rights vacuums" as to the geographical applicability of the relevant instruments. Yet, when acting within foreign territory under agreement or with the direct involvement of another state, it becomes much more alluring to fall back on the principle of territorial jurisdiction.

This return to the basic Westphalian order of responsibility-sharing may inadvertently support a growing commercialization of sovereignty, as states exploit jurisdiction shopping by negotiating arrangements to perform migration control inside other states' sovereign land or sea territory.

Regime Shifting: From Interdiction to Rescue at Sea

Reading the press statements from Frontex or the political justifications for increased funding to patrol the Mediterranean and West African coasts one finds surprisingly few references to a stated aim of migration control.[39] Rather, these operations primarily seem to be framed as efforts to dissuade migrants from the perilous journey toward Europe and the need to ensure rescue for those in distress at sea. There is much to say in favor of such aspirations. Many vessels embarking on the journey have no or limited navigation aids, insufficient engines, fuel, and safety equipment onboard. Overcrowded ships entail a number of sanitary and health issues and there is a substantial risk of diseases, debilitation, or psychological stress spreading among those aboard during the voyage (Pugh 2004, 56).

Hardly a week goes by without dead bodies are found washing up on the shores between EU and its southern neighbors. According to International Centre for Migration Policy Development (ICMPD), more than 10,000 persons have died trying to cross the Mediterranean from 1994 to 2004.[40] In addition, Spanish authorities estimate that approximately 6,000 persons, mainly Senegalese, died last year alone trying to reach the Canary Islands.[41] The growing human tragedy may in part be seen as a result of the reinforcement of migration control at EU's external borders. As the easier routes, such as the Strait of Gibraltar and the Spanish enclaves in Morocco, are reinforced, pressure moves toward less accessible and typically more dangerous routes, such as the one from West Africa to the Canary Islands.

Consequently, interest in reinforcing search and rescue cooperation between EU/member states and North African states has been given high priority on the agenda and in the relations between relevant coastal states within the MEDA and European Neighbourhood Policy (ENP) frameworks. Even in states with whom EU cooperation is scarce, such as Libya, EU missions have been launched, a "Libyan search and rescue area" defined, and operational cooperation in this field established.[42] Yet, beyond a humanitarian imperative, the recent interest in rescue at sea may also be viewed as a sovereignty game for the purpose of migration control in its own right. First, performing a rescue mission at sea supersedes the otherwise established norm prohibiting an acting state to intercept and board a vessel flying the flag, and thus subject to the jurisdiction, of another state.[43] Second, cooperation agreements in the context of search and rescue operations, such as the framework established with Libya, may provide a context for shifting asylum and human rights obligations to third states.

Performing rescue operations at sea is a long-established duty under international maritime law.[44] It contains a responsibility for private, commercial, and state vessels to respond to persons in distress at sea. Traditionally, the maritime rescue regime has been marred by lack of a mechanism to decide where rescued persons should be put ashore and an explicit obligation for states to allow disembarkation. This became a particular problematic issue following the rise of "boat refugees," which made states concerned that asylum processing and protection responsibilities would follow from the hitherto relatively trivial issue of disembarkation and subsequent return to the country of origin.

Thus, for much of the last decades the issue of rescue at sea has been playing out as a variation of the classic problem between self-interested states and international cooperation (Barnes 2004, 11). The opaqueness in the intersection between refugee and maritime law meant that the nearest coastal states (whether within territorial waters or on the high sea), flag states of the rescue vessels and states of the next port of call for merchant vessels were all arguing against having to take a responsibility themselves. The result has been a number of problematic stalemates and costly delays for vessels, eventually leading to a disincentive to undertake rescue obligations at all.[45]

Only recently amendments to the 1979 Convention on Maritime Search and Rescue (SAR) and the 1974 International Convention for the Safety of Life at Sea (SOLAS) have attempted to establish mechanisms for identifying which coastal state is responsible for allowing disembarkation.[46] Under this regime the world's oceans are divided into 13 Search and Rescue Regions (SRR). In each region the affected states are responsible for establishing coordination, which effectively has translated into drawing a map partitioning the high sea zones in which each coastal state is responsible in addition to their territorial waters. While third state or private vessels may undertake the rescue missions themselves, the state in whose zone the operation takes place holds main responsibility for ensuring that distress calls are responded to and, importantly, allow disembarkation.[47]

While these amendments have been broadly celebrated as closing a vital gap in the search and rescue regime, one should appreciate how these amendments may also favor new interdiction strategies by altering the locus of international protection obligations. The intensified Frontex patrols and cooperation agreements with North and West African countries means that EU ships are increasingly operating inside foreign search and rescue zones, whether on the high sea or inside foreign territorial waters. Under the new disembarkation rules, the respective African states will be responsible for allowing disembarkation and therefore, presumably, provide asylum procedures or enforce return to the country of origin. This argument was made by Malta when refusing to let the Spanish trawler La Valletta, carrying 51 migrants, dock at Maltese ports. Malta was supported by EU Commissioner Franco Frattini, stating that "the vessel had picked up illegal immigrants in Libya's Search and Rescue Area and that therefore Malta is under no obligation to take them in."[48]

The potential for jurisdiction shopping in such instances is exacerbated by the fact that none of the maritime conventions provide a solid definition of what constitutes "distress" (Pugh 2004, 58). Instead, the master of the intercepting ship has been given authority to evaluate when a vessel is in need of rescue or when a vessel is merely unseaworthy by modern standards. In the context of Frontex or other European vessels operating migration control at sea this seems to provide a system where situations may usefully be defined differently to divert responsibilities for asylum-seekers at different points in their journey toward Europe; if boats are intercepted inside a foreign state's Search and Rescue zone the incentive would be to define it as a rescue operation and thereby shift any disembarkation obligation to that state. If, on the other hand, interdiction is conducted inside the European search and rescue zone there would be an interest in defining it as migration control and thereby evade any direct disembarkation responsibilities and instead deal with the issue in the context of varying interpretations of jurisdiction, as discussed earlier.

The question remains, of course, whether defining a situation as a rescue mission legally supersedes any direct responsibilities vis-à-vis asylum-seekers on behalf of the acting state. This is somewhat unclear. A case could be made that the rescuing state is still exercising jurisdiction in performing the rescue mission or by virtue of taking onboard rescued persons on a state vessel. While not legally binding, the guidelines adopted by the Maritime Safety Committee of the International Maritime Organization on the treatment of persons rescued at sea emphasizes that consideration should be given "to avoid disembarkation in territories where the lives and freedoms of those alleging a well-founded fear of persecution would be threatened."[49]

In practice, however, it seems that by defining the operation within the search and rescue regime, questions regarding refugee protection are moved away from the acting state and responsibilities solely assigned according to territorial or zone divisions, as agreed among the states in the region. The Valletta case mentioned earlier illustrates this quite clearly. Libya is not a signatory to the 1951 Refugee Convention and has a track record of onward expulsion of asylum-seekers and migrants returned from Europe to unsafe countries where persons risk torture or persecution.[50] To the extent that it could be established that these persons had been under European jurisdiction, a case could be made that such chain-*refoulement* would constitute a breach of article 3 of the European Convention of Human Rights. Yet, both the EU commissioner and the Maltese government argue that responsibility rested solely with Libya and no considerations were seemingly made as to any protection issues.

Before the SAR and SOLAS amendments, rescue at sea could be described as a traditional noncooperative sovereignty game, where every coastal state had the possibility to "free ride" by denying disembarkation with reference to their sovereign right of migration control. This clearly disfavored the flag states not being able to put rescued persons ashore and perhaps, more importantly, created a substantial negative economic externality by delaying commercial vessels. Under the present regime, this is replaced by a cooperative sovereignty game in which the international legal framework in principle provides a positive obligation for a single state at any point in the Mediterranean or the Atlantic Ocean outside West Africa. The sovereignty game thus shifts from one of territorial retraction to one in which African coast states may commercialize their territorial waters and high sea rescue zones as venues, where Frontex ships can effectively intercept migrants without incurring correlate responsibilities for disembarkation, and thus asylum processing.

Conclusions

In its communication on "Reinforcing the management of the EU's Southern Maritime Borders" the commission noted the lack of "clarity and predictability" as regards member state obligations under international law and thus the need to:

> ...analyse the circumstances under which a State may be obliged to assume responsibility for the examination of an asylum claim as a result of the application of international refugee law, in particular when engaged in joint operations or in operations taking place within the territorial waters of another State or in the high sea.[51]

The present chapter has attempted to do exactly this. Yet, the earlier analysis does not paint a "clear" picture of international law in this area or establish "predictable" mechanisms for designating state responsibilities. Rather, it has tried to elucidate how different interpretations of the concept of jurisdiction and interlocking legal regimes has made the exact nature of state obligations toward asylum-seekers and refugees a field of contestation, in which the extraterritorial applicability of refugee rights is open to different interpretations, new cooperation schemes emerge and it is possible for states to frame issues within various legal regimes with rather different game rules.

The result seems to be an increased maneuverability for states. Whether *de facto* or *de jure*, the extraterritorialization of migration control works to the advantage of European states when it comes to deconstructing or shifting responsibilities owed to refugees and asylum-seekers. In particular, moving regulation into foreign jurisdiction or casting operations within the international search and rescue regime seem to improve the likelihood that legal responsibilities are settled by falling back on the basic Westphalian notion of territorial jurisdiction.

This again has given rise to the increasing commercialization of sovereignty for the purpose of migration control. The present chapter has confined itself to situations in which European states are directly involved in performing offshore migration control. Yet, both the practical and legal difficulties in asserting state responsibility in such instances are presumably only exacerbated when interstate cooperation entails a complete outsourcing of migration control to third states.[52] In sum, we may be witnessing the beginning of a new offshore human rights economy through which "protection in the region" and "cooperation with third countries" are both hides for attempts to capitalize on foreign territorial jurisdictions and lower national human rights standards to shift and reduce burdens of refugee protection away from Europe (Gammeltoft-Hansen 2008).

So far there has been a tendency among human rights lawyers and refugee advocates to reject the restrictive and territorially based interpretations of extraterritorial jurisdiction as stemming from both state practice and international case law as bad reasoning or policy-driven misinterpretations. While such misdemeanors are certainly conceivable in this field of international law, this chapter has tried to point to a more structural explanation for the difficulty in exactly defining the extent of extraterritorial human rights responsibilities. Within the late sovereign order this difficulty does not simply amount to a systematic attempt to undermine the applicability of international human rights and refugee law, but rather points to the inherent duality in the way that sovereignty has been conceived within international legal discourse.

From the viewpoint of refugee protection this conclusion may seem disappointing. To the extent that Europe hails its human rights regime as an attempt to codify universal norms, the least we would expect would be for European states to abide by the same human rights standards when acting abroad. In this sense, the increasing trend of extraterritorialization warrants further reconsideration of the primarily territorial framing of state jurisdiction and consequently human rights standards. Whether this will happen and the late sovereignty order thus continue to develop, time will tell; indeed one could agree with the assessment of Richard O'Boyle of the ECtHR when in relation to *Bankovic* he noted that "the law on 'jurisdiction' is still in its infancy" (O'Boyle 2004, 139).

Notes

1. This was the title accompanying the photograph when published in the New York Times, July 10, 2001.
2. For an overview of the history of migration flows and control initiatives in the Mediterranean see Lutterbeck 2006.
3. UNHCR (2000). Interception of Asylum-Seekers and Refugee: The International Framework and Recommendations for a Comprehensive Approach. *UN Doc. EC/50/SC/CRP.17.* June 9, 2000, p. 10.
4. *The Case of the S.S. "Lotus."* Judgment of September 7, 1927. Permanent Court of International Justice. PCIJ Series A No. 10, p. 14.

5. *Case of the Island of Palmas.* Judgment of April 4, 1928. Permanent Court of International Justice. R.I.I.A. Vol. II.

6. *Case concerning the Barcelona Traction, Light and Power Company, Ltd.* Judgment of February 5, 1970 (Second Phase). International Court of Justice. ICJ Reports 1970.

7. The *non-refoulement* principle is set out in a number of international human rights instruments, most notably in art. 33 of the 1951 Refugee Convention, art. 3 of the Convention against Torture, and art. 3 of the European Convention on Human Rights (ECHR).

8. Since refugee status is declaratory, not constitutive, the *non-refoulement* principle must be applied presumptively to asylum-seekers before refugee-hood is established. See further UNHCR (2007). Advisory Opinion on the Extraterritorial Application of Non-Refoulement Obligations under the 1951 Convention relating to the Status of Refugees and its 1967 Protocol. Geneva. January 26, 2007, par. 8.

9. The most pertinent rights under the 1951 Refugee Convention that are specifically granted without reference to being present or staying at the territory include art. 33 (*non-refoulement*), art. 16 (access to courts), and art. 3 (non-discrimination). Of somewhat lesser importance, Articles 13 (property), 22 (education) and 20 (rationing) also apply extraterritorially (Hathaway 2005: 160–171).

10. Jurisdiction as the *ratione loci* of international human rights treaties is spelled out in a number of instruments, see in particular art. 1 of the European Convention on Human Rights, art 2(1) in the International Covenant on Civil and Political Rights (ICCPR) and in art 2(1) in the Convention Against Torture. Similarly, it has been convincingly argued that the core principles of refugee law, such as the *non-refoulement* principle enshrined in art. 33 of the 1951 Refugee Convention, is similarly applicable in all cases where a refugee falls under a state's jurisdiction (Hathaway 2005: 339; Lauterpacht and Bethlehem 2003, 110; Goodwin-Gill 1996, 141f). It should be noted that a number of human rights instruments, for example, the Genocide Convention, contains no territorial restrictions but puts an obligation upon states to prevent and punish genocide everywhere (Coomans and Kamminga 2004, 2). Similarly, some rights may be reserved for persons strictly within the territory of a state or having a particular relationship to the state. As noted earlier, this is the case for the more substantial rights flowing from the Refugee Convention.

11. For example, *Cyprus v. Turkey (Appl. No. 25781/94).* Judgment of May 10, 2001. European Court of Human Rights.

12. *Issa and Others v. Turkey (appl. No. 31821/96).* Judgment of November 16, 2004. European Court of Human Rights, par. 71

13. This has been expressed in, for example, *Bankovic*, arguing that "from the standpoint of public international law, the jurisdictional competence of a State was primarily territorial" and that extraterritorial jurisdictions "were, as a general rule, defined and limited by the sovereign territorial rights of

the other relevant States." *Bankovic and Others v. Belgium, Czech Republic, Denmark, France, Germany, Greece, Hungary, Iceland, Italy, Luxembourg, Netherlands, Norway, Poland, Portugal, Spain, Turkey, and the United Kingdom* (Appl. No. 5207/99). Judgment of December 12, 2001. European Court of Human Rights, par 71.

14. *Bankovic,* ibid.

15. *López Burgos v. Uruguay.* Judgment of June 6, 1979. Human Rights Committee. UN Doc. A/36/40. *Issa and Others v. Turkey,* ibid. *Öcalan v. Turkey (Appl. no. 46221/99).* Judgment of March 12, 2003. European Court of Human Rights. But see *Xhavara and fifteen v. Italy and Albania (Appl. No. 39473/98).* Judgment of January 11, 2001. European Court of Human Rights.

16. See in particular the Australian "Pacific Solution" and in Europe, though never realized, the United Kingdom plans for a New Vision for Refugees (Pugh 2004; Kneebone 2006; Gammeltoft-Hansen 2007).

17. See note 45 of this chapter.

18. Notably, no references were made as to whether the vessels presumably intercepted and in particular if any asylum-seekers were turned back toward North Africa or allowed disembarkation in other EU states. Agence Europe, November 1, 2006.

19. Frontex. (2006). "Longest Frontex coordinated operation—HERA, the Canary Islands." News Releases, December 19, 2006 retrieved March 16, 2007, from http://frontex.europa.eu.

20. 113 US Supreme Court 2549 (1993).

21. Ibid. at 2565.

22. See in particular the dissenting opinion by Justice Blackmum, the *amicus curiae* and the external comments reprinted in *International Journal of Refugee Law.* 6 (1). (1994), 69–109. Further Hathaway (2005, 336–340) and Goodwin-Gill (1996, 143–144).

23. The case was, however, declared inadmissible on grounds of nonexhaustion of national remedies. *Xhavara,* ibid.

24. *Amuur v. France.* Judgment of June 25, 1996. European Court of Human Rights. Reports 1996-III, No. 11.

25. See for example, UNHCR Press Release. "UNHCR deeply concerned over Lampedusa deportations." March 18, 2005; Amnesty International (2005). "Spain: The Southern Border." EUR 41/008/2005; and Human Rights Watch. "The Other Face of the Canary Islands: Rights Violations against Migrants and Asylum Seekers." February 2002.

26. Amnesty International. (2005). "Spain: The Southern Border." EUR 41/008/2005.

27. The territorial waters may extend 12 nautical miles (22 km) from the low water mark or internal waters. This belt is regarded as the sovereign territory of a state, except that foreign ships are allowed innocent passage. Control over an additional contiguous zone extending up to 24 nautical miles may further be claimed by states to "prevent infringement of its customs, fiscal, immigration or sanitary laws and regulations." (Art 24(1) of the Geneva

Convention on the Territorial Sea and Contiguous Zone). Although this zone for other purposes are considered high seas, it reflects a functional extension of territorial sovereignty for the above purposes.

28. ISN Security Watch, January 7, 2007. See further http://frontex.europa.eu.
29. International Law Commission (1975). *Yearbook of the ILC.* Vol. II, p. 83.
30. *López Burgos*, ibid.
31. *Öcalan*, ibid.
32. *López Burgos*, ibid. par. 12.3. See the similar reasoning in *Issa* cited earlier.
33. *Bankovic*, ibid.
34. Ibid. par. 43.
35. Ibid.
36. See in particular *Ilascu and Others v. Moldova and Russia (Appl. No. 48787/99)*. Judgment of July 8, 2004. European Court of Human Rights.
37. Ibid. For the premises of effective extraterritorial jurisdiction in the territorial sense, see further *Loizidou v. Turkey (Merits)*. Judgment of December 18, 1996. European Court of Human Rights. Reports 1996-VI and *Cyprus v. Turkey*, ibid.
38. Whether this is a legitimate argument could again be contested; as long as ships are captained by EU officials, these could be claimed to hold effective authority.
39. See for example, COM (2006) 733, Reinforcing the management of the European Union's Southern Maritime Borders, November 30, 2006.
40. ICMPD, Irregular transit migration in the Mediterranean—some facts, futures, and insights, Vienna, 2004.
41. ISN Security Watch, January 12, 2007.
42. Department of Information, Malta, Press Release no. 1094: "Agreed Conclusions of Seminar on 'Saving Life at Sea and in the Desert' held in Malta on 20th July 2005," available from www.doi.gov.mt.
43. 1958 Geneva Convention on the Territorial Sea and the Contiguous Zone, art. 19.
44. The issue first emerged in international instruments in 1910. Since then it has been codified in various forms in the four 1958 Conventions on the Law of the Seas, the 1982 United Nations Convention on the Law of the Sea (superseding the 1958 Conventions), the 1974 International Convention for the Safety of Life at Sea, the 1979 International Convention on Maritime Search and Rescue, and the 1989 International Convention on Salvage. It is further established as a general principle of international law (Miltner 2005).
45. One of the more recent examples in the European context is the "Marine 1" that broke down in international waters and was rescued by the Spanish Coast Guard. The ship was towed to Nouadhibou, the nearest port in Mauritania, but the Mauritanian government refused disembarkation on the grounds that the shipped likely originated from Guinea and should be returned there. Following negotiations, Mauritania allowed disembarkation in return for guarantees from the Spanish government that all migrants and refugees would be returned or resettled elsewhere. However, repatriation proved equally difficult. Most of the approximately 200 passengers were believed

to come from the Kashmir area but do not want to reveal their identities. Afghanistan and Pakistan have been reluctant to cooperate. Similarly, a plane with 35 migrants had to return in midair because Guinea-Bissau would not receive them (ECRAN Weekly Update, February 9, 2007 and February 17, 2007).

Outside Europe the most notorious example of such a détente concerned the Norwegian ship "MV Tampa" that in 2001 responded to the Australian Search and Rescue authorities' request to investigate a distress call from an Indonesian vessel, which turned out to carry 433 Afghan asylum-seekers. Australia refused to let the Tampa enter Australian waters. Health problems onboard made the Tampa ignore this and the ship was subsequently boarded by Australian troops. Following another week of negotiations, Australia struck a deal with Papua New-Guinea and Nauru where the asylum-seekers were taken for processing. The incident gave rise to Australia's plans for interception and offshore asylum processing, what is now commonly referred to as the Pacific Solution. For more information on this case, see Barnes 2004, Pugh 2004, and Kneebone 2006.

46. The amendments to both Conventions were adopted by the International Maritime Organisation in 2004 and entered into force on July 1, 2006. See MSC 78/26/Add. 1, Annex 3 and 5 respectively.

47. Ibid.

48. Department of Information, Malta, Press Release no. 1094, ibid. It should be noted, however, that Libya refused to take on any responsibilities in this matter, and that the migrants were disembarked in Spain after being stranded off the Maltese coast for eight days.

49. This language closely resembles that used in articles 1 and 33 of the 1951 Refugee Convention prohibiting *refoulement*. See Maritime Safety Committee, Guidelines on the treatment of persons rescued at sea, Resolution MSC.167(78), adopted on May 20, 2004, par. 6.17.

50. Notably, on the basis of Red Crescent information the Italian journalist Fabrizio Gatti reported that more than 100 people had died following Libya's expulsion of "illegal migrants" through the Saharan desert. A number of these had previously been deported to Libya from the Italian island detention centre Lampedusa (L'Espresso, March 24, 2005).

51. COM (2006) 733, 30.11.2006, par. 34.

52. For some perspectives on the scope of such outsourcing in the EU context, see Gammeltoft-Hansen 2006 and Lutterbeck 2006.

11

Epilogue: Three Layers of a Contested Concept

Rebecca Adler-Nissen and
Thomas Gammeltoft-Hansen

Closing our pursuit of sovereignty games we hope to have sketched a number of both theoretical and practical examples for others to add additional illustrations and perspectives. Throughout the volume, we have argued for the emergence of new and the return of old games in which sovereignty, or claims to sovereignty, have been instrumentalized by states and other players for a multitude of purposes. In the analysis of both vertical and horizontal sovereignty games, we have demonstrated how new scenarios may be emerging, rules twisted, and new moves contemplated. The majority of the chapters have thus been devoted to analyzing the implications of these sovereignty games for the world we live in.

The empirical outlook of the preceding chapters has been predominantly European. Yet, the overarching dynamics that have been pursued are far from limited to any one region or continent. European policies to interdict immigrants on the high seas or foreign territorial waters have found inspiration in similar policies enacted by the United States and Australia. In its underlying logic, Chinese deregulation of Shanghai and Hong Kong to allow outsourcing by Western companies share certain traits with the facilitation of CIA interrogation facilities and rendition flights in a number of European countries; both constitute cooperative sovereignty games, in which the territorial state barters off sovereign prerogatives for the outsourcing state or company to avoid constraints imposed by national or international law (Ong 1999). Similarly, parallels to the vertical sovereignty games played out among the European Union

(EU) and its member states can be found, though in rather different variations, in the struggles over the legitimate level authority between the state of Israel and the claim for Palestine or in the struggles between sovereignty claims at both the subnational and international level in the case of "failed states" and international occupations.

The question less explicitly tackled is the converse relationship, namely the implication of this analysis for the conceptual framework set out. Although sovereignty games may change the daily lives of legal and political practitioners, how do sovereignty games themselves change? To be sure, sovereignty games are not a new phenomenon, yet all our contributions have suggested a dynamic component to these games. Where disagreement remains, however, is in regards to the deeper transformative potential of the present structure for the concept of sovereignty. In particular, the analysis points to the need for a more refined approach in terms of where such transformation takes place. Although sovereignty practices are constantly taking new forms, do the rules of the sovereignty game or even the epistemic core prove equally fluid? Put plainly, is sovereignty all there is?

Thus, rather than trying to simply summarize the preceding chapters, this chapter will take the opportunity to revisit the theoretical underpinnings set out in the first part of the volume and pit them against some of the conclusions reached in the more applied analyses. In doing so, we may challenge our arguments against competing ways of thinking about sovereignty and its future. Our exploration of sovereignty games addresses the ways in which established meanings and functions of sovereignty are accepted, contested, or transformed in theory as well as practice.

The contributions to this volume have examined three levels or layers of sovereignty: the first and deepest is the foundational institution of sovereignty, the second layer is sovereignty as a legal and political concept of ultimate and indivisible authority, and the third layer is sovereignty as social practice. The three layers of sovereignty are interrelated, but they have a relative autonomy. Each layer of meaning has given rise to specific legal and political debates that contribute to the contestedness of sovereignty. The subsequent sections set out to explore these layers before turning to the broader question of transformation in and between them.

Sovereignty as a Foundational Institution

Discussing the meaning of sovereignty involves tackling its both constitutive and functional dimensions. Sovereignty constitutes the state system as the "meta-political authority in world politics" (Thomson 1995:

214). But once this constitution has taken place, or rather is taken for granted, it also functions as a framework of action; it regulates international relations and law, and it provides the rules of the game. This is the double character of sovereignty. Sovereignty is already instituted, but it also needs to be maintained through political, legal, and social practices.

The first contest over sovereignty emerges because of this binary conceptualization. Who constitutes sovereignty and how? And what makes it legitimate? The ontological status of sovereignty has not been resolved and is not likely to be so. It is intrinsically ambivalent because it is ontologically before our imagination of the political and legal world. Sovereignty constitutes the world as we know it in the sense that it provides us with the possibility of distinguishing between internal and external politics, national, and international polities. Sovereignty is a frame, which cannot be given an a priori meaning outside the context of its articulation. It is an interpretive concept, just as equality and liberty, a concept that is subject to interpretation and hence contestation (*Tanja Aalberts and Wouter Werner; Rebecca Adler-Nissen*). But does the status of sovereignty as an *interpretative* concept mean that sovereignty is an empty box, an *essentially contested* concept (Sarooshi 2004)?

Some of the chapters (e.g. *Tanja Aalberts and Wouter Werner*), point to a lack of foundation for sovereignty, which shares the image of an empty space where society has to understand itself with another related and contested concept, democracy (Lefort 1986). The site, *locus*, of power is in principle empty. Politics is therefore continuous, but in the end constitutes futile attempts to take the place of the absolutist King and fill out the space where totalitarian ideologies placed the unity of the people. Following Claude Lefort, the site of power can no longer belong to anyone; it is and should be impersonal. According to this line of thinking, the "sovereign people" is an abstraction and democratic sovereignty is based on a paradoxical uncertainty about its own foundation. If sovereignty is built on this presence of an absence, then all essentialist ideas about sovereignty are problematic. Drawing on such insights and taking them further, Chantal Mouffe has argued that democracy must then be seen as the constitutional site where antagonisms or choices with no rational solution will be played out (Mouffe 1999). As a claim to authority, sovereignty in modern democracy will be a claim, the content of which has to be filled out through debates and struggles. As such, sovereignty constitutes an unresolved basis for authority in the forms of power, law, and knowledge.

Other contributions (*Neil Walker; Jens Bartelson*) take the opposite position. According to Walker, sovereignty is not empty; it is a metaphysical understanding of political presence and organization. By treating it simply as a speech-act and analyzing only what sovereignty *does*, not what it *is* or what it *should be*, the "real" problem of sovereignty is confiscated; the normative questions about how sovereignty should be exercised are not asked. In this sense, there seems to be a trade-off between on the one hand, philosophical debates on sovereignty, its constitutive dimension and on the other hand, more applied studies of the function of sovereignty in world politics. Since the meaning of sovereignty as a foundational institution is contested, it follows that the determination of the functions of sovereignty cannot be distinguished from the values it entails and from the normative discussion in which it is embedded (Besson 2004). This would warrant a double research strategy of both analysis and critique. As Bartelson elucidates, however, any critical analysis of the foundational structures of sovereignty tends to presuppose and institutionalize the very object of critique. To investigate sovereignty, we inevitably start by imposing a set of definite meanings to the concept.

Although each of these approaches undoubtedly has merit, the reciprocal critique interestingly points to a mutual difficulty in writing, and even thinking, beyond sovereignty. Under the former, claims to sovereignty may be increasingly stretched in regards to whom and what is claimed for sovereignty. Yet, the question remains whether the epistemic starting point for such claims can ever make sense outside a reference to existing power structures and thus a statist framework. Even claims to power and the legitimate use of force by nonstate actors, seen by many as a key challenge to state sovereignty, has a way of referring back to the state as the necessary starting point for speaking about these issues (*Anna Leander*). Under the latter approach, a critical stance may be launched toward the foundational core of the concept, yet in search for the Archimedean point necessary to turn around the existing, a fixture of meaning is almost inevitably presupposed. Thus, while the legal framework of human and refugee rights are borne by an underlying idea to move beyond the state as the sole holder of entitlements in the international arena, its institutionalization and formulation is solidly reaffirming state sovereignty and seemingly anachronistic principles of territoriality (*Thomas Gammeltoft-Hansen*).

In conclusion, it seems difficult to move beyond sovereignty at the foundational level. Unlike some of the more radical and critical theories of international law and politics, none of the contributions in the present volume suggest that we should or can abandon sovereignty altogether. In fact, such attempts only seem to reproduce the fundamental importance of sovereignty; as Spiermann pointedly puts it "[...] nobody would care about striking off an irrelevant word" (*Ole Spiermann*).

Sovereignty as Legal and Political Authority

The second layer has sovereignty conceived as authority or the rules regulating all sovereignty games. We may define these rules in both legal and political terms, as norms prescribed by sovereignty or as an institutionalization of political power. In political terms, sovereignty at this level signifies the political structures projecting power within and between boundaries. In legal terms, sovereignty is the ordering principle; it points toward the state as the source of political authority and sets out its prerogatives, internally and externally. At the most general level, this ordering institution spell out the principle to allow ab-solute, meaning un-bound, power for the polity to command within the commonwealth, and externally principles for the mutual recognition of the polity qua polity (N. Walker 2003). In the spheres of international law and politics these manifest themselves in a multitude of explicit and implicit rules for the entitlement and constraints of sovereigns, be it the coordinating principle of nonintervention or the cooperative doctrine of *pacta sunt servanda*—international agreement must be respected. Although the different disciplines of law and politics may express these rules in slightly different languages, they point to the same understanding of sovereignty as an institution setting out and distributing authority.

A particular issue at this level of analysis concerns the role of the state and the extent to which sovereignty gives primacy to this particular type of polity. As we have seen in the preceding chapters new players are emerging in the sovereignty games, be it private organizations or supranational institutions such as the EU. This may challenge the ability of states to effectuate their monopoly of power; however, it does necessarily imply a fundamental shift in the game rules. As sovereignty is not about the actual control, but rather the claimed authority, new players on the world stage do not automatically impact on the state's status as sovereign. As Glencross demonstrates, current strategies to sideline sovereignty claims by member states in the context of the EU have failed to do anything but reinforce their importance (*Andrew Glencross*). Similarly, despite the multiplication of nonstate actors on the world scene, international law remains a tool of coordination and cooperation, rather than the subordination or disintegration, of equal sovereignties. If there is change at the level of authority because of new actors it is taking more subtle guises—those looking down from the state might point to the increasing possibilities of individual representation before international courts, those looking up to the accession of supranational organizations to instruments like the European Convention on Human Rights.

The second issue relates to the possibility of game rules to change as a consequence of new practices. In some cases, international law has adapted quite rapidly to the "new world order" (Held, McGrew, Goldblatt, and Perraton 1999, 70). Horizontally, the principle of nonintervention, establishing the right for states to conduct their affairs without outside interference, is challenged both by the prevalence of so-called humanitarian interventions and by practices whereby states "invite" intervention in otherwise domestic issues, such as when handing over sovereign competence in particular policy areas to supranational organizations. Importantly, however, the principle of nonintervention is not simply abandoned but rather complemented by what Georg Sørensen calls "regulated intervention" to which new rules clearly apply (2004, 115). International law is still concerned with the protection of sovereignty in these cases, but the object of protection is less the power base of the dictator or the apparatus of a totalitarian political order, but the state as an international law subject and the continuing capacity of a population freely to express and affect choices about the identities and policies of its governors (Sarooshi 2004). Importantly, authority and popular democracy is still claimed and exercised in terms of sovereignty, there is no "end of sovereignty," but international law and the double structure of sovereignty provides a framework for shifts in its particular meaning and regulatory effects (Spiermann 1995).

Further, not all developments necessarily spawn new game rules. As dealt with in several of the preceding chapters, the current-day framework of international exchanges is not entirely governed by international law or political principles. International legal and political rules are inherently backward looking: they reflect needs as they arose in games played in the past. Today, some economic, legal, and political practices are not subject to any international regulation and hence escape the control of states as well as international organizations. This may give rise to different strategies in the sovereignty games. One such strategy may be to intentionally suppress development of new rules to reassert power in the regulatory lacunas that emerge as new practices develop (*Thomas Gammeltoft-Hansen*). Another strategy could be to retreat from the very ambition of establishing solid game rules for all areas of international life. Hence, many seem to have accepted the proposition that it is utterly unrealistic to expect monetary and financial markets to be regulated to the extent that a single state or a group of states actually control what goes on (*Christoph Herrmann*).

This leads us to our third consideration, namely the extent to which seeming changes at the level of authority and rules are fixed or fluid. As pointed out earlier, many of the current moves in the sovereignty game imply that sovereignty is exercised outside its "normal" sites. These moves have usually been addressed in terms of globalization and transnational interactions thereby hiding their fundamental strategic character. However, many of these moves are state-driven, and when states delegate the exercise of certain policies to international organizations or private actors, they do not give away sovereignty, but they transfer political and legal control. Hence, from a legal point of view it is contestable whether the transfer of authority over monetary policy to, for instance, the European Central Bank is definitive (*Rebecca Adler-Nissen*). However, de facto, transfer of competencies can be definitive in that the legal right is only hypothetic. To withdraw from the Euro zone and recapture economic sovereignty may be legally imaginable, but politically and economically out of the question (*Christoph Herrmann*). We would argue that much of the existing literature on globalization and cosmopolitanism fails to come to terms with this dynamic dimension of sovereignty and ignores that concrete strategic actors and moves are often behind the instrumentalization of sovereignty.

What emerges is an opportunity for bargaining sovereign authority among the players, which is increasingly exploited. Climbing up or down the ladder of authority between national, regional, and global levels, or moving sideways across state borders, are tactical maneuvers in sovereignty games. These vertical and horizontal moves make it more difficult to understand and monitor both the content and the consequences of state decisions. This may be exactly the idea behind the moves when state executives delegate authority to supranational organizations or private companies and hence blur the question of responsibility, yet often remaining in de facto control (*Anna Leander*). This dispersion of sites where sovereignty is exercised is an important part of contemporary sovereignty games. The way politics may be disguised as law, and hence depoliticize the moves in these sovereignty games points to the third level of sovereignty—practice—as a privileged site for the study of sovereignty games.

Sovereignty as Practice

The most visible layer of sovereignty is found in the social, legal, and political practices. Here, sovereignty is practiced by real-life actors from immigration officials to constitutional monarchs in everyday situations. This moves us from the idea of sovereignty as an ontological ground for power and order and its institution as political and legal authority to the more tentative claims and discourses of sovereignty that are performed by individuals, state representatives, and private companies on a day-to-day basis. On this layer, the academic debates take a sociological turn oriented toward the interpretation of *praxis*, rituals, and symbols. This daily face of sovereignty comes up when competing sovereign claims are made as part of struggles over power, identity, and law. Campaigns by secession movements in the Basques regions and Greenland are example of such sovereign practices where the conflicts over political authority and the rightful expression of a collective political will are at stake. Here, sovereignty is linked to the way people conceive of legitimate power. The practical, everyday use of concepts such as "state" and "sovereignty" derive their meaning from the specific context and the commonsense ideas and knowledge of those participating in the practice (Wight 2006, 270). In this sense, practitioners operate within a certain scope or knowledge of the epistemic core and authority rules defined at the deeper layers. Yet, while the international lawyer may pay homage to a broad range of adjudicative history, the ongoing application will be a balancing act to suit the case at hand and thus in itself holds the potential of renewal. In this way, concrete games may have an effect on the "deeper" layers of sovereignty, its regulative functions and on a longer term, though in our view unlikely, perhaps even shake sovereignty as the foundational institution of international relations. We shall return to this idea in the last section of this chapter.

In the sovereignty games, we see how state authorities play and manipulate with ideas about legitimate authority and power. The quality of the relationship between individuals and the state can be severely affected by the transfer of power to unaccountable and seemingly distant international institutions such as the European institutions in Brussels or private security companies in North Carolina. We can see the impact of changes in legislative authority and the relationship between domestic populations and their political representatives in the resurgence of demands for referenda to decide on important changes to the European cooperation project. The French and Dutch *"non"* and *"nee"* to the Constitutional Treaty of the EU in 2005 were at first sight the exercise of a sovereign will, but they also signified a crisis of democracy. Despite the rejection of the Constitutional Treaty, the treaty may be surviving almost untouched with the new and less controversial label of the Lisbon Treaty. To some observers this expresses that the principle of popular sovereignty is sabotaged because the "will" of the political authority is imposed on the people (Baudrillard 2005). To others, contemporary demands for referenda do not represent so much the reassertion of the sovereign power of member states on the integration process; rather, it is a lack of faith with national processes of representations and accountability that is creating the demands for referenda. In any event, the strategic renegotiations of democracy by state executives and supranational bureaucracies represent an elusion of what many would take to be an expression of the voice of the sovereign people.

Such strategic moves may disturb commonsense understandings of sovereignty and its legitimate exercise and raise the question of responsibility. Who are to be rendered accountable when sovereignty is played around? Take the example of the outsourcing of military tasks—is it the private military company or the outsourcing state who is responsible if civilians are killed during a mission? Or is it simply naïve to talk of responsibilities because of the rudimentary character of international law? To render private military actors directly accountable under international law would require a change in the rules that constitute the sovereignty game. Indeed, what is often suggested instead is soft law, codes of conducts, and transparent legal contract between states and companies, which would supplement the original model of sovereignty that characterized the nation-state (*Anna Leander*). By codifying this grey zone of state-private action, the rules of the game are being rewritten. This is the official reason for why states have so far avoided codifying private-military actor responsibilities in conventions. However, as Aalberts and Werner suggest, perhaps the real reason is rather that intervening states prefer to hide behind the stretched principle of sovereignty (and legitimate self-defense) to avoid responsibility?

Each time the norms are modified or developed, actors adapt their strategies. New holes in the international legal regime will be found. The interrelatedness between the philosophical, legal, political, and social dimensions of sovereignty suggests that despite decades of attempts to bring order and discipline into the study of sovereignty, we must accept that there is a limit to this order.

The Dynamic Structure of Sovereignty Games: Layer by Layer

In the beginning of this book, we wondered about the transformative potential in the sovereignty games. Is world politics changing to a degree that sovereignty is seriously challenged as the metaframe for understanding politics and law? Put differently, how much can sovereignty change without becoming something else? Inevitably, the shape of things to come is hazy, but it is possible to detect the contours of the immediate to medium-term landscape. Our argument is that changes in the way sovereignty games are played may impact the organization of political and legal authority, which again may affect the epistemic core of sovereignty.

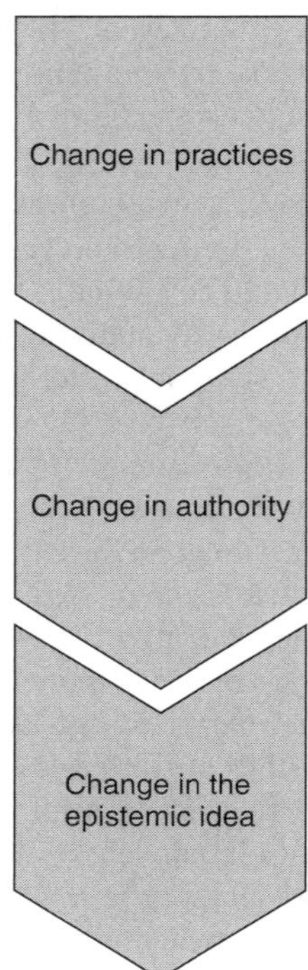

Figure 11.1   Three layers of sovereignty

There is no automacity to these shifts, but changes at one layer can splash down to the next. The deeper the layer, the more stabilized is the meaning of sovereignty (figure 11.1).

Change in *practices* related to sovereignty occurs all the time in the form of more or less strategic moves. Sometimes these practices force us to think of authority in new ways. The outsourcing of military actions, interventions in failed states, and the European integration process may lead to change in the *authority* structure. Domestically, changing social practices involves asking new questions about which form of political rule is legitimate and how popular sovereignty should be organized. Internationally, new ways of exercising authority relate to disputes on controversial phenomena such as neoimperialism, military interventions, and global hierarchies. If new practices lead to a rethinking of sovereignty as authority, they may also in the end affect the deepest level of sovereignty, sovereignty as an *epistemic* idea. This is indirectly what Neil Walker refers to with the concept of "late sovereignty" (N. Walker 2003). Walker describes a fundamental shift in the way we think of sovereignty, a new condition, just as "late modernity," from where the world can never be the same again.

However, there is a real disagreement as to both the transformative potential and the assessment of our current stage. Some argue that we already live in a "post-Westphalian order" (Albert, Jacobson, and Lapid. 2001). The claim is often made as a rejection of the essentialist positions, both in the *traditionalist* version in which sovereignty remains an absolute and indivisible property—either the state has sovereignty or it does not (Sørensen 2004, 104)—and in the increasingly popular *relativist* positions, where sovereignty is cut up and measured along its proclaimed constituent parts (Krasner 1999). Further, little agreement exists as to what shall be the successor of sovereignty. On one end of the spectrum, cosmopolitans argue that new rules should apply in new types of responsibilities and rights on new actors in the evolving word community and future world order (Held 2002). The EU and EU law has in this perspective been seen as a cosmopolitan laboratory for a new polycentric system of rights and duties, which takes the individual, rather than the state, as its point of departure (Habermas 1998; Morgan 2005, 3). On the other end of the spectrum, but equally dissatisfied, critical theorists argue that imperialism or "Empire" is the shape of the future world system and sovereignty has to be understood accordingly and critically. Hence, while the Westphalian definition of sovereignty may have provided for equality among Western states, it does not extend the same status to the non-Western world (Schmitt 2006; Hardt and Negri 2000, 70). Sovereignty in this context acts to reinforce inequality between the developed and developing world. Inequality, in turn, provides a justification for the interference, exploitation, or conquest of the "other" by the West to fulfill a multitude of missions—exploitation of resources for industrialization, civilizing the uncivilized, and so on (Grovogui 2002). Instead of viewing the development of international law as providing order among sovereign equals, it is seen as a tool used by the West to embed structural inequality into the international system (Anghie 2005). Sovereignty becomes a mere cover for the real thing: imperialism.

However, in our view, many of these alternative approaches fail to grasp the epistemic and symbolic dimensions of sovereignty. Sovereignty is a powerful institution and *instituting* phenomenon, it may be instrumentalized, but it is not simply an empty shell. What the analysis of the previous chapters all seem to suggest is that while sovereignty games are abundant at the level of practices and may result in a number of changes at the regulatory layer and in the emergence of new international legal and political norms, transition is much harder to imagine to the foundational or epistemic layer.

As R.B.J. Walker has aptly put it,

> State sovereignty works because it has come to seem to be simply there, out in the world, demarcating the national orders of here and there. But the lessons that theorists of international relations have consistently refused to learn since Hobbes is that sovereignty is never simply there. And what was never simply there can never simply disappear. (1995, 322)

In this sense those proclaiming the end of sovereignty seem to fall prey to the same reductionism as the essentialists to whom they react. While it is correct that new moves, players and even game rules may substantially alter how the game is being played, sovereignty, strangely enough, remains largely intact as "the only game in town" (Krasner 2004b, 1077). On this basis we suggest to move beyond both the essentialist and the post-Westphalian trench wars in search of an understanding of sovereignty that spends less time pondering what sovereignty "really" is, but instead looks at what functions sovereignty serves in our contemporary legal and political lives. It is in this sense that the framework of sovereignty games might prove useful.

This is not to say that sovereignty games may not result in wide ranging and important transformations in the intertwined realm of international law and world politics. First of all, horizontal shifts have seen the emergence of new players and new locations. Nonstate actors are increasingly taking over tasks the state will not or cannot engage in, from illegal groups, over private military companies, to international organizations. These practices have been situated within a continuum of legitimacy, "ranging from tranquil conviviality to open challenges of state sovereignty" (Blom-Hansen and Stepputat 2006, 306). States may maintain international presence and the machinery and ideology to sustain this. But as pointed out by Leander, the nonstate world may be instrumental to the state authorities who delegate certain tasks and policies to for instance private companies, which occupy strategic positions between state institutions and the population.

The horizontal shifts in sovereignty do not only cover offshore interrogation centers or migration control on the high seas, but also a virtual and vertical extension ranging from the Internet to outer space. Online communities, such as the growing game world of Second Life, do hold a potential to challenge the ordering principle of sovereign territoriality. The World Wide Web represents an area where ideas of world community and extreme individualism are blossoming; here the state is only one among other players. However, it would be mistaken to suppose that there are white spots on the map where the state has not, or will not seek to, control—be it Antarctica, planet Mars, or the Internet. Treaties between state parties regulate their actions on and in relation to Antarctica as well as Mars. Chinese authorities have introduced scores of regulations, closed Internet cafés and blocked e-mails, search engines, foreign news, and politically sensitive Web sites. There may be technical difficulties in this, but the state has so far been able to catch up with nonstate inventions that challenge its authority. New representations of sovereignty will present themselves as new actors, rules, and moves—ready and available codes for deciphering the world. Yet, to understand these evolving forms of sovereignty requires us to think out of the state box and examine some of the paradoxes in the way sovereignty games are played out (Weldes 1999).

On the vertical dimension, state governments and institutions provide a clear limit to how dramatic the changes caused by sovereignty games will be. States are still eager to limit and control the expansion of the competencies of international and regional organizations. In the EU, more tasks will be transferred to the supranational level and this may lead to a redefinition of what is implied as responsibilities lying under state authority in the sense of who does what, when, and how. This may create legitimacy deficits as authority is moved out of the state, and areas traditionally important for the domestic conception of national interest are depoliticized. In the current multispeed integration process, Europe is characterized by a sovereignty surplus in the sense that many conflicting sovereignty claims are made at the same time. Judging from these competing attempts of claiming ultimate authority, neither the state nor the EU comes out as a winner (Goetschel 2007).

Ultimately, our reading of sovereignty could be labeled *neoclassical*, because contrary to much of the existing literature, we do not claim to study a post-sovereign order. Instead, a central proposition in this book has been that sovereignty plays a genuine part in the current changes of legal and political practices in international relations. Sovereignty is part of, not external to, processes of globalization and Europeanization. It is the sovereignty games, the instrumentalization of sovereignty, that give much of world politics its dynamic quality. Sovereignty is constitutive of both international relations and international law, but when sovereignty games are played out and new practices are invented, the tensions between these realms and the deeper meanings of sovereignty come to the fore and affect our world imaginaries. Understanding these imaginaries demands the backward journey of continually probing the practices, principles, and epistemic core of the concept around which we organize both law and politics.

References

Aalberts, Tanja E. 2004. The Sovereignty Game States Play: (Quasi-)States in the International Order. *International Journal for the Semiotics of Law* 17 (2): 245–257.

———. 2006. Sovereignty as Discipline. Paper presented at the 31st Annual BISA Conference, Cork, December 18–20, 2006.

Abrahamsen, Rita, and Michael C. Williams. 2006a. *The Globalization of Private Security: Country Report Nigeria.* Aberystwyth: University of Wales.

———. 2006b. *The Globalization of Private Security: Country Report Sierra Leone.* Aberystwyth: University of Wales.

Adler-Nissen, Rebecca. 2008a. Behind the Scenes of Differentiated Integration: Circumventing National Opt-Outs in Justice and Home Affairs. *Journal of European Public Policy,* forthcoming.

———. 2008b. The Diplomacy of Opting Out: A Bourdieudian Approach to National Integration Strategies. *Journal of Common Market Studies* 46 (2): 663–684.

Agamben, Giorgio. 1998a. *Homo Sacer: Sovereign Power and Bare Life.* Stanford: Stanford University Press.

———. 1998b. *Potentialities: Collected Essays in Philosophy.* Stanford: Stanford University Press.

Agnew, John. 2005. Sovereignty Regimes: Territoriality and State Authority in Contemporary World Politics. *Annals of the Association of American Geographers* 95 (2): 437–461.

Akeh, J.M. Migai. 2007. *Breaking the Cartel of Power: Democracy, Public Law Values, and the Governance of Privatization in the Weak State in Africa.* Unpublished manuscript. Nairobi.

Albert, Mathias, David Jacobson, and Yosef Lapid, eds. 2001. *Identities, Borders, Orders: Rethinking International Relations Theory.* Minneapolis: University of Minnesota Press.

Altig, David and Ed Nosal. 2005. Dollarization—What's in It for the Issuing Country. *Current Developments in Monetary and Financial Law* 3: 807–816.

Andersen, Svein and Tom Burns. 1996. The European Union and the Erosion of Parliamentary Democracy: A Study of Post-Parliamentary Governance. In *The European Union: How Democratic Is It?,* ed. Svein Andersen and Kjell Eliassen, 227–252. London: Sage.

Andersen, Stine and Andrew Glencross. 2007. Pre-Empting the Court: Member State Expectations, Political Oversight and the Nexus of Law and Politics in the EU. Paper presented at the European Union Studies Association Biennial Conference, May 17–19, in Montreal, Canada.

Anghie, Anthony. 2005. *Imperialism, Sovereignty and the Making of International Law.* Cambridge: Cambridge University Press.

Antonowicz, Lech. 1966–1967. Definition of State in International Law. *Polish Yearbook of International Law* 1: 195–207.

Anzilotti, Dionisio. 1958. *Corso di Diritto Internazionale.* 4th edition. Padova: Cedam.

Ashley, Richard K. 1987. The Geopolitics of Geopolitical Space: Towards a Critical Social Theory of International Politics. *Alternatives* 12 (2): 403–434.

———. 1995. The Powers of Anarchy: Theory, Sovereignty, and the Domestication of Global Life. In *International Theory: Critical Investigations,* ed. James Der Derian, 94–128. Basingstoke: Macmillan.

Assemblée Nationale, France. 2003. *Loi n° 2003–340 du 14 avril 2003 relatif à la répression de l'activité de mercenaire.* France: Assemblée Nationale.

Auer, Andreas. 2007. National Referendums in the Process of European Integration: Time for a Change. In *The European Constitution and National Constitutions: Ratification and Beyond,* ed. Anneli Albi and Jacques Ziller, 261–272. The Hague: Kluwer Law International.

Austin, J.L. 1961. *Philosophical Papers.* Oxford: Oxford University Press.

Avant, Deborah. 2005. *The Market for Force: The Consequences of Privatizing Security.* Cambridge: Cambridge University Press.

Ayoob, Mohammed. 2002. *Humanitarian Intervention and State Sovereignty. International Journal of Human Rights* 6 (1): 81–102.

Baliño, Tomás. 2003. Dollarization: A Primer. *Current Developments in Monetary and Financial Law* 2: 613–628.

Barnard, Catherine. 2000. Flexibility and the Social Policy. In *Constitutional Change in the EU: From Uniformity to Flexibility?,* ed. Gráinne de Búrca and Joanne Scott, 197–218. Oxford: Hart.

Barnes, Richard. 2004. Refugee Law at Sea. *International and Comparative Law Quarterly* 53 (1): 47–77.

Bartelson, Jens. 1995. *A Genealogy of Sovereignty.* Cambridge: Cambridge University Press.

———. 2006. The Concept of Sovereignty Revisited. *European Journal of International Law* 17: 463–474.

———. 2007. Philosophy and History in the Study of Political Thought. *Journal of the Philosophy of History* 1 (1): 101–124.

Bartolini, Stefano. 2005. *Restructuring Europe: Centre Formation, System Building and Political Structuring between the Nation-State and the European Union.* Oxford: Oxford University Press.

———. 2006. Should the Union Be Politicized? Prospects and Risks. In *Politics: The Right or the Wrong Sort of Medicine for the EU?,* ed. Simon Hix and Stefano Bartolini, 29–50. Brussels: Notre Europe Policy Paper, no. 19.

Bassett, Thomas J. 2003. Dangerous Pursuits: Hunter Associations (Donzo ton) and National Politics in Cote D'Ivoire Africa. *Journal of the International African Institute* 73 (1): 1–30.

Baty, Thomas. 1934. Can an Anarchy be a State? *American Journal of International Law* 28 (3): 444–455.

Baudrillard, Jean. 2005. Holy Europe. *New Left Review* 33 (May–June): 24–25.

Bayart, Jean François, Stephen Ellis, and Béatrice Hibou. 1997. *La criminalisation de l'Etat en Afrique.* Paris: Editions Complexe.

Beaulac, Stéphane. 2004. *The Power of Language in the Making of International Law: The Word Sovereignty in Bodin and Vattel and the Myth of Westphalia.* Leiden: Martinus Nijhoff.

Benn, Stanley I. 1969. The Uses of "Sovereignty." In *In Defense of Sovereignty*, ed. W.J. Stankiewicz, 67–85. London: Oxford University Press.

Bernanke, Ben. 2005. Monetary Policy in a World of Mobile Capital. *Cato Journal* 25 (1): 1–12.

Besson, Sandra. 2004. Sovereignty in Conflict. *European Integration online Chapters (EIoP)* 8 (15): http://eiop.or.at/eiop/pdf/2004–015.pdf. (accessed December 17, 2007).

Bickerton, Christopher, Philip Cunliffe, and Alexander Gourevitch, eds. 2006. *Politics without Sovereignty: A Critique of Contemporary International Relations.* London: Palgrave.

Biersteker, Thomas J. and Cynthia Weber, eds. 1996a. *State Sovereignty as a Social Construct.* Cambridge: Cambridge University Press.

———. 1996b. The Social Construction of State Sovereignty. In *State Sovereignty as a Social Construct*, ed. Thomas J. Biersteker and Cynthia Weber, 1–21. Cambridge: Cambridge University Press.

Bigo, Didier. 2000. When Two Become One: Internal and External Securitisations in Europe. In *International Relations Theory and the Politics of European Integration. Power, Security and Community*, ed. Morten Kelstrup and Michael Williams. 171–204. London and New York: Routledge.

Bigwood, Jeremy. 2001. DynCorp in Colombia: Outsourcing the Drug War. *www. corporatewatch.org*, March 23.

Bishai, Linda. 2004. Liberal Empire. *Journal of International Relations and Development* 7 (1): 48–72.

Bislev, Sven, Hans Krause Hansen, and Dorte Salskov-Iversen. 2002. The Global Diffusion of Managerialism: Transnational Discourse Communities at Work. *Global Society* 16 (2): 199–212.

Blom-Hansen, Thomas and Finn Stepputat. 2006. Sovereignty Revisited. *Annual Review of Anthropology* 35: 295–315.

Bodin, Jean. 1977 [1583]. *Les six livres de la République.* Aalen: Scientia.

Börzel, Tanja. 2005. Mind the Gap! European Integration between Level and Scope. *Journal of European Public Policy* 12 (2): 217–236.

Boucher, David. 2005. The Rule of Law in the Modern European State. *European Journal of Political Theory* 4 (1): 89–107.

Bourdieu, Pierre. 1992. *Language and Symbolic Power.* Cambridge: Polity.

Brauer, Jürgen. 1998. An Economic Perspective on Mercenaries: Military Companies and the Privatisation of Force. *Cambridge Review of International Affairs* 13 (1): 130–146.

Brownlie, Ian. 1991. *International Law and the Use of Force by States*. Oxford: Clarendon.

Busch, Andreas. 2003. Die politische Ökonomie der Inflation. In *Politische Ökonomie*, ed. Herbert Obinger, Uwe Wagschal, and Bernhard Kittel, 175–197. Opladen: Leske und Budrich.

Buur, Lars. 2006. Reordering Society: Vigilantism and Sovereign Expressions in Port Elizabeth's Townships. *Development and Change* 37 (4): 735–757.

Buur, Lars, Steffen Jensen, and Finn Stepputat, eds. 2007. *The Security-Development Nexus*. Capetown: HSRC Press.

Buzan, Barry, Ole Wæver, and Jaap De Wilde. 1998. *Security: A New Framework for Analysis*. Boulder, CO: Lynne Rienner.

Byers, Michael. 2002. Terrorism, the Use of Force and International Law after 11 September. *International and Comparative Law Quarterly* 51 (2): 401–414.

Camilleri, Joseph A. and Jim Falk. 1992. *The End of Sovereignty? The Politics of a Shrinking and Fragmenting World*. Aldershot: Edward Elgard.

Cassesse, Antonio. 1989. The International Community's "Legal" Response to Terrorism. *International and Comparative Law Quarterly* 38 (3): 589–608.

Chevrier, Yves. 2004. Postface: Privatisation and the Historical Paths of the Political. In *Privatizing the State*, ed. Béatrice Hibou, 241–258. New York: Columbia University Press.

Chown, John. 2003. *A History of Monetary Unions*. London: Routledge.

Church, Clive and David Phinnemore. 2006. *Understanding the European Constitution: An Introduction to the EU's Constitutional Treaty*. London: Routledge.

Claes, Monica and Bruno de Witte. 1998. Report on the Netherlands. In *The European Court and National Courts—Doctrine and Jurisprudence. Legal Change in Its Social Context*, ed. Anne-Marie Slaughter, Anne Stone Sweet and Jospeh H.H. Weiler, 171–194. Oxford: Hart.

Clapham, Christopher. 1996. *Africa and the International System: The Politics of State Survival*. Cambridge: Cambridge University Press.

———. 1999. Sovereignty and the Third World State. *Political Studies* 47 (3): 522–537.

Clark, Ian. 1999. *Globalization and International Relations Theory*. Oxford: Oxford University Press.

Clark, William. 2005. *Petrodollar Warfare: Oil, Iraq and the Future of the Dollar*. Gabriola Island: New Society.

Cohen, Benjamin. 1999. The New Geography of Money. In *Nation-States and Money*, ed. Emily Gilbert and Eric Helleiner, 121–138. London: Routledge.

Cohen, Jean L. 2004. Whose Sovereignty? Empire versus International Law. *Ethics and International Affairs* 18 (3): 1–24.

Committee on Oversight and Government Reform. 2007. Hearing: Private Security Contracting in Iraq and Afghanistan. October 2.

Coomans, Fons, and Menno T. Kamminga, eds. 2004. *Extraterritorial Application of Human Rights Treaties*. Antwerp: Intersentia.

Corden, Warner X. 2002. *Too Sensational: On the Choice of Exchange Rate Regimes*. Cambridge: MIT Press.

Coultrap, John. 1999. From Parliamentarism to Pluralism: Models of Democracy and the European Union's "Democratic Deficit." *Journal of Theoretical Politics* 11 (1): 107–135.

Crawford, James. 2006. *The Creation of States in International Law.* Oxford: Clarendon.

Curtin, Dierdre. 1993. The Constitutional Structure of the Union: A Europe of Bits and Pieces. *Common Market Law Review* 30 (1): 17–69.

Dahl, Robert. 2001. *How Democratic Is the American Constitution?* New Haven, CT: Yale University Press.

de Burca, Gráinne. 2003. Sovereignty and the Supremacy Doctrine of the European Court of Justice. In *Sovereignty in Transition,* ed. Neil Walker, 449–460. Oxford: Hart.

de la Grotte, Michel. 1929. Les Affaires Traitées par la Cour Permanente de Justice Internationale Pendant la Periode 1926–1928. *Revue de Droit International et de Legislation Comparée* 10: 387.

de Witte, Bruno. 1995. Sovereignty and European Integration: The Weight of Legal Tradition. *Maastricht Journal of European and Comparative Law* 2: 145–173.

———. 2002. Anticipating the Institutional Consequences of Expanded Membership of the European Union. *International Political Science Review* 23 (3): 235–248.

———. 2004a. The Process of Ratification of the Constitutional Treaty and the Crisis Options: A Legal Perspective. European University Institute Working Paper, 04/16.

———. 2004b. Treaty Revision in the European Union: Constitutional Change through International Law. *Netherlands Yearbook of International Law* 35: 51–84.

Danish Institute for International Studies. 2008. *De danske forbehold over for Den Europæiske Union. Udviklingen siden 2000,* Copenhagen: DIIS.

Dean, Mitchell. 1999. *Governmentality, Power and Rule in Modern Society.* London: Sage.

Dehousse, Renaud. 1994. Community Competences: Are There Limits to Growth? In *Europe after Maastricht. An Ever Closer Union?* ed. Renaud Dehousse, 103–125. Munich: Beck.

———. 2005. We the States: Why the Anti-Federalists Won. In *With Us or against US? European Trends in American Perspective,* ed. Nicolas Jabko and Craig Parsons, 105–121. New York: Oxford University Press.

———. 2006. The Unmaking of a Constitution: Lessons from the European Referenda. *Constellations* 13 (2): 151–164.

Delcourt, Barbara. 2006. Pre-emptive Action in Iraq: Muddling Sovereignty and Intervention? *Global Society* 20 (1): 47–67.

Derlugian, Georgi. 2005. *Bourdieu's Secret Admirer in the Caucasus: A World System Biography.* Chicago: University of Chicago Press.

Deutsche Bundesbank. 2007. *Devisenkursstatistik Februar 2007.* http://www.bundesbank.de/download/volkswirtschaft/devisenkursstatistik/2007/devisenkursstatistik022007.pdf (accessed July 17, 2008).

Didion, Joan. 2006. Cheney: The Fatal Touch. *New York Review of Books* 53 (15).

Dinstein, Y. 2003. 'Ius ad Bellum Aspects of the "War on Terrorism." In *Terrorism and the Military*, ed. W.P. Heere, 13–21. The Hague: T.M.C. Asser Institute.

Donahue, John and Mark Pollack. 2001. Centralization and Its Discontents: The Rhythms of Federalism in the United States and the European Union. In *The Federal Vision: Legitimacy and Levels of Governance in the United States and the European Union*, ed. Nicolaidis Kalypso and Robert Howse, 73–118. New York: Oxford University Press.

Donner, A.M. 1974. The Constitutional Powers of the Court of Justice of the European Communities. *Common Market Law Review* 11: 127.

Dorn, Nicholas and Michael Levi. 2007. European Private Security, Corporate Investigation and Military Services: Collective Security, Market Regulation and Structuring the Public Sphere. *Policing & Society* 17 (3): 213–238.

Doty, Roxanne Lynn. 1996. Sovereignty and the Nation: Constructing the Boundaries of National Identities. In *State Sovereignty as a Social Construct*, ed. Thomas J. Bierstecker and Cynthia Weber, 121–147, Cambridge: Cambridge University Press.

Duffield, Mark. 2001. *Global Governance and the New Wars: The Merging of Development and Security*. London and New York: Zed Books.

———. 2007. *Development, Security and Unending War: Governing the World of Peoples*. Oxford: Polity.

Dworkin, Ronald M. 1986. *Law's Empire*. London: Fontana.

Ehrenreich Brooks, Rosa. 2005. Failed States or the State as Failure? *University of Chicago Law Review* 71 (4): 1159–1196.

Eichengreen, Barry. 1994. *International Monetary Arrangements for the 21st Century*. Washington: Brookings Institution Press.

Elizalde, Hector. 2005. The International Monetary Fund and Current Account Convertibility. *Current Developments in Monetary and Financial Law* 4: 17–39.

Engström, Agneta. 2007. Ecuador: Oil and Militarized Corporate Terrorism. *Upside Down World*, November 14.

Erk, Jan. 2003. Federalism and Mass Media Policy in Germany. *Regional and Federal Studies* 13 (2): 107–127.

———. 2004. Austria: A Federation without Federalism. *Publius: The Journal of Federalism* 34 (1): 1–20.

Espersen, Ole, Frederik Harhoff, and Ole Spiermann. 2003. *Folkeret: De internationale retsforhold*. Copenhagen: Christian Ejlers' Forlag.

European Court of Justice. 2006. C-514/03 Commission v Spain: ECJ.

Fainaru, Steve. 2007a. For Abducted Guards, Iraq Wasn't about Money. *Washington Post*, September 30.

———. 2007b. Guards in Iraq Cite Frequent Shootings: Companies Seldom Report Incidents. *Washington Post*, October 3.

———. 2007c. Iraq Contractors Face Growing Parallel War. *Washington Post*, June 16.

———. 2007d. Where Military Rules Don't Apply. *Washington Post*, September 20.

Fainaru, Steve and Alec Klein. 2007. In Iraq, a Private Realm of Intelligence Gathering. *Washington Post*, July 1.

Falkner, Gerda, Miriam Hartlapp, Simone Leiber, and Oliver Treib. 2004. Non-Compliance with EU Directives in the Member States: Opposition through the Back Door? *West European Politics* 27 (3): 452–473.

Fastenrath, Ulrich. 1995. States, Extinction. In *Encyclopedia of Public International Law*, ed. R. Bernhardt, 669–672. Amsterdam: North Holland.

Ferguson, Roger. 2006. Monetary Credibility, Inflation, and Economic Growth. *Cato Journal* 26 (2): 223–230.

Finnis, John. 1980. *Natural Law and Natural Rights*. Oxford: Oxford University Press.

Fischer, Stanley. 1999. Capital Account Liberalization. *Current Developments in Monetary and Financial Law* 1: 1–6.

Foreign and Commonwealth Office. 2002. *Response of the Secretary of State for Foreign and Commonwealth Affairs to the Ninth Report of the Foreign Affairs Committee: Private Military Companies (session 2001–2002)*: http://www.fco.gov.uk/Files/kfile/cm5642.pdf. (accessed July 27, 2008).

———. 2004. Regime-Collisions: The Vain Search for Legal Unity in the Fragmentation of Global Law. *Michigan Journal of International Law* 25: 999–1045.

Fitzpatrick, J. 1996. Revitalizing the 1951 Refugee Convention. *Harvard Human Rights Journal* 9: 229–253.

Follesdal, Andreas and Simon Hix. 2005. Why There Is a Democratic Deficit in the EU: A Response to Majone and Moravcsik. *European Governance Papers* C-05-02: 1–27.

Foreign and Commonwealth Office. 2002. *Private Military Companies: Options for Regulation*. London: http://www.fco.gov.uk/Files/kfile/mercenaries,0.pdf. (accessed July 27, 2008).

Forster, Anthony. 2000. Britain. In *The Foreign Policies of European Union Member States*, ed. Ian Manners and Richard G. Whitman, 44–63. Manchester: Manchester University Press.

Forsyth, Murray. 1981. *Unions of States: The Theory and Practice of Confederation*. Leicester: Leicester University Press.

Forsythe, David P. 2000. *Human Rights in International Relations*. Cambridge: Cambridge University Press.

Foucault, Michel. 2004. *Sécurité, territoire, population. Cours au Collège de France (1977–1978)*. Paris: Gallimard, Seuil.

Franck, Thomas M. 1995. *Fairness in International Law and Institutions*. Clarendon Press: Oxford.

Fraser, N. 2005. Reframing Justice in a Globalizing World. *New Left Review* 36: 69–88.

Freeden, Michael. 2006. Ideology and Political Theory. *Journal of Political Ideologies* 11 (1): 3–22.

Frege, Gottlob. 1984a. On Concept and Object. In *Gottlob Frege: Collected Papers on Mathematics, Logic and Philosophy*, ed. Brian McGuinness, 182–194. Oxford: Basil Blackwell.

Frege, Gottlob. 1984b. On Sense and Meaning. In *Gottlob Frege: Collected Papers on Mathematics, Logic and Philosophy,* ed. Brian McGuinness, 157–177. Oxford: Basil Blackwell.

Friedmann, Wolfgang. 1964. *The Changing Structure of International Law.* London: Stevens & Sons.

Gamble, Andrew and Gavin Kelly. 2002. Britain and the EMU. In *European States and the Euro: Europeanization, Variation, and Convergence,* ed. Kenneth Dyson, 97–119. Oxford: Oxford University Press.

Gammeltoft-Hansen, Thomas. 2006. Outsourcing Migration Management: EU, Power, and the External Dimension of Asylum and Immigration Policy. DIIS Working Paper, 2006/1. Copenhagen: Danish Institute for International Studies.

———. 2008. The Extraterritorialisation of Asylum and the Advent of "Protection Lite." In *The International Politics of Immigration in Europe,* ed. Virginie Guiraudon. Cheltenham: Edward Elgar, forthcoming.

GAO. 2007. *Defense Budget: Trends in Operation and Maintenance Costs and Support Services Contracting.* Washington: United States Government Accountability Office.

Garrett, Geoffrey. 1995. From the Luxembourg Compromise to Codecision: Decision Making in the European Union. *Electoral Studies* 14 (3): 289–308.

Geddes, Andrew. 2005. Getting the Best of Both Worlds? Britain, the EU and Migration Policy. *International Affairs* 81 (4): 17–23.

Gianviti, François. 1999. The International Monetary Fund and the Liberalization of Capital Movements. *Current Developments in Monetary and Financial Law* 1: 7–16.

———. 2003. Liberalization of Capital Movements: A Possible Role for the IMF. *Current Developments in Monetary and Financial Law* 2: 217–231.

———. 2005a. Current Legal Aspects of Monetary Sovereignty. *Current Developments in Monetary and Financial Law* 4: 1–16.

———. 2005b. Use of a Foreign Currency under the IMF's Articles of Agreement. *Current Developments in Monetary and Financial Law* 3: 817.

Gifford, Chris. 2006. The Rise of Post-imperial Populism: The Case of Right-wing Euroscepticism in Britain. *European Journal of Political Research* 45 (4): 851–869.

Gil-Bazo, Maria-Teresa. 2006. The Practice of Mediterranean States in the Context of the European Union's Justice and Home Affairs External Dimension: The Safe Third Country Concept Revisited. *International Journal of Refugee Law* 18 (3–4): 571–600.

Gilbert, Emiliy and Eric Helleiner, eds. 1999. *Nation-States and Money.* London: Routledge.

Givens, Terri and Adam Luedtke. 2004. The Politics of European Union Immigration Policy: Institutions, Salience and Harmonisation. *Policy Studies Journal* 32 (1): 145–165.

Glencross, Andrew and Alexander H. Trechsel. 2007. First or Second Order Referendums? Understanding the Votes on the Constitutional Treaty in Four

Member States. Paper Presented at the European Consortium for Political Research General Conference, September 6–8, in Pisa, Italy.

Goetschel, Laurent. 2007. Continuities Within Change : The Background of Swiss Relations with Europe. In *Switzerland and the European Union: A Close, Contradictory and Misunderstood Relationship*, ed. Clive C. Church, 169–185. London and New York: Routledge.

Goldstein, Leslie. 2001. *Constituting Federal Sovereignty: The European Union in Comparative Context*. Baltimore, MD: Johns Hopkins University Press.

Goodman, John B. 1992. *Monetary Sovereignty: The Politics of Central Banking in Western Europe*. Ithaca, NY: Cornell University Press.

Goodman, Nelson. 1978. *Ways of Worldmaking*. Indianapolis: Hackett.

Goodman, Nelson and Willard V. Quine. 1947. Steps towards a Constructive Nominalism. *Journal of Symbolic Logic* 12 (4): 105–122.

Goodwin-Gill, Guy. 1996. *The Refugee in International Law*. Oxford: Clarendon.

Grant, Thomas D. 1999. Defining Statehood: The Montevideo Convention and Its Discontents. *Columbia Journal of Transitional Law* 37 (2): 403–457.

Greenfeld, Liah. 1992. *Nationalism: Five Roads to Modernity*. Cambridge, MA: Harvard University Press.

Grewe, Wilhelm G. 2000. *The Epochs of International Law*. Berlin: De Gruyter.

Grimm, Dieter. 2005. The Constitution in the Process of Denationalization. *Constellations* 12: 447–463.

Grovogui, Siba N. 2002. Regimes of Sovereignty: International Morality and the African Condition. *European Journal of International Relations* 6 (2): 315–338.

Gruson, Michael. 2003. Dollarization and Euroization. *Current Developments in Monetary and Financial Law* 2: 629–640.

Guillory, Major Michael E. 2001. Civilianizing the Force: Is the United States Crossing the Rubicon? *Air Force Law Review* 51: 111–142.

Guiraudon, Virginie. 2000. European Integration and Migration Policy: Vertical Policy-Making as Venue Shopping. *Journal of Common Market Studies* 38 (2): 251–271.

Habermas, Jürgen. 1996. The European Nation State. Its Achievements and Its Limitations: On the Past and Future of Sovereignty and Citizenship. *Ratio Juris*: 125–37.

———. 1998. *The Inclusion of the Other: Studies in Political Theory*. Cambridge: Polity.

———. 2001. Why Europe Needs a Constitution. *New Left Review* 11 (September-October): 5–26.

Hacking, Ian. 1999. *The Social Construction of What?* Cambridge, MA: Harvard University Press.

Hagan, Sean. 1999. The Design of the International Monetary Fund's Jurisdiction over Capital Movements. *Current Developments in Monetary and Financial Law* 1: 68–77.

Hamilton, Alexander, John Jay, and James Madison. 2003. *The Federalist*. Cambridge: Cambridge University Press.

Hanf, Dominik. 2001. Flexibility Clauses in the Founding Treaties, from Rome to Nice. In *The Many Faces of Differentiation in EU Law*, ed. Bruno de Witte, Dominik Hanf, and Ellen Voos, 3–26. New York: Intersentia.

Hansen, Lene. 2002. Sustaining Sovereignty: The Danish Approach to Europe. In *European Integration and National Identity: The Challenge of the Nordic States*, ed. Lene Hansen and Ole Wæver, 50–87. London: Routledge.

Hansen, Thomas Blom and Finn Stepputat. 2005. *Sovereign Bodies: Citizens, Migrants, and States in the Postcolonial World*. Princeton, NJ: Princeton University Press.

Hansen, Troels B. and Bruno Scholl. 2002. Europeanization and Domestic Parliamentary Adaptation—A Comparative Analysis of the Bundestag and the House of Commons. *European Integration online Chapters (EIoP)* 6, http:// eiop.or.at/eiop/texte/2002–015a.htm. (accessed December 17, 2007).

Hardt, Michael and Antonio Negri. 2000. *Empire*. Cambridge, MA: Harvard University Press.

Hart, Herbert L.A. 1994. *The Concept of Law*. 2nd edition. Oxford: Oxford University Press.

Hartley, Trevor C. 1999. *Constitutional Problems of the European Union*. Oxford: Hart.

Hathaway, James. 2005. *The Rights of Refugees under International Law*. Cambridge: Cambridge University Press.

Hayek, Friedrich. 1977. *Entnationalisierung des Geldes*. Tuebingen: Mohr.

Hayes-Renshaw, Fiona and Helen Wallace. 2006. *The Council of Ministers*. Basingstoke: Palgrave.

Heald, Suzette. 2007. Controlling Crime and Corruption from Below: Sungusungu in Kenya. *International Relations* 21 (4): 183–199.

Heaton, J. Ricou. 2005. Civilians at War: Reexamining the Status of Civilians Accompanying the Armed Forces. *Air Force Law Review* 57: 157–208.

Hedetoft, Ulf. 2000. The Interplay between Mass and Elite Attitudes to European Integration in Denmark. In *Denmark's Policy towards Europe after 1945: History, Theory and Option*, ed. Hans Branner and Morten Kelstrup, 282–304. Odense: Odense University Press.

Held, David. 2002. Law of States, Law of Peoples: Three Models of Sovereignty. *Legal Theory* 8 (1): 1–44.

———. 2004. *Global Covenant: The Social Democratic Alternative to the Washington Consensus*. Cambridge: Polity.

Held, David, Anthony McGrew, David Goldblatt, and Jonathan Perraton. 1999. *Global Transformations: Politics, Economics, and Culture*. Stanford: Stanford University Press.

Helleiner, Eric. 2003. *The Making of National Money: Territorial Currencies in Historical Perspective*. Ithaca, NY: Cornell University Press.

Henkin, Louis. 1995. *International Law: Politics and Values*.

———. 1999. That "S" Word: Sovereignty, and Globalization, and Human Rights, Et Cetera. *Fordham Law Review* 68 (1): 1–14.

Herdegen, Matthias. 1996. Der Wegfall effecktiver Staatgewalt im Völkerrecht: "The Failed State". In *Der Wegfall effectiver Staatsgewalt:*

"The Failed State" (The Breakdown of Effective Government), ed. Thürer, Daniel, Matthias Herdegen, and Gerhard Hohloch, 49–85. Heidelberg: C.F. Müller Verlag.

Hibou, Béatrice. 2004. From Privatising the Economy to Privatising the State: An Analysis of the Continual Formation of the State. In *Privatizing the State*, ed. Béatrice Hibou, 1–47. New York: Columbia University Press.

Hindess, Barry. 2004. Liberalism—What's in a Name? In *Global Governmentality: Governing International Spaces*, ed. Wendy Larner and Warner P. Walters, 23–39. London: Routledge.

Hinsley, Fancis H. 1969. The Concept of Sovereignty and Relations between States. In *In Defense of Sovereignty*, ed. W.J. Stankiewicz, 275–290. London: Oxford University Press.

Hix, Simon. 2006. Why the EU Needs (Left-Right) Politics? Policy Reform and Accountability are Impossible without It. In *Politics: The Right or the Wrong Sort of Medicine for the EU?* ed. Simon Hix and Stefano Bartolini, 1–28. Brussels: Notre Europe Policy Paper, no. 19.

———. 2007. *What's Wrong with the European Union and How to Fix It?* Oxford: Polity.

Hobson, John and J.C. Sharman. 2005. "The Enduring Place of Hierarchy in World Politics: Tracing the Social Logics of Hierarchy and Political Change," *European Journal of International Relations* 11 (1): 63–98.

Holsti, Kalevi J. 1996. *The State, War, and the State of War*. Cambridge: Cambridge University Press.

Hont, Istvan. 1994. Permanent Crisis of a Divided Mankind: The Contemporary Crisis of the Nation-State in Historical Perspective. *Political Studies* 42: 166–231.

Howarth, David. 2007. The Domestic Politics of British Policy on the Euro. *Journal of European Integration* 1 (29): 47–68.

Howe, Herbert M. 2001. *Ambiguous Order: Military Forces in African States*. Boulder, CO: Lynne Rienner.

Huber, Max. 1928. *Die soziologischen Grundlagen des Völkerrechts*. Berlin: Verlag Dr. Walther Rothschild.

———. 1936. Observations. *Annuaire de l'Institut de Droit International*.

———. 1974. *Denkwürdigkeiten, 1907–1924*. Zürich: Orell Fussli.

Hughes, Kirsty and Edward Smith. 1998. New Labour-New Europe? *International Affairs* 74 (1): 93–103.

Huysmans, Jeff. 2003. Discussing Sovereignty and Transnational Politics. In *Sovereignty in Transition*, ed. Neil Walker, 209–227. Oxford: Hart.

ICISS. 2001. *The Responsibility to Protect*. Ottawa: International Development Research Centre.

ICMPD. 2004. *Irregular Transit Migration in the Mediterranean—Some Facts, Futures and Insights*. Vienna: ICMPD.

IMF. 2007. *Annual Report on Exchange Arrangements and Exchange Restrictions*. Washington: IMF.

Ingham, Geoffrey. 2004. *The Nature of Money*. Cambridge: Polity.

———. 2005. *Concepts of Money*. Cheltenham: Edward Elgar.

Ize, Alain. 2003. Strongly Anchored Currency Arrangements. *Current Developments in Monetary and Financial Law* 2: 641–656.

Jackson, Robert H. 1990. *Quasi-States: Sovereignty, International Relations and the Third World*. Cambridge: Cambridge University Press.

———. 1999a. Introduction: Sovereignty at the Millennium. In *Sovereignty at the Millennium*, ed. Robert Jackson, 1–8. Oxford: Blackwell.

———. 1999b. Sovereignty in World Politics: A Glance at the Conceptual and Historical Landscape. *Political Studies* 47 (3): 431–456.

James, Alan. 1999. The Practice of Sovereign Statehood in Contemporary International Society. *Political Studies* 47 (3): 457–473.

Joly, Eva avec la contribution de Laurent Beccaria. 2003. *Est-ce dans ce monde-là que nous voulons vivre?* Paris: Editions des Arènes.

Jonung, Lars. 2004. The Political Economy of Monetary Unification: The Swedish Euro Referendum of 2003. *Cato Journal* 24 (1–2): 123–149.

Kaldor, Mary. 1998. *Restructuring the Global Military Sector: New Wars*, ed. Mary Kaldor and B. Vashee, 1–23. London: Pinter.

Kelsen, Hans. 1928. *Das Problem der Souveränität und die Theorie des Völkerrechts*. 2nd edition. Tübingen: J.C.B. Mohr.

———. 1960. Sovereignty and International Law. *Georgetown Law Journal* 48: 627–640.

———. 1969. Sovereignty and International Law. In *Defense of Sovereignty*, ed. W.J. Stankiewicz, 115–131. London: Oxford University Press.

Kelstrup, Morten and Michael C. Williams. 2000. Introduction: Integration and the Politics of Community in the New Europe. In *International Relations Theory and the Politics of European Integration: Power, Security and Community*, ed. Morten Kelstrup and Michael C. Williams, 1–13. London: Routledge.

Kennedy, David. 1987. *International Legal Structures*. Baden-Baden: Nomos Verlagsgesellschaft.

Keohane, Robert O. 1995. Hobbe's Dilemma and Institutional Change in World Politics: Sovereignty in International Society. In *Whose World Order? Uneven Globalization and the End of the Cold War*, eds. Hans Henrik Holm and Georg Sørensen, 165–186. Boulder, CO: Westview.

———. 2002. Ironies of Sovereignty: The European Union and the United States. *Journal of Common Market Studies* 40 (4): 743–765.

Kessing, Peter Vedel. 2007. Skal danske styrker i udlandet overholde Danmarks menneskeretlige forpligtelser? *Juristen* 1.

Keynes, John Maynard. 1935. *The General Theory of Employment, Interest and Money*. New York: Macmillan.

Kingsbury, Benedict. 1998. Sovereignty and Inequality. *European Journal of International Law* 9: 599–625.

Kirschner, Jonathan. 1995. *Currency and Coercion*. Princeton, NJ: Princeton University Press.

Klabbers, Jan. 1998. Clinching the Concept of Sovereignty: Wimbledon Redux. *Austrian Review of International and European Law* 3: 345.

Knapp, Georg. 1923. *Staatliche Theorie des Geldes.* 4th edition. Munich: Duncker & Humbolt.

Kneebone, Susan. 2006. The Pacific Plan: The Provision of "Effective Protection"? *International Journal of Refugee Law* 18 (3/4): 696–722.

Knop, K. 1993. Re/statements: Feminism and State Sovereignty in International Law. *Transnational and Contemporary Legal Problems* 3: 293–344.

Koskenmäki, Riikka. 2004. Legal Implications Resulting from State Failure in Light of the Case of Somalia. *Nordic Journal of International Law* 73 (1): 1–36.

Koskenniemi, Martti. 1989. *From Apology to Utopia: The Structure of International Legal Argument.* Helsinki: Lakimiesliiton Kustannus.

———. 1991. The Future of Statehood. *Harvard International Law Journal* 32 (2): 397–410.

———. 2002. *The Gentle Civilizer of Nations: The Rise and Fall of International Law 1870–1960.* Cambridge: Cambridge University Press.

Krahmann, Elke. 2005. Controlling Private Military Companies in the UK and Germany: Between Partnership and Regulation. *European Security* 13 (2): 277–295.

Krasner, Stephen D. 1999. *Sovereignty: Organized Hypocrisy.* Princeton, NJ: Princeton University Press.

———. 2001a. Abiding Sovereignty. *International Political Science Review* 22 (3): 229–251.

Krasner, Stephen D. 2001b. Problematic Sovereignty. In *Problematic Sovereignty: Contested Rules and Political Possibilities,* ed. Stephen D. Krasner, 1–23. New York: Columbia University Press.

———. 2004a. Sharing Sovereignty: New Institutions for Collapsed and Failed States. *International Security* 29 (2): 85–120.

———. 2004b. The Hole in the Whole: Sovereignty, Shared Sovereignty, and International Law. *Michigan Journal of International Law* 25: 1075–1101.

Kratochwil, Friedrich V. 1989. *Rules, Norms, and Decisions: On the Conditions of Practical and Legal Reasoning in International Relations and Domestic Affairs.* Cambridge: Cambridge University Press.

Kreijen, Gerard. 2004. *State Failure, Sovereignty and Effectiveness: Legal Lessons from the Decolonization of Sub-Saharan Africa.* Leiden: Martinus Nijhoff.

Kutscher, Hans. 1976. Methods of Interpretation as Seen by a Judge at the Court of Justice. Offprint of paper delivered at *Judicial and Academic Conference,* September 27–28, 1976. Luxemburg.

Ladrech, Robert. 2004. Europeanization and the Member States. In *Developments in the European Union,* ed. Maria Green Cowles and Desmond Dinan, 47–64. Houndmills: Palgrave.

Lake, David A. 2003. The New Sovereignty in International Relations. *International Studies Review* 5 (3): 303–323.

Lastra, Rosa Maria. 2006. *Legal Foundations of International Monetary Stability.* Oxford: Oxford University Press.

Lauterpacht, Elihu, and Daniel Bethlehem. 2003. The Scope and Content of the Principle of *Non-refoulement*: Opinion. In *Refugee Protection in International*

Law: UNHCR's Global Consultations on International Protection, ed. E. Feller, Volker Türk, and Frances Nicholson. Cambridge: Cambridge University Press.

Lawson, Rick. 2004. Life after Bankovic: On the Extraterritorial Application of the European Convention on Human Rights. In *Extraterritorial Application of Human Rights Treaties*, ed. F. Coomans and M.T. Kamminga, 83–123. Antwerp: Intersentia.

Leander, Anna. 2005a. The Market for Force and Public Security: The Destabilizing Consequences of Private Military Companies. *Journal of Peace Research* 42 (5): 605–622.

———. 2005b. The Power to Construct International Security: On the Significance of Private Military Companies. *Millennium Journal of International Studies* 33 (3): 803–826.

———. 2006. *Eroding State Authority? Private Military Companies and the Legitimate Use of Force.* Rome: Centro Militare di Studi Strategici.

———. 2007. Re-Configuring Security Practices: On the Power of the Private Security Business. CBS Working Paper.

Leander, Anna and Rens van Munster. 2007. Private Security Contractors in Darfur: Reflecting and Reinforcing Neo-Liberal Governmentality. *International Relations* 21 (2): 201–216.

Lee Lanning, Michael. 2002. *Blood Warriors: American Military Elites.* New York: Presidio Press.

Lefort, Claude. 1986. *Essais sur le politique. XXIe. XXe siècles,* Paris: Seuil.

Legomsky, Stephen H. 2006. The USA and the Caribbean Interdiction Programme. *International Journal of Refugee Law* 18 (3/4): 677–696.

Lenihan, Niall. 1998. *The Legal Implications of the European Monetary Union under U.S. and New York Law.* Brussels: Directorate General for Economic and Financial Affairs, European Commission.

Levy, Mickey. 2006. Sound Monetary Policy, Credibility, and Economic Performance. *Cato Journal* 26 (2): 231–242.

Lindahl, Hans. 1997. Sovereignty and Symbolization. *Rechtstheorie* 28: 347–371.

———. 2003. Acquiring a Community: The *Acquis* and the Institution of European Legal Order. *European Law Journal* 4 (9): 433–450.

Lindahl, Rutger and Daniel Naurin. 2005. Sweden: The Twin Faces of a Euro-Outsider. *European Integration* 27 (1): 65–87.

Lippens, Ronnie. 2004. Surgical Strikes, Viral Contagion and Anti-Terrorism. Notes on Medical Emergency, Legality and Diplomacy. *International Journal for the Semiotics of Law* 17 (2): 125–139.

Locke, John. 1991. *An Essay Concerning Human Understanding.* London: Everyman's.

Lönnberg, Åke. 2005. Restoring and Transforming Payment and Banking Systems in Postconflict Economies. *Current Developments in Monetary and Financial Law* 3: 725–753.

Loucaides, Loukis G. 2006. Determining the Extra-territorial Effect of the European Convention: Facts, Jurisprudence and the Bankovic Case. *European Human Rights Law Review* 4: 391–407.

Loughlin, Martin. 2003. *The Idea of Public Law.* Oxford: Oxford University Press.

Lovering, John. 1998. Rebuilding the European Defense Industry in a Competitive World. In *Restructuring the Global Military Sector: The End of Military Fordism*, ed. Mary Kaldor, U. Albrecht, and G. Schméder. London and Washington: Pinter.

Lowenfeld, Andreas. 2002. *International Economic Law.* Oxford: Oxford University Press.

Lutterbeck, Derek. 2006. Policing Migration in the Mediterranean. *Mediterranean Politics* 11 (1): 59–82.

MacCormick, Neil. 1993. Beyond the Sovereign State. *Modern Law Review* 56: 1–19.

———. 1999. *Questioning Sovereignty: Law, State and Nation in the European Commonwealth.* Oxford: Oxford University Press.

Madigan, Nick. 2007. 13 People Taking the Oath of Allegiance at Fort McHenry Had Served Their Country Even before It Was Their Country. *Baltimore Sun*, September 25.

Magnette, Paul. 2005. *What Is the European Union? Nature and Prospects.* Basingstoke: Palgrave.

Mair, Peter. 2005. Popular Democracy and the European Polity. *European Governance Papers*, no. C-05-03.

———. 2007. Political Opposition and the European Union. *Government and Opposition* 42 (1): 1–17.

Majone, Giandomenico. 2005. *Dilemmas of Integration: The Ambiguities and Pitfalls of Integration by Stealth.* Oxford: Oxford University Press.

———. 2006. The Common Sense of European Integration. *Journal of European Public Policy* 13 (5): 607–626.

Malanczuk, Peter. 1993. *Humanitarian Intervention and the Legitimacy of the Use of Force.* Amsterdam: Spinhuis.

Malmvig, Helle. 2006. *State Sovereignty and Intervention: A Discourse Analysis of Interventionary and Non-interventionary Practices in Kosovo and Algeria.* London: Routledge.

Mancini, G. Federico. 1989. The Making of a Constitution for Europe. *Common Market Law Review* 26: 595–614.

Mancini, G. Federico and David T. Keeling. 1994. Democracy and the European Court of Justice. *Modern Law Review* 57: 175–190.

Manners, Ian, ed. 2000. *Substance and Symbolism: An Anatomy of Cooperation in the New Europe.* Ashgate: Aldershot.

Marcussen, Martin. 2005. Denmark and European Monetary Integration: Out but Far From Over. *Journal of European Integration* 27 (1): 743–763.

Marcussen, Martin and Mette Zolner. 2001. The Danish EMU Referendum 2000: Business as Usual. *Government and Opposition* 36 (3): 379–401.

Markusen, Ann R. 2003. The Case against Privatizing National Security. *Governance: An International Journal of Policy, Administration, and Institutions* 16 (4): 471–501.

Marx, Karl. 1970. *A Contribution to a Critique of Political Economy.* Moscow: International Publishers.

Mattli, Walter. 2000. Sovereignty Bargains in Regional Integration. *International Studies Review* 2 (2): 149–180.

McKay, David. 2001. *Designing Europe: Comparative Lessons from the Federal Experience.* Oxford: Oxford University Press.

Mihaljek, Dubravko. 2005. Free Movement of Capital, the Real Estate Market and Tourism: A Blessing or a Curse for Croatia on its Way to European Union? In *Croatian Accession to the European Union: Facing the Challenges of Negotiations*, ed. Katarina Ott, vol. 3, 185–228. Zagreb: Institute of Public Finance.

Miles, Lee. 2005. Introduction: Euro-outsiders and the Politics of Asymmetry. *Journal of European Integration* 27 (1): 73–23.

Miles, Lee and Gabriel Doherty. 2005. The United Kingdom: A Cautious Euro-outsider. *Journal of European Integration* 27 (1): 89–109.

Mill, John Stuart. 1909. *Principles of Political Economy.* London: Longmans, Green.

Miller, Christian. 2003. U.S. pair's role in bombing shown. *Los Angeles Times*, March 16.

Miller, Vaughne. 2002. The Danish Referendum on Economic and Monetary Union, House of Commons Research Chapter. London: House of Commons, http://www.parliament.uk/commons/lib/research/rp2000/rp00-078.pdf (accessed December 18, 2007).

Minow, Martha. 2003. Public and Private Partnerships: Accounting for the New Religion. *Harvard Law Review* 116 (March): 1229–1270.

Moravcsik, Andrew. 1993. Preferences and Power in the European Community: A Liberal Intergovernmentalist Approach. *Journal of Common Market Studies* 31 (4): 473–523.

———. 1998. *The Choice for Europe: Social Purposes and State Power from Messina to Maastricht.* Ithaca, NY: Cornell University Press.

Morefield, Jeanne. 2005. States Are Not People: Harold Laski on Unsettling Sovereignty, Rediscovering Democracy. *Political Research Quarterly* 58 (4): 659–669.

Morgan, Glyn. 2005. *The Idea of a European Superstate.* Princeton, NJ: Princeton University Press.

Mouffe, Chantal. 1999. Deliberative Democracy or Agnostic Pluralism. *Social Research* 66: 745–758.

MPRI: MPRI Index. http://www.mpri.com.

Neff, Stephen. 2005. *War and the Law of Nations.* Cambridge: Cambridge University Press.

Nijman, Janne. 2004. *The Concept of International Legal Personality: An inquiry into the History and Theory of International Law.* The Hague: T.M.C. Asser Institute.

Noll, Gregor. 2003. Visions of the Exceptional: Legal and Theoretical Issues Raised by Transit Processing Centres and Protection Zones. *European Journal of Migration Law* 5 (3): 303–341.

Nolte, Ina. 2007. Ethnic Vigilantes and the State: The Oodua People's Congress in South-Western Nigeria. *International Relations* 21 (4): 217–235.

Nordland, Rod, Mark Hosenball, and Larry Kaplow. 2007. Blackwater Is Soaked: An Arrogant Attitude Only Adds Fuel to the Criticism. *Newsweek*, October 15.

O'Boyle, Richard. 2004. The European Convention on Human Rights and Extraterritorial Jurisdiction: A Comment on Life after Bankovic. In *Extraterritorial Application of Human Rights Treaties*, ed. F. Coomans and M.T. Kamminga, 125–141. Antwerp: Intersentia.

Ogden, C.K. and I.A. Richards. 1936. *The Meaning of Meaning: A Study of the Influence of Language upon Thought and of the Science of Symbolism*. London: Kegan Paul.

Ong, Aiwa. 1999. *Flexible Citizenship: The Cultural Logics of Transnationality*. Durham, NC: Duke University Press.

Onuf, Nicholas. 1991. Sovereignty: Outline of a Conceptual History. *Alternatives* 16 (4): 425–446.

Orford, Anne. 1999. Muscular Humanitarianism: Reading the Narratives of the New Intervention. *European Journal of International Law* 10 (4): 679–711.

———. 2003. *Reading Humanitarian Intervention: Human Rights and the Use of Force in International Law*. Cambridge: Cambridge University Press.

Padoa-Schioppa, Tommaso. 2006. *Europe, a Civil Power: Lessons from EU Experience*. London: Federal Trust.

Palan, Ronen. 2002. Tax Havens and the Commercialization of State Sovereignty. *International Organization* 56 (1): 151–176.

———. 2003. *The Offshore World: Sovereign Markets, Virtual Places and Nomad Millionaires*. Ithaca, NY: Cornell University Press.

Parsons, Craig. 2003. *A Certain Idea of Europe*. Ithaca, NY: Cornell University Press.

Patomäki, Heikki. 2002. State Is Not a Person: On the Theoretical and Practical Consequences of State-Antropomorphism. Paper for 43rd Annual International Studies Association, New Orleans.

Paton Walsh, Nick. 2004. US Privatizes Its Military Aid to Georgia. *Guardian*, January 6.

Payne, Dexter. 2000. Policy-making in Nested Institutions: Explaining the Conservation Failure of the EU's Common Fisheries Policy. *Journal of Common Market Studies* 38 (2): 303–24.

Percy, Sarah. 2007. Mercenaries: Strong Norm, Weak Law. *International Organization* 61 (2): 367–397.

Philpott, Daniel. 2001. *Revolutions in Sovereignty: How Ideas Shaped Modern International Relations*. Princeton, NJ: Princeton University Press.

Pilkington, Colin. 1995. *Britain in the European Union*. Manchester: Manchester University Press.

Plato. 1955. *The Republic*. Harmondsworth: Penguin.

Proctor, Charles. 2005. *Mann on the Legal Aspect of Money*. 6th edition. Oxford: Oxford University Press.

Pugh, Michael. 2004. Drowning not Waving: Boat People and Humanitarianism at Sea. *Journal of Refugee Studies* 17 (1): 50–68.

Raepenbusch, Sean van, and Dominik Hanf. 2001. Flexibility in Social Policy. In *The Many Faces of Differentiation in EU Law*, ed. Bruno de Witte, Dominik Hanf, and Ellen Voos, 65–82. New York: Intersentia.

Rasmussen, Hjalte. 1986. *On Law and Policy in the European Court of Justice.* Dordrecht: Martinus Nijhoff Publishers.

Rasor, Dina and Robert Bauman. 2007. *Betraying Our Troops: The Destructive Results of Privatizing War.* New York: Palgrave.

Raunio, Tapio. 1999. Always One Step Behind? National Legislatures and the European Union. *Government and Opposition* 34 (2): 180–202.

Raustiala, Kal. 2005. The Geography of Justice. University of California, Los Angeles School of Law Public Law & Legal Theory Research Paper no. 05-7.

Reno, William. 1998. *Warlord Politics and African States.* Boulder, CO and London: Lynne Rienner.

Reus-Smit, Christian. 1999. *The Moral Purpose of the State: Culture, Social Identity, and Institutional Rationality in International Relations.* Princeton, NJ: Princeton University Press.

Riese, Otto. 1966. Über den Rechtsschutz innerhalb der Europäischen Gemeinschaften. *Europarecht* 1: 24.

Risse, Thomas. 2003. The Euro between national and European identity. *Journal of European Public Policy* 10 (4) : 587–505.

Rodden, Jonathan. 2002. Strength in Numbers? Representation and Redistribution in the European Union. *European Union Politics* 3 (2): 151–175.

Rosanvallon, Pierre. 2000. *La démocratie inachevée.* Paris: Gallimard.

Rose, Nikolas and Peter Miller. 1992. Political Power beyond the State: Problematics of Government. *British Journal of Sociology* 43 (2): 173–202.

Ross, Alf. 1947. *A Textbook in International Law.* London: Longmans, Green.

———. 1961. *Lærebog i Folkeret.* København: Munksgaards Forlag.

Rotte, Ralph, and Klaus Zimmermann. 1998. Fiscal Restraint and the Political Economy of EMU. *Public Choice* 94 (3): 385–406.

Rufin, Jean-Christophe. 1993. Les économies de guerre dans les conflits internes. In *Économie des guerres civiles*, ed. F. Jean and J.C. Rufin. Paris: Hachette.

Ruggie, John G. 1983. Continuity and Transformation in the World Polity: Towards a Neorealist Synthesis. *World Politics* 35 (2): 276–279.

———. 1993. Territoriality and Beyond: Problematizing Modernity in International Relations. *International Organization* 47 (1): 139–174.

Russell, Bertrand. 1962. *Problems of Philosophy.* Oxford: Oxford University Press.

Sakellaropoulos, Spyros. 2007. Towards a Declining State? The Rise of the Headquarters State. *Science and Society* 71 (1): 7–34.

Santos, B de Sousa. 1995. *Towards a New Common Sense.* London: Routledge.

Sapone, Montgomery. 1999. I Have Rifle with Scope, Will Travel: The Global Economy of Mercenary Violence. *California Western International Law Journal* 30 (fall): 1–43.

Sarooshi, Dan. 2004. The Essentially Contested Nature of Sovereignty: Implications for the Exercise by International Organizations of Delegated

Powers of Government. *Michigan Journal of International Law* 25 (summer): 1107–1139.

Sassen, Saskia. 1995. *Losing Control? Sovereignty in an Age of Globalization.* New York: Columbia University Press.

———. 2006. *Territory, Authority, Rights: From Medieval to Global Assemblages.* Princeton, NJ: Princeton University Press.

Scahill, Jeremy. 2007a. *Blackwater: The Rise of the World's Most Powerful Mercenary Army.* Washington: Nation Books.

Scahill, Jeremy. 2007b. Out in the Open: CNN September 24, 8:00 PM EST.

Schméder, Geneviève. 1998. Global Trends in Military Efforts and Activities. In *Restructuring the Global Military Sector: The End of Military Fordism,* ed. by Mary Kaldor, U. Albrecht, and G. Schméder, 11–35. London and Washington: Pinter

Schmidt, Vivien A. 1997. European Integration and Democracy: The Differences among Member States. *Journal of European Public Policy* 4 (1): 28–45.

———. 2004. The European Union: Democratic Legitimacy in a Regional State. *Journal of Common Market Studies* 42 (5): 975–997.

———. 2006. *Democracy in Europe: The EU and National Polities.* Oxford: Oxford University Press.

Schmitt, Carl. 1974. *Der Nomos der Erde in Völkerrecht des Jus Publicum Europaeum.* Berlin: Duncker & Humblot.

———. 1992. The Constitutional Theory of Federalism. *TELOS* 91 (spring): 26–56.

———. 2006. *The Nomos of the Earth in the International Law of the Jus Publicum Europaeum.* New York: Telos Press.

Schuler, Kurt. 2005. Some Theory and History of Dollarization. *Cato Journal* 25 (1): 115–125.

Schumpeter, Joseph A. 1917. Das Sozialprodukt und die Rechenpfennige. Glossen und Beiträge zur Geldtheorie. *Archiv für Sozialwissenschaft* 44: 627–715.

———. 1954. *History of Economic Analysis.* London: Allen & Unwin.

———. 1970 [1930]. *Das Wesen des Geldes.* Göttingen: Vandenhoeck u. Ruprecht.

Schwartz, Anna. 2004. The Uselessness of Monetary Sovereignty. *Cato Journal* 24 (1–2) : 107–121.

Schwebel, Stephen. 1980. Second Report on the Law of Non-navigational uses of International Watercourses. *Yearbook of the International Law Commission* II (1): 159.

Searle, John R. 1969. *Speech Acts.* Cambridge: Cambridge University Press.

———. 1995. *The Construction of Social Reality.* Hammondsworth: Penguin.

Shaw, Jo. 1998. The Treaty of Amsterdam: Challenges of Flexibility and Legitimacy. *European Law Journal* 4 (1): 63–86.

Shaw, Martin N. 2003. *International Law,* 5th edition. Cambridge: Cambridge University Press.

Shaw, Martin. 1991. *Post-Military Society: Militarism, Demilitarization and War at the End of the Twentieth Century.* Cambridge: Cambridge University Press.

Simmel, Georg. 1930. *Philosophie des Geldes.* 5th edition. Munich: Duncker & Humblot.

Simpson, Gerry. 2004. *Great Powers and Outlaw States, Unequal Sovereigns in the International Legal Order.* Cambridge: Cambridge University Press.

Singer, Peter W. 2003. *Corporate Warriors: The Rise of the Privatized Military Industry.* Ithaca, NY and London: Cornell University Press.

———. 2007. Can't Win with 'Em, Can't Go to War without 'Em: Private Military Contractors and Counterinsurgency. *Foreign Policy at Brookings. Policy Papers* (4).

Skinner, Quentin. 2002. *Visions of Politics 1: Regarding Method.* Cambridge: Cambridge University Press.

Sørensen, Georg. 1999. Sovereignty: Change and Continuity in a Fundamental Institution. *Political Studies* 47 (3): 590–604.

———. 2004. *The Transformation of the State: Beyond the Myth of Retreat.* New York: Palgrave Macmillan.

Spiermann, Ole. 1995. *Enten & Eller: Studier i suverænitetsbegreber.* Copenhagen: Jurist- og Økonomforbundets Forlag.

———. 2003. A National Lawyer Takes Stock: Professor Ross' Textbook and Other Forays into International Law. *European Journal of International Law* 14: 675–702.

———. 2005. *International Legal Argument in the Permanent Court of International Justice: The Rise of the International Judiciary.* Cambridge: Cambridge University Press.

Spruyt, Hendrik. 1994. *The Sovereign State and Its Competitors.* Princeton, NJ: Princeton University Press.

Stampp, Kenneth. 1978. The Concept of a Perpetual Union. *Journal of American History* 65 (1): 5–33.

Streeck, Wolfgang and Philippe Schmitter. 1991. From National Corporatism to Transnational Pluralism: Organized Interests in the Single European Market. *Politics and Society* 19 (2): 133–164.

Sukiennicki, Wiktor. 1927. *La souveraineté des états en droit international moderne.*Paris: A. Pedone.

Sur, Serge. 1997. The State between Fragmentation and Globalization. *European Journal of International Law* 8 (3): 421–435.

Sweeney, Richard, Clas Wihlborg, and Thomas Willett. 1999. *Exchange-Rate Policies for Emerging Market Economies.* New York: Westview.

Tavlas, George. 2004. Costs and Benefits of Entering the Eurozone. *Cato Journal* 24 (1–2): 89–106.

Taylor, C. 2004. *Modern Social Imaginaries.* Durham, NC: Duke University Press.

Tesón, Ferdinand. 1992. The Kantian Theory of International Law. *Columbia Law Review* 92 (1): 53–102.

Thompson, Janice. 1995. State Sovereignty in International Relations: Bridging the Gap between Theory and Empirical Research. *International Studies Quarterly* 39 (2): 213–233.

Thomson, Janice E. 1994. *Mercenaries, Pirates, and Sovereigns: State-building and Extraterritorial Violence in Early Modern Europe.* Princeton, NJ: Princeton University Press.

———. 1995. State Sovereignty in International Relations: Bridging the Gap between Theory and Empirical Research. *International Studies Quarterly* 39 (2): 213–233.

Thürer, Daniel, Matthias Herdegen, and Gerhard Hohloch, eds. 1996. *Der Wegfall effectiver Staatsgewalt: "The Failed State" (The Breakdown of Effective Government)*. Heidelberg: C.F. Müller Verlag.

Tierney, S. 2005. Reframing Sovereignty? Sub-state National Societies and Contemporary Challenges to the Nation-State. *International and Comparative Legal Quarterly* 54: 161–183.

Tigner, Brooks. 2007. Intelligence: The Risks of Going Private. *ISN Security Watch*, April 3.

Tipton, Diane. 1969. *Nullification and Interposition in American Political Thought*. Albuquerque: University of New Mexico.

Tocqueville, Alexis de. 1994. *Democracy in America*, trans. Henry Reeve. London: David Campbell.

Toews, John E. 1987. Intellectual History after the Linguistic Turn: The Autonomy of Meaning and the Irreducibility of Experience. *American Historical Review* 92 (4): 879–907.

Tokar, Adrian. 2001. Something Happened. Sovereignty and European Integration. *Extraordinary Times: IWM Junior Visiting Fellows Conferences* 11/2.

Trechsel, Alexander H. 2005. How to Federalize the EU…and Why Bother. *Journal of European Public Policy* 12 (3): 401–418.

UN. 2001. *Report of the Panel of Experts on the Illegal Exploitation of Natural Resources and Other Forms of Wealth of the Democratic Republic of Congo (S/2001/357)*. New York: UN Security Council.

UN, General Assembly. 2007. *Report on the Question of the Use of Mercenaries as a Means of Violating Human Rights and Impeding the Exercise of the Right of Peoples to Self-Determination (A/62/150)*. New York: UN.

van Dun, Frank. 1998. National Sovereignty and International Monetary Regimes. In *Money and the Nation State*, ed. Kevin Dowd and Richard H. Timberlake, 47–76. New Brunswick: Transaction.

Van Roermund, B. 2003. Sovereignty: Unpopular and Popular. In *Sovereignty in Transition*, ed. N. Walker, 33–54. Oxford: Hart.

Vattel, Emerich de. 1758. *The Law of Nations or the Principles of Natural Law*. Washington: Carnegie Institution.

Vaubel, Roland. 1994. The Public Choice Analysis of European Integration: A Survey. *European Journal of Political Economy* 10 (1): 227–249.

Vedsted-Hansen, Jens. 2004. Denmark. In *Migration and Asylum Law and Policy in the European Union. FIDE 2004 National Reports*, ed. Imelda Higgens and Kay Hailbronner, 65–88. Cambridge: Cambridge University Press.

Verdross, Alfred. 1950. *Völkerrecht*. 2nd edition. Wien: Springer.

Verkuil, Paul. 2007. *Outsourcing Sovereignty: Why Privatization of Government Functions Threatens Democracy and What We Can Do about It*. Cambridge: Cambridge University Press.

Vincent, R. John. 1974. *Non-Intervention and International Order.* Princeton, NJ: Princeton University Press.

von Trotha, Trutz. 2000. Die Zukunft liegt in Afrika. *Leviathan* 28: 253–279.

Wade, William. 1996. Sovereignty – Revolution or Evolution? *Law Quarterly Review* 112: 568–578.

Wæver, Ole. 1995. Identity, Integration and Security: Solving the Sovereignty Puzzle in E.U. Studies. *Journal of International Affairs* 48 (2): 389–431.

———. 2000. The EU as a Security Actor: Reflections from a Pessimistic Constructivist on Post-sovereign Security Orders. In *International Relations Theory and the Politics of European Integration: Power, Security and Community,* ed. Morten Kelstrup and Michael C. Williams, 250–294. London: Routledge.

Wagner, Peter. 2002. As Intellectual History Meets Historical Sociology: Historical Sociology and the Linguistic Turn. In *Handbook of Historical Sociology,* ed. Gerard Delanty, Engin Isin, and Margaret Somers, 168–179. London: Sage.

Waldock, Humphrey. 1980. The Effectiveness of the System Set up by the European Convention on Human Rights. *Human Rights Law Journal* 1: 1–12.

Walker Neil. 2003. Late Sovereignty in the European Union. In *Sovereignty in Transition,* ed. Neil Walker, 3–33. Portland: Hart.

———. 2006. Sovereignty, Global Security and the Regulation of Armed Conflict: The Possibilities of Political Agency. In *The Politics of Protection,* ed. J. Huysmans, A Dobson and R Prokhovnik, 154–174. London: Routledge.

———. 2007. Europe at 50: A Mid-Life Crisis? National University of Ireland, Galway, Faculty of Law Annual Distinguished Lecture, May 23.

Walker, Robert B.J. 1990. Sovereignty, Identity, Community: Reflections on the Horizons of Contemporary Political Practice. In *Contending Sovereignties: Redefining Political Community,* ed. R.B.J. Walker and Saul H. Mendlovitz, 159–185. Boulder, CO: Lynne Rienner.

———. 1995. International Relations and the Possibility of the Political. In *International Relations Theory Today,* ed. Ken Booth and Steve Smith, 306–327. Cambridge: Polity.

Wallace, William. 1999. The Sharing of Sovereignty: The European Paradox. *Political Studies* 47 (3): 503–521.

Wallace, Helen 1997. At Odds With Europe. *Political Studies* 45 (4): 677–690.

Wallace-Bruce, Nii Lante. 2000. Of Collapsed, Dysfunctional and Disoriented States: Challenges to International Law. *Netherlands International Law Review* 47 (1): 53–73.

War on Want. 2006. *Corporate Mercenaries.* London: War on Want.

Waxman, Henry. 2007. Letter to the Inspector General, Honorable Howard J. Krongard, on Behalf of the Committee on Oversight and Government Reform, September 18. Washington: Congress of the United States.

Weber, Cynthia. 1995. *Simulating Sovereignty: Intervention, the State and Symbolic Exchange.* Cambridge: Cambridge University Press.

Wegner, Manfred. 1998. EMU and the World Economy. *European Foreign Affairs Review* 3: 451–457.

Weiler, Joseph H.H. 1999. *The Constitution of Europe: Do the New Clothes Have an Emperor? And other Essays on European Integration*. Cambridge: Cambridge University Press.

Weldes, Jutta. 1999. *Constructing National Interests: The United States and the Cuban Missile Crisis*. Minneapolis: University of Minnesota Press.

Werner, Wouter G. 2001. Speech Act Theory and the Concept of Sovereignty: A Critique of the Descriptivistic and Normativistic Fallacy. *Hague Yearbook of International Law* 14: 73–84.

———. 2004. State Sovereignty and International Legal Discourse. In *Governance and International Legal Theory*, ed. Wouter Werner and Ige F. Dekker, 125–158. Leiden: Brill Academic Publishers.

Werner, Werner G. and Jaap H. de Wilde. 2001. The Endurance of Sovereignty. *European Journal of International Relations* 7 (3): 283–313.

Wheeler, Nicholas J. 2000. *Saving Strangers: Humanitarian Intervention in International Society*. Oxford: Oxford University Press.

Whelan, Theresa. 2003. (Deputy Assistant Secretary of Defense for African Affairs) Remarks to IPOA Dinner. Washington D.C., November 19, 2003.

Wiener, Antje. 1999. Forging Flexibility—The British 'No' to Schengen. *European Journal of Migration and Law* 1(4): 441–463.

Wight, Colin. 2006. *Agents, Structures and International Relations: Politics as Ontology*. Cambridge: Cambridge University Press.

Wilde, Ralph. 2005. Legal "Black Hole"? Extraterritorial State Action and International Treaty Law on Civil and Political Rights. *Michigan Journal of International Law* 26: 739–806.

Wind, Marlene. 2001. *Sovereignty and European Integration: Towards a Post-Hobbesian Order*. Basingstoke: Palgrave.

Winfield, Percy. 1922. "The History of Intervention in International Law." *British Yearbook of International Law* 1922–1923: 130–149.

Wulf, Herbert. 2005. *Internationalizing and Privatizing War and Peace*. Basingstoke and New York: Palgrave.

Yack, Bernard. 2001. Popular Sovereignty and Nationalism. *Political Theory* 29 (4): 517–536.

Yeager, Leland. 2004. The Euro Facing Other Moneys. *Cato Journal* 24 (1–2): 27–40.

Zamparelli, Colonel Steven J. 1999. Competitive Sourcing and Privatization: Contractors on the Battlefield. *Air Force Journal of Logistics* 23 (3): 1–17.

Zedner, Lucia. 2006. Liquid Security: Managing the Market for Crime Control. *Criminology and Criminal Justice* 6 (3): 267–288.

Zelizer, Viviana. 1994. *The Social Meaning of Money*. New York: BasicBooks.

Index